The
BUSINESS of
BUSINESS
VALUATION

The BUSINESS of BUSINESS VALUATION

Gary E. Jones
Dirk Van Dyke WITHDRAWN

McGraw-Hill
New York   San Francisco   Washington, D.C.   Auckland
Bogotá   Caracas   Lisbon   London   Madrid   Mexico City
Milan   Montreal   New Delhi   San Juan   Singapore
Sydney   Tokyo   Toronto

Library of Congress Cataloging-in-Publication Data

Jones, Gary E.
    The business of business valuation / by Gary Jones
and Dirk Van Dyke.
        p. cm.
        ISBN 0-7863-0487-1
        1. Business enterprises—Valuation. I. Van Dyke, Dirk.
    II. Title
    HG4028.V3J66 1998
    658.15—dc21   97-37423
                                                       CIP

McGraw-Hill

A Division of The McGraw-Hill Companies

Copyright © 1998 by The McGraw-Hill Companies, Inc. All rights reserved.
Printed in the United States of America. Except as permitted under the
United States Copyright Act of 1976, no part of this publication may be reproduced or distributed in any form or by any means, or stored in a data base
or retrieval system, without the prior written permission of the publisher.

1 2 3 4 5 6 7 8 9 0 DOC/DOC 9 0 2 1 0 9 8 7

ISBN 0-7863-0487-1

The sponsoring editor for this book was Stephen Isaacs, the editing supervisor was Donna Namorato, and the production supervisor was Suzanne W. B.
Rapcavage. It was set in Palatino by Hendrickson Creative Communications.

Printed and bound by R. R. Donnelley & Sons Company.

This publication is designed to provide accurate and authoritative information in regard to the subject matter covered. It is sold with the understanding that neither the author nor the publisher is engaged in rendering legal,
accounting, or other professional service. If legal advice or other expert
assistance is required, the services of a competent professional person
should be sought.

> *—From a Declaration of Principles jointly adopted by a Committee of
> the American Bar Association and a Committee of Publishers*

McGraw-Hill books are available at special quantity discounts to use as
premiums and sales promotions, or for use in corporate training programs.
For more information, please write to the Director of Special Sales,
McGraw-Hill, 11 West 19th Street, New York, NY 10011. Or contact your
local bookstore.

 This book is printed on recycled, acid-free paper containing a minimum of 50% recycled de-inked fiber.

C O N T E N T S

Chapter 3

The Components of a Business Valuation   31

This book is designed to assist those who are entering the world of valuation or performing a limited number of valuations and are looking for some insight into the issues contained herein. The book is meant to serve as an introduction to an exciting professional niche that is just beginning to flourish.

Dirk and I wish to thank our families, friends, and other professionals at ValueNomics Research, Inc. for their contribution of time, energy, and patience toward the completion of *The Business of Business Valuation*. We appreciate very much the extra effort given by John Gutman and Benjamin Chiu and the assistance from Paul Jones and Germaine Hunter.

I want to personally thank James J. Pertrinovich, CPA, for his years of patience with me as his protégé and partner. During those years I learned much from him and retain many of those lessons with enthusiasm and gratitude.

Other key individuals who have played a role in my development as a professional are Eva M. Jones (mom), Charles T. Catalan, Joseph R. Megna, Blake L. Downing, Samuel C. Grinels, Norman Glickman, Esq., Alan Koltin, Bob Greene, Parnell Black, Armon Mills, Chuck Heschmeyer, and Peter F. Murray. To these people I extend my appreciation.

But most of all to my wife Barbara, who can only be described as a true saint for putting up with me. I love you and can only hope that you never give up.

My son Trevor and daughter Lauren have contributed much to my quest for life and success. Their sense of humor, smiles, and hugs bring sunshine to an otherwise drab day. Remember, kids, life is truly a Movable Feast.*

Gary E. Jones

---

* Ernest Hemingway

Two roads diverged in a wood, and I—
I took the one less traveled by,
And that has made all the difference.

Robert Frost

I would like to thank those people who have helped me along the road less traveled: Jim, Mallory, John, Scott, John, Art, Tom, Jim, Dave, and others too numerous to mention but very much appreciated.

I want to thank my parents for their continous loving support and encouragement. I thank my sister and brother for encouraging me to read, which has contributed to my writing skills.

I am grateful to my coauthor for his many insights and valuable lessons. I also am indebted to Jimmy Olsson, Professors Carl Christ and Brett Trueman, and Dave Peterson for their guidance in my professional and personal development.

I am glad that I can call Tim Browning, Greg Czumak, Michelle Hiskey, Alex Holder, Dave Gregory, Kelly McGuckin, and Andy Patrick my friends.

I want to thank Carlyn and Kelsey Van Dyke; Sara, Brian, and Kelly Bush; and Andrew Allen for reminding me of what is truly important in life.

To my wife Karen, whom I love more than words can tell. I am grateful for the wonderful years we have had together, and I am still totally psyched to be married to you.

Dirk Van Dyke

Dear Readers:

Although valuing a business might not be on the top of your clients' to-do list, there are many excellent business and investment reasons to undertake the valuation process: as part of a business plan, as a platform in a loan package for expansion capital, as the basis for an employee stock ownership plan (ESOP), buy/sell agreements, and many more. Unfortunately, there are also situations in which clients may have little choice: They may suddenly find themselves a party to an insurance claim, in the midst of an ownership dispute with a minority shareholder, or the respondent in a divorce action.

To many, confronting these circumstances may appear overwhelming. But as we walk through the logical steps for valuing a business, you will gain information and a better understanding of the business valuation process, how to negotiate the engagement, manage support staff, and complete the project in a timely and cost-effective manner.

This new insight into the valuation process should increase the worth of your client's company, improve its competitive edge, and assist in negotiating a fair deal, whether it be buying or selling a business or gift and estate planning. Valuing a business can ultimately bring financial rewards far beyond the cost of undertaking the process.

For the past few years, we have been searching for simple tools that would help our colleagues understand how various aspects of the business valuation process work. *The Business of Business Valuation* is the first in what we hope will be a series of books that can offer an introduction to and/or new perspectives on this exciting field. High on our list of objectives is to help consumers receive the right value for their businesses by engaging qualified valuation analysts, those who assume a neutral position and strive to determine the best estimate of value. This book will also provide educators, students, and professional candidates with a learning tool and an overview of some of the misconceptions consumers and others may have about the process.

This clear-cut book should provide you with a level of comfort as you work through a business valuation. We have strived to make it an easy-to-follow guide to smoothly steer your course as you navigate the process. It outlines what you need to know as you study how to perform business valuation services so that there should be few surprises. *The Business of Business Valuation* will describe the following:

- Why and when a client should have a business valuation
- What the valuation process entails
- What you should expect during the process
- How long it should take, barring unforeseen and/or changed circumstances
- What the consumer's role is
- What the valuation report should contain
- How the valuation process serves to increase the value of a business
- What qualifications a good valuator should have
- The pitfalls involved in the valuation process
- How to achieve a reasonable value for the business
- How much it costs and how you manage the costs

The pages of this book are designed to assist professionals who are considering entering the field of business valuations, either by expanding their client services or by making a career change. We also hope that it will be useful to those who want to reach a comfort zone and face the business valuation process head on with less anxiety, as well as those looking for perspective on the valuation process.

We have included sample written reports and engagement letters in the Appendix. We believe that these reports will provide the reader with examples of what a sound valuation report looks like.

These materials, along with the Valuation Process Chart in Chapter 4, have been included in the book with the hope that they will stimulate ideas and new approaches to valuation, rather than simply serve as a template, and will help you receive value for your investment.

CHAPTER 1

An Overview of Business Valuation

WHAT IS A BUSINESS VALUATION?

A business valuation determines the estimated market value of a business entity. A thorough, robust valuation consists of an in-depth analysis by a qualified, independent professional who combines (1) proven techniques, (2) analysis and understanding of a specific company and its associated industry, (3) research and analysis of industry, association, and other publications; academic studies; the national and local economy; and on-line databases with (4) judgment honed by education, training, and experience, and (5) intuition. A valuation estimates the complex economic benefits that arise from combining a group of physical assets with the intangible assets of the business enterprise as a going concern. The resulting valuation, part science and part art, is a well-founded estimate that represents the price that hypothetical informed buyers and sellers would negotiate at arm's length for an entire business or for a partial equity interest.

WHY PERFORM A BUSINESS VALUATION?

Establishing and documenting the value of a business is a savvy decision for several reasons. First, a high-quality valuation can be the cornerstone of a successful business plan to increase the firm's value, it can reduce the risk of future legal problems, and it can decrease unnecessary expenses. Second, by establishing a price for a business, a valuation can assist business owners in negotiating a fair deal in situations as varied as a buy/sell agreement, a merger, sale, or acquisition, or a joint venture or strategic partnership. Third, given estate and other transfer taxes that combined can be greater than 50 percent, a valuation is a crucial initial step for gift and estate tax planning and charitable giving. Finally, certain valuations are mandated by government and judicial authorities, including eminent domain takings, employee stock ownership plans (ESOPs), S corporation election, and marital dissolution. Chapter 2 describes these issues in more detail.

VALUATION VS. APPRAISAL: HOW DO THEY DIFFER?

While valuations and appraisals are similar in some ways, they are not interchangeable. Most people are familiar with appraisals as part of their personal lives, even if they do not encounter appraisals in their business or profession. For instance, many individuals have had personal assets like houses, cars, jewelry, or works of art appraised. The key difference between a valuation and an appraisal is that a valuation includes the tangible *and* intangible assets of a business as a going concern, while an appraisal is solely for tangible, or physical, assets.

In many cases, physical asset appraisal(s) can supplement a valuation. For instance, a company may have physical assets with an aggregate tangible net worth greater than the earning power of the company. Such assets may include inventory, property, plant, and equipment. In these situations, a valuation analyst calls upon appraisers who specialize in specific types of physical assets, and the estimated value of the business may thus depend more on the company's tangible net assets than on the company's projected earnings.

THE SCIENCE AND ART OF VALUATION

At first glance, business valuation may appear to be solely a set of numbers added up in a formulaic way. While business valuation certainly uses the science of quantitative analysis, it combines science with the art of qualitative evaluation and the interpretation of human and business behavior. So, while it is based on factual information and sound methodology, a valuation consists of more than plugging numbers into a formula to arrive at an answer.

The science of valuation combines the set of complex internal and external factors that affect a business, its industry, and the overall economy. Together, these factors influence value at any given point in time. Chapter 3 describes these factors in more detail.

The art of valuation comes from taking the relevant facts gathered during the scientific part of the valuation and combining them with the valuator's knowledge, training, experience, and professional judgment to arrive at a reasonable estimate of value. The valuator has to search for real-world experiences and market comparisons and has to challenge his or her preliminary conclusions continually. This side of the valuation process, the art form, depends on the valuator's ability to synthesize facts and perceptions from disparate sources into a meaningful, quantified estimate of value. Chapter 4 describes this process in more detail.

Throughout this book, the fragile balance between the science and the art of valuation will be a recurrent theme. Too often, computerized tools that are allegedly easy to use can overshadow the basic building blocks of sound reasoning and intuition that must guide a valuation. The numbers are very important, but it is equally important to remember the broader picture.

A PERSONAL ANECDOTE ABOUT BUSINESS VALUATION FROM GARY JONES

A valuator can learn general principles of valuation through education and training, but it often takes a mentor to help the novice valuator hone—and trust—the intuitive skills used in valuation.

I still recall vividly my first realization of the differences between the science and art of valuation. Early in my career in the 1970s, I was asked to prepare a detailed projection of earnings and cash flow for a retail business with $2.5 million in annual revenues. The business owner was considering transferring some of the shares in the firm to his two sons, but he first needed an estimate of the value of the shares.

My boss was a trusting person who gave me the latitude to learn from my mistakes. He explained simply what he wanted, handed me the documents, and left me on my own. Although I had been introduced to the discounted earnings/cash flow method of valuing a business through textbooks and in the classroom, this incident proved to be a real-world lesson in applying my formal education.

Since this was back in the days before personal computers, I created a spreadsheet with paper and pencil and projected earnings and cash flows over 25 years. I made assumptions about inflation and built models of complex scenarios with components like cost of goods sold, compensation, and sales growth. I then calculated a reasonable discount rate and the net present value of the earnings results. Hundreds of calculations later, I turned off my smoking calculator and presented my boss with what I thought was a masterpiece of financial handiwork.

Walking into my boss's office was always a treat; he was never harsh or unduly critical. His review method was to have a subordinate sit and watch as he studied the document through his half-eye reading glasses. During the 10-plus years I worked with him before he retired, his eyes and demeanor never gave away the thoughts and responses he was formulating. His skills in negotiation and human relations were matched, incidentally, by his poker face around the card table.

What I gave my boss that day was an example of the *science of valuation*—a detailed set of numbers and projections. What he added was the *art of valuation*, developed over his years of experience.

The main point that I learned from his review was that projecting into the future, even for a few years, had to be done carefully. Willing buyers of a business would pay primarily for cash returns over relatively short periods of time that would permit them to recoup their investment and earn a fair return.

My boss explained that sellers of most private, closely held businesses could not avail themselves of a public market. An owner of a privately held business cannot call a stockbroker and sell his or her shares in a day or two. Shareholders in companies that trade on stock markets can almost always find a buyer for their shares if they are willing to sell at the current market price. Although I calculated a valuation number that could be defended from a textbook approach, I ignored the effects of market forces and other external factors that could have a significant impact on the value of a business, such as the lack of a market where the shares of a company's stock can be sold.

I learned that the worth of a business was more than an analysis of a company's financial information and other internal documents. I began to see the art form that comes from incorporating other elements into the valuation result. These elements include economic and industry conditions, ownership control, relative size of the company, liquidity of the equity interest under consideration, market comparables, and current merger and acquisition trends.[1] I learned that these issues and trends often surface only through research and interviews with the client and key industry players.

On that day, I began the transition from a numbers person to a valuator prepared to consider both the science and the art of the valuation process. I added my boss's input to the report, which eventually was audited and accepted by the Internal Revenue Service.

The moral of this first valuation experience is that a good valuator needs to have the talent to run the numbers as well as the willingness to challenge the result on the basis of professional judgment and intuition. The results of the quantification and analysis must be articulated in an oral or written report to communicate the conclusion of estimated value. Finally, it is difficult to overemphasize the importance of clearly communicated and presented final reports; all the finest science and art of valuation slips away if the results cannot be understood by the intended audiences.

A BRIEF HISTORY OF VALUATION AND APPRAISAL[2]

Ever since humans first started to exchange goods and services, they have needed to consider—implicitly or explicitly—how to value items to be traded. People needed a sense of value both to barter goods and to sell goods in return for coins. Historians believe that the first coins were made by the Greeks several centuries before Christ.

The ideas and practice underlying modern-day business valuation depend on a complex infrastructure of accounting techniques and practices that have grown up over many centuries. In the Western world, historical records show that a very early use of accounting was as a means to control agricultural production on manorial estates in the Middle Ages. In a period when trade was infrequent, overseers of estates needed to keep track of production on relatively self-sufficient estates.

As trade blossomed during the Renaissance, Italian merchants in Venice, Genoa, and Florence developed what would today be considered rudimentary accounting techniques to separate personal affairs from business affairs. Further stages of sophistication utilized the innovations of double-entry bookkeeping to assist in the determination of the profitability of separate trading ventures. Pacioli's *Summa de Arithmetica, Geometria, Proportioni, et Proportionalita*,[3] published at the end of the fifteenth century, is widely considered to be the first accounting textbook.

In the seventeenth century, as the locus of business innovation moved to northern Europe, English merchants developed accounting mechanisms to protect shareholders and to allocate profits among shareholders. Two factors drove these changes: large investor losses and the notion that the privilege of incorporation had to be reciprocated by the obligation to disclose financial information. In the succeeding three centuries, various companies acts enacted by the English Parliament played a significant role in pushing forward accounting practice.

In conjunction with the transition from agriculture and trading to manufacturing and distribution that embodied the Industrial Revolution, advances in concepts such as cost accounting and depreciation developed. With the need to raise large amounts of capital in public arenas, standards for accounting and auditing evolved so that investors could have higher degrees of confidence in investment opportunities. In addition, the introduction of the income tax (in 1913 in the United States) necessitated increased precision and refinements in accounting practice to meet expanding governmental requirements. To meet these demands, business valuations became increasingly important, and, over time, widely accepted valuation practices have begun to evolve.

Today, stock markets and commodities exchanges provide the opportunity to develop publicly the relevant valuations for businesses, products, and services. The most noteworthy opinion from the Internal Revenue Service on valuation issues, Revenue Ruling 59–60, disseminated in 1959, is more oriented toward valuation of estates and closely held businesses.[4] Running a mere seven pages, it outlines the basic principles that formed the foundation for business valuations in the United States today.

As this cursory review has documented, the needs to control business activities, determine profitability, and meet investor and governmental requirements all created the accounting infrastructure that is an essential part of business valuation. At its broadest level today, the practice of business valuation serves as a bridge among the sophisticated and somewhat distinct methodologies of securities analysis, management, financial, and tax accounting, finance, and economics to arrive at a coherent view of the estimated worth of a business enterprise.

THE VALUATION INDUSTRY

The business valuation industry in the United States is not tracked by any single organization. The industry includes valuations performed by accounting firms and valuation firms ranging in size from the Big Six international firms to small, one- or two-person firms. In addition, it includes the internal valuations by companies, investors, commercial banks, venture capital firms, and investment banks. The valuators themselves include securities analysts, economists, certified public accountants (CPAs), chartered financial analysts (CFAs), investment bankers, and venture capitalists, in addition to businesspeople with a variety of other types of training.

Several trade associations represent the interests of valuators, issue their standards, and provide forums for the discussion of valuation issues. These organizations include the American Institute of Certified Public Accountants (AICPA), the American Society of Appraisers (ASA), the Appraisal Foundation, the Association for Investment Management and Research (AIMR), the Institute of Business Appraisers (IBA), and the National Association of Certified Valuation Analysts (NACVA). Each of these associations provides training, publishes newsletters and conducts annual meetings and conventions. Unlike the Financial Accounting Standards Board (FASB), which issues the accepted authority of Generally Accepted Accounting Principles (GAAP) for corporate financial reporting, no single private-sector or governmental organization serves as the generally accepted authority on business valuation standards.

SUMMARY

A business valuation determines the estimated market value of a business entity. The resulting valuation, part science and part art, is a well-founded estimate that represents the price that hypothetical informed buyers and sellers might negotiate at arm's length for an entire business or for a partial equity interest. A high-quality valuation can help increase the firm's value and meet government requirements, can assist business owners in negotiating a fair deal for a variety of situations, and can serve as a crucial base step for gift and estate tax planning and charitable giving. The remaining chapters in the book describe these issues in more detail.

NOTES

1. Good sources of information about these issues and trends include suppliers, customers, competitors, firm principals, professional service firms, industry experts, research-oriented professors, government

officials, and association analysts. A good reference tool to guide this type of information gathering is Michael Porter's *Competitive Strategy*, New York, NY: The Free Press, 1985.

2. Michael Chatfield, *A History of Accounting Thought*, Hinsdale, IL: Dryden Press, 1974; Coffman, Edward, Raoul H. Tondkar, and Gary John Previts, eds., *Historical Perspectives of Selected Financial Accounting Topics*, Homewood, IL: Irwin, 1993.

3. Luca Pacioli, *Summa de Arithmetica, Geometria, Proportioni, et Proportionalita*, 1494. P. Crivelli, *An Original Translation of the Treatise on Double Entry Bookkeeping by Frater Lucas Pacioli*, London: Institute of Bookkeepers, 1924.

4. Jeff A. Schnepper, *The Professional Handbook of Business Valuation*, Reading, MA: Addison-Wesley, 1982, p. Ap16–22. This section includes a copy of Internal Revenue Service Revenue Ruling 59–60.

CHAPTER 2

Why Do a Valuation?

THE IMPORTANCE OF VALUATION

Valuations can serve many purposes—to establish a price, to help increase value, to attract capital, to aid in estate planning, and to meet governmental requirements. With a broad variety of business and legal situations triggering the need to know the value of a business—strategic partnerships, merger or acquisition of a business, estate planning, eminent domain issues, marital disputes, employee stock ownership plans (ESOPs), and joint ventures—it is important to have a professional estimate the value of a business and to have periodic valuation updates. From the perspective of a valuator, a business owner, or an interested financial party, a valuation provides a useful baseline to establish a price for a business or to help increase a company's value and attract capital.

Planning for estate, gift, and other taxes is demanding and complicated, and a professional valuation is one of the most important tools to assist a specialist in these areas. Because tragedy can strike without warning, it is important to estimate the value of a business in advance so that a business owner's family can be prepared to deal with third parties, such as partners, shareholders, and governmental authorities like the IRS. Otherwise, family members may be left at a disadvantage without the same knowledge and wisdom as the business owner. The war stories surrounding estate taxes abound; some examples are presented later in this chapter.

In certain situations, the government steps in and mandates a business valuation. For marital dissolutions, the establishment and management of employee stock ownership plans (ESOPs), eminent domain issues, minority shareholder actions, election of S corporation status, corporate divorce, and estate taxes, governmental regulations are the driving forces behind the standard of value.

Two other broad factors also create the need for valuations. First, as business owners try to sell a business, there is no efficient market to help buyers and sellers connect; thus, there is no analog for small companies to the role that major stock exchanges play for public companies. Second, many business owners need an exit strategy to obtain value from their companies when they desire to sell.

The Lack of an Efficient Market

Despite the commonly held belief that markets are efficient, an efficient market does not exist for private businesses and for certain fractional equity interests. Without a private business analog to the New York Stock Exchange or NASDAQ, there is no place to buy and sell private businesses in whole or in part, aside from a business brokerage community that is small in scope. As a result, it is very difficult to determine what a private business is worth in the marketplace, and because of the lack of an efficient market, there is a critical need for business valuation services.

Real Estate—An Intermediate Stage Between Efficient and Inefficient Markets

Between the relatively efficient markets for stocks, bonds, and commodities and the inefficient market for private business equity interests, there lies a market with a different profile—the real estate market. Our viewpoint comes from experience in developing, purchasing, and selling real estate and from consulting on numerous real estate transactions. Our roles have included salesman, accountant, tax adviser, financial adviser, and principal.

Professionals in the real estate market have artfully blended marketing strategy, emotion, and analytical skill to create a quasi-efficient marketplace. The real estate brokerage community deserves most of the credit for having created and provided the fuel for the real estate market. It is the brokerage community which provides the liquidity for most of us who wish to buy or sell in a controlled environment. For instance, the real estate community made home ownership such an emotional experience that it has become linked to a sociological phenomenon—"The American Dream"—that appears to withstand severe recessions and strong negative factors such as the 1986 Tax Reform Act and the late 1980s savings and loan crisis.

Why, then, has this talented group of professionals failed to create a similar market for closely held businesses or partial equity interests in real estate? The reasons, we believe, are that the market for these interests is unstable and riddled with risk, that the market cannot be controlled by external influences, and that the market has little liquidity unless there is a primary motivation specific to the situation at hand. Overall, real estate is an amazingly resilient business; however, real estate professionals have failed to create a similar market for private business and fractional equity interests.

The Role of Entrepreneurs and Inefficient Markets

There is another reason such a market has not materialized. There is an influence so powerful and vibrant that it has a greater power than the efforts of any group trying to master it. That influence is the entrepreneur, whose unpredictability and variation in style make it a challenge to place an efficient market value on a privately held business.

The entrepreneurial concept is most likely the part of the American Dream that is so difficult for other nations to emulate. In fact, the entrepreneur is a natural resource that the United States, with its unparalleled freedom and educational system, nurtures so well. In our society, this character proliferates but is not fully understood. It manifests itself in government, religion, science, and the arts, but its primary spawning ground is private business.

This influence of the entrepreneur drives the inefficient marketplace. It is likely to remain for one reason—its independent strengths are greater than any whole. It needs to be recognized and respected for what it is: the forum for invention, economic growth, improved international competitiveness for American businesses, and improved living standards for American citizens.

The lack of an efficient marketplace for partial real estate interests is similar to the lack of an efficient marketplace for private businesses that American entrepreneurs confront. Because of the amazing diversity of objectives and styles of entrepreneurs, it is difficult to place efficient market values easily on privately held businesses.

Entrepreneurs who make a conscious decision to keep their businesses private are often trying to avoid the influences and second-guessing from external parties. The entrepreneur who owns the majority of the company retains control and limits the influence of a minority owner or owners.

Unlike complete interests in real estate, for which brokers create the market, there are few market makers for private companies and fractional interests. The sale of a small business is not like listing a house whose value is influenced by what the market will bear; instead, entrepreneurs have a large impact on value by leaving their imprint on the company, and entrepreneurs negotiate for the most part over how to buy and sell these types of businesses. There are no real referees, and the contestants control the outcome.

Who, then, are the largest winners in these negotiations? Those entrepreneurial businesses with *organizational capital*[1] consisting of a quality workforce, a proprietary interest in their product or service, a source of equity, organized systems, protected distribution, good prospects for earnings and returns on investment, and solid business ethics are the ones that will command the highest premiums. On the other hand, those businesses which are mediocre and unethical will be worth far less, if marketable at all. The liquidity of the inefficient marketplace is driven by the elements of this complex formula for success. Thus, because of the lack of an efficient market, there is a critical need for business valuation services. The concept of organizational capital is discussed in more detail later in the chapter.

The Exit Strategy

In addition to the lack of an efficient market for private businesses, there is another reason for ensuring that valuations are performed: The need for an exit strategy for the owners of private businesses. If a potential buyer is able to invest fewer dollars on his or her own and reasonably duplicate the seller's business, then the buyer would generally be better off to start a new business than buy an existing one. So, the business owner needs a strategy to be able to obtain value from the company when he or she desires to sell.

This scenario can be frustrating for the seller, because he or she has a lot of pride in the business. Unless the seller has established a proprietary interest in the overall business system, it's not likely that an informed purchaser will pay a substantial premium; however, for the seller who has positioned the business properly, the rewards can be substantial.

Consider the situation when a key employee of a company approaches management with the question: "What is my future and how can I get a piece of the equity?" The two owners, a father and his son, look at each other. They want to keep this person; if she were to leave, her departure would have a substantial cost to the company in dollars and in morale.

It is a familiar scenario. What are the owners to do? First, they will need to know the value of the business if they intend to share ownership with the employee or to sell the company. In fact, just about any reasonable option the owners face will involve the need to know the value. In general, this pair of owners more than likely ignored a vital issue—how to exit the company successfully and profitably. The employee's request reminded the two of the need to develop an exit strategy.

An integral part of exit strategy planning is knowing the value of the business. With a well-crafted buy/sell agreement and a method to determine a reasonable estimate of value, the ownership transition should become easier for all parties concerned. Perhaps the solution to the father-and-son team's dilemma is to consider an employee stock ownership plan (ESOP). Again, this requires current and ongoing valuations of the business.

The common theme here is obvious. In contrast to shareholders in publicly traded companies who can find valuations of their shares on a daily basis, owners of interests in privately held companies have many fewer opportunities to learn or determine market valuations of their interests. No matter which direction business owners pursue, they should know the value of their current business interests and get periodic updates. If the owners choose not to develop a strategy, then they are leaving their future to chance.

By creating a solid exit plan, business owners can maximize their return on investment. Look at this simple hypothetical example. Through creative tax planning in the past, a company's owners have been able to adjust income legally to reduce the annual taxable income of the corporation. If the owners took a different approach and reported an extra $50,000 per year of earnings, they would have to pay more corporate income taxes, but they would increase their company's earnings and liquidity and increase the equity in the company. Given a price or value multiple of five times pretax earnings, they would increase the value of the company by $250,000. That's no small change and well worth the investment. In addition, there are the bonuses of a potentially lower tax on capital gains, rather than the tax on the personal income that would have be paid on the owner's compensation, lower payroll taxes, and added working capital.

It must be said, as well, that along with almost any exit strategy comes the need to do some housecleaning—cleaning up the balance sheet and income statement. A little planning now can mean a big payoff in the future. Conversely, those business owners who maximize their compensation each year to avoid paying corporate income taxes are in general increasing their current standard of living while jeopardizing their retirement and the value of perhaps their largest personal asset.

The rest of this chapter discusses in more depth the general purposes of business valuation. The topics in the next section are oriented to reasons for valuations in the near term. Later in the chapter, the reasons for valuations focus on ways to increase the value of a company and raise capital for the future.

ESTABLISHING A PRICE

When buy/sell agreements, ownership issues, and insurance claims are at hand, an up-to-date valuation can reduce doubt about the value of the business and may provide protection for partners, shareholders, and spouses who want to ensure that their interests are fairly represented. Unfortunately, the need for the types of valuations in this section often arise out of unpleasant circumstances: death, divorce, or business dissolution.

Ownership Issues

When it comes time to sell a business, it is particularly helpful to have an independent valuation performed to satisfy everyone's interests before closing the deal. Consider a hypothetical situation in which the owner of a candy manufacturing company with minority shareholders is considering a merger with Jane Doe's Delectable Foods. The owner sets a value for the stock and a compensation/retirement package to be attained. In many states, minority shareholders have the right to file a dissenting shareholder action to protest a value that they suspect is unfair. In addition, an astute shareholder in a minority position should demand an independent valuation from a disinterested consultant or specialist prior to consenting to a merger. In these types of situations, a valuation furnishes all interested parties with an independent estimate of the value of the business.

Buy/Sell Agreements

Naturally, for anything to be bought or sold, it has to have a price, and often squabbling over that price can make or break a potential deal. A buy/sell agreement sets the price for a particular equity interest under specific circumstances. A disinterested opinion should help buyers better understand what their dollars are purchasing. In addition, the valuation should be regularly updated to reflect the estimated value of a business as it changes.

Partners, shareholders, spouses, and other heirs may have an interest in knowing the value of a business. A potential problem arises when the valuation is not updated after it has been completed. For a real-life example, consider a co-owner/partner who died prematurely, leaving a retail business whose value had been set 19 years earlier. To the widow's dismay, her deceased husband's partner held firm to the outdated value of the business and secured a windfall by adhering to the 19-year-old document. The decedent's heirs lost hundreds of thousands of dollars. Good professional advice and a regular update of the value might have prevented this unfortunate circumstance for the widow.

Another example to consider is the man who, in the 1970s, retired and sold his $1 million manufacturing business to his two children. When his son died without warning 15 years later, the daughter was required to pay her brother's widow and children for their share of the business. Unfortunately, a buy/sell value on the business had been established 15 years earlier, and the buy/sell agreement did not provide for an updated valuation. Thus, the brother's wife and family received millions of dollars less than anticipated—a very painful lesson for the widow and her children resulting from the business owner's failure to keep the value of his business current.

Insurance Claims

A current valuation is also an important first step in obtaining the right amount of insurance coverage and in facilitating maximum insurance claims coverage. For instance, a fire can devastate a software firm and can cause not only an interruption of business, but ultimately bankruptcy from the loss of competitive momentum. An insurance company may refuse to pay what the software firm claims its business is worth. Without an independent valuation and well-kept records backed by an audit trail, an insurance company and an after-the-fact valuation analyst will have little information to rely on. Both an insurance company and a valuator need records representing the true financial position and results of operations for a business in order to deliver a claim that is merited. Not knowing the value of a business is an internal control weakness that could lead to a loss of assets through undervaluation.[2]

Furthermore, a reasonably current business valuation along with reviewed or audited financial statements can help ensure adequate insurance coverage. It is a waste of resources to carry $2.5 million of insurance for a business that is worth only $750,000, or, in reverse, it is unwise to insure a $2.5 million business for only $750,000. Sometimes, purchasers of insurance take a "leap of faith" by relying on an inappropriate rule of thumb, such as a gross multiple of earnings for the target industry. By knowing the proper amount of coverage for business interruption insurance and total loss from a catastrophic event, a company can buy the insurance coverage that it needs.

INCREASING VALUE AND RAISING NECESSARY CAPITAL

A valuation can paint a picture of the worth of a business and can provide critical analysis for a business seeking financing or a new partner through a joint venture, a strategic partnership, a merger or an acquisition, or the sale of the business. In addition to the benefits of value planning and management or an emerging growth value analysis, a valuation can position a business strategically. The rest of this section presents a set of examples that illustrate situations of increasing a company's value and attracting capital.

Value Planning and Management

First, consider an individual who has owned a distribution business for five years and is investigating ways to position the company for a sale, a merger, or a partnership, and who requires an appropriate strategy. A full-scope valuation may be premature, because the company has not yet reached its full potential. A valuation consultant, as the respected adviser to the business, can assist in positioning the business strategically to enhance value. This ongoing process, known as managing the value of the business entity, is unfamiliar to most people (see Chapter 5).

Emerging Growth Value Analysis

Consider another situation in which an owner wants to build up her growing office supply business and then have it be acquired. Periodic valuations can demonstrate the ongoing growth of the business to potential investors, buyers, strategic partners, and lenders. A consistent pattern of documented valuations indicates that the owner is a savvy businessperson who stays on top of material business issues.

Strategic Partnerships

A three-office real estate brokerage firm survived the real estate crash of the early 1990s but realizes that in order to grow, it must expand its resources. The owners have explored the possibility of forming an alliance with a national firm to take advantage of its substantial geographical range and leveraged resources. Both parties will need to know what value the three-office brokerage will contribute to this strategic alliance.

A detailed analysis of the brokerage's business, industry, and competition by an independent valuator will add a fresh perspective for the smaller firm and perhaps even for the larger concern. A full written valuation report with footnotes, exhibits, and bibliography can serve as an eye-opener in the present and an excellent reference source in the future.

Joint Ventures

Another possibility is that both a business owner and his cousin each own successful auto parts stores and figure it may be beneficial to expand by jointly opening a third store in a nearby community. As with buying or selling any business, there should be an agreed-upon value in writing to make an informed decision and protect everyone's best interests.

Sale of a Business

Do you notice from time to time that business owners, nearing retirement, instead of closing down a second-generation family business, want to pass it along to the third generation? After all, it has been in the family for over 50 years and has much in the way of organizational capital. The owners would like to keep it in the family, but the child who would logically assume control of the business has no interest in it.

A valuation should place a realistic measure of worth on the company and help all concerned determine a reasonable asking price. Investors, shareholders, and family members will have a vested interest in the establishment of a reasonably estimated price for the business. A professionally estimated price should minimize the negotiation over value and make the process easier for everyone.

Mergers and Acquisitions

A doctor wants to merge her health care practice with a thriving local clinic. Placing a value on the two businesses puts all the players—investors, shareholders, and even employees—on a level playing field and ensures that all parties receive appropriate value for their business interests. Not only does a valuation determine a price for the acquiring or merging of companies, but it also provides assurance that the business owner and others followed due diligence in representing a company's fair market value. This action may reduce litigation risk.

Private Funding or Financing

A business owner wants to add a new piece of sophisticated technical equipment to his food processing business but needs a loan or lease for hundreds of thousands of dollars. Here is a perfect chance for a valuator to add value. Left to their own devices and without a current valuation of the business, lenders will make their own assumptions about the value of the company through behind-the-scenes, internal analysis balanced by little or no hands-on experience. Parts of the value of the company may never be appreciated by members of the loan committee, who may have little understanding of the business.

It is even possible that the bank's valuation could later end up in court through the discovery process or in the hands of the IRS via subpoena. It could cost a great deal of money to prove that the bank analyst was incorrect in the assumptions made or in the application of valuation methodology.

ESTATE PLANNING

When issues of gift giving and estate planning arise, the short-term cost of a valuation can provide long-term benefits by clarifying intricate situations and by furnishing peace of mind. Appropriate wealth planning to deal with matters intelligently before an owner's death will save an owner's loved ones time, worry, and money. In addition, if an owner chooses to take a tax deduction for a charitable gift of a business interest, a valuation is mandatory and a valuator (a "qualified appraiser") must attest to it. (See IRS Form 8283 and Reg.1.170A–13 (c)(3)(B).)[3]

Gift and Estate Planning

Consider the following situation: A company has prospered in a booming economy, so an owner decides to give a generous gift of ownership to his three grandchildren. Since the gift tax is based on the value of the assets at the time of the gift, the value has to be determined. In addition, when someone dies, a posthumous valuation of the closely held business to determine the estate tax is almost inevitable. Knowing the value of a business can reduce controversy at the time of death and can also provide an effective planning tool when the business is a substantial part of the estate.

There is a high probability of an IRS audit when the estate's tax return includes the value of even a fairly modest private, closely held business, especially if a valuation has not been performed or if appropriate references to the valuation report in the tax returns have been omitted. What is considered "modest" is up for grabs. Many professionals in the area of valuation believe that an estate with a value between $1 million and $5 million has a 50 percent chance of audit. If it's over $5 million, the probability of being audited is probably over 90 percent. The IRS currently reviews all gift and estate tax returns by hand and is looking for specific items for audit. Business valuations with adjustments for economic conditions, control, and marketability are at the top of this review list. It is well worth the trouble to do a valuation right the first time.

If a business owner plans to transfer business ownership to family members, the transaction should be at the estimated fair market value. The IRS is particularly diligent about auditing to ensure a fair market value, since family members may have an incentive to transfer equity interests below fair market value, causing a material transfer of wealth with less tax liability than should have been paid.

Overall, the best advice is to determine the estimated fair market value before preparing either a gift or estate tax return. This value should pass two tests: It should be quantifiable, and it should be supported by relevant evidence.

Charitable Giving

As a country, America relies extensively on the generosity of financially successful individuals to help fund many of the social services and cultural activities that governments pay for directly in other countries. As people contemplate the end of their lives, the theme of returning something to the community, especially for those people who benefited from the generosity of others, can become important. Thus, issues of charitable giving often accompany gift and estate planning.

An up-to-date valuation provides a business owner with a current estimate of his or her wealth, even if charitable giving is not associated directly with estate planning. By incorporating an estimate of business value into an assessment of total wealth, an individual can develop a better understanding of how charitable giving may affect his or her total assets and taxable estate.

VALUATIONS MANDATED BY GOVERNMENT

In addition to estate and gift tax matters, there are other circumstances when government authorities require valuations. For eminent domain, a marital divorce, the election of S corporation status, or corporate dissolution or dissenting shareholder action, a business owner should choose to invest the time and money for a thorough valuation. For employee stock ownership plans (ESOPs), federal law mandates that any ESOP have an initial and timely independent valuation as well as annual updates.

Eminent Domain

Consider a popular café, gift shop, and motel complex adjacent to an interstate highway. The government decides to expand the highway to 10 lanes, exercising its power of eminent domain to take the property. We can almost imagine all the trucks racing through the café's kitchen into the motel garden. The state, of course, is required to pay compensation for what the business is worth. But how much is that?

This situation presents a complex set of circumstances. First, there is the issue of the value of the real estate, which will most likely be determined by a real estate appraiser. Second, there is the issue of the going-concern value of the business that is to be closed. Opinion differs, however, as to whether the real estate is merely a functional element of the going concern or the foundation of value. To the extent the real estate does not have a higher and better use or that it is a single-purpose facility, it is merely a functional element of the business. A single-purpose facility and the physical assets are certainly material to the generation of revenue. However, physical assets may still need to be appraised separately from the intangible ones when they are material to the outcome of an estimate of value.

What if the real estate is under lease? In this situation, the landowner will be involved and will receive a portion of the state's eminent domain compensation. Here is another reason to engage a real estate appraiser. Depending on the terms of the lease, the business seller may have an off-balance-sheet asset in the form of a favorable lease.

Employee Stock Ownership Plan (ESOP)

ESOPs facilitate and encourage ownership of equity interests in companies by their employees. To correct a common misperception, employees do not directly own shares in their company; a trust, established for the benefit of employees, owns the shares on behalf of the employees who qualify as owners. Although ESOPs are set up for a variety of corporate financial purposes, the legislative intent for ESOPs was to provide retirement benefits for a company's employees.

A key provision of the Economic Recovery Tax Act of 1981 permitted ESOPs to deduct all the interest costs associated with purchases of stock in the company for which the employees work. Please be advised that Congress could change the deductibility at a future date. Both the U.S. Department of Labor and the IRS, under provisions of ERISA (Employee Retirement Income Securities Act of 1974), require an initial valuation during the formation of an ESOP and periodic valuation updates during the existence of the plan. Also, the Tax Reform Act of 1986 mandates that ESOP stock be appraised annually by a qualified independent valuator; some ESOPs have their stock appraisals updated as often as every quarter or every month. A valuation is also necessary whenever there is a transaction with a controlling stockholder or the company itself or when the ESOP sells its stock position.[4]

There is a debate as to whether a company's certified public accountant has a conflict of interest by performing the audit, other consulting services for the client, and the valuation of the shares of stock for the ESOP. When an independent business valuation firm values the company's shares for the ESOP, it may reduce the litigation risk for the company, since there is clearly no conflict of interest. As the adviser to the company, a valuator should seek advice in writing about potential conflicts of interest from the loss prevention department of his or her liability insurance carrier and/or from legal counsel as needed.

Marital Dissolution

Consider a situation in which a 20-year marriage has just come to an end, and state statute, common law, or local family law court rules require that an independent valuation of the business in written report form be in the hands of opposing counsel 30 days before trial. The court is generally interested in protecting the out-spouse[5] and any children, who are income and estate beneficiaries.

The conflict-of-interest issue must be considered in this situation as well as in the ESOP situation. The valuator has an obligation to both the spouse who is not involved in the business and to the children to remain objective and independent with an estimate of value. Advocacy is permissible in certain situations if the interested parties are made aware of the advocacy position and acknowledge the conflict; however, this type of situation requires a valuator to remain committed to his or her objectivity and integrity. If the valuator has doubts, he or she should withdraw and recommend a colleague who will perform a good job for the client.

In some cases, judges may set the value of the business equal to the other assets of the marital estate even though value of the business may differ substantially from the value of other assets (e.g., the family home, stock holdings, cash). In the long run, this judicial choice can cost the estate a significant amount of money, even as the in-spouse or out-spouse earnestly tries to establish the right value. For example, if the value of the business is inflated by the court and there is a shareholder dispute at a later date, this inflated value will most likely surface during discovery, and it could actually serve to have a negative impact on the business and the in-spouse. Where, then, will the dollars come from to pay child support and alimony? Usually, this type of result is not contemplated at the outset by the court.

Election of S Corporation Status

The value of assets at the date of election to convert from a C corpo-ration to an S corporation is a serious concern because of the built-in gains rule. A C corporation is the conventional type of corporation with an unlimited number of shareholders and with taxes assessed at the corporate level and on shareholder dividends. An S corpora-tion is a "small business corporation with a statutorily limited num-ber of shareholders, which has elected to have its taxable income taxed to its shareholders at regular income tax rates."[6] S corporations are limited to 35 shareholders at the time of this writing.

When an S election is made, the corporate taxpayer is com-mitted to paying a tax on that portion of gain recognized on the disposition of any asset, where appreciation existed prior to the S election date, in accordance with the C rules for taxation of those assets for 10 years after the election. The valuator and the tax coun-sel should make sure that this potentially substantial exposure to tax liability is taken into consideration at the time of valuation.

The way to ensure some peace of mind is to have a valuation performed as of the election date. This valuation should establish the value of goodwill and other intangible assets that should be disclosed and documented with the election. Failure to arrive at an independent valuation as of this date places the taxpayer at risk to tax exposure. If there are other shareholders, management may not have fulfilled its fiduciary responsibility if it chooses to forgo an independent valuation.

Corporate Dissolution

If a minority shareholder decides to file for a corporate dissolution and sell his or her shares, but the other shareholders want to con-tinue running the company, certain state governments require a val-uation of the business. Many state statutes outline specific require-ments for determining how the business is valued.

COMPLEXITIES OF VALUATION

A good valuation builds on the raw data available to analyze a business and supplements the numbers with an appreciation of the less tangible issues that make a business tick. The phrase *organiza-tional capital* embodies many of these less quantitative measures. In addition, different standards of value are used depending on the purposes of a valuation.

Organizational Capital

Organizational capital, which includes intangible assets and goodwill, creates added value above and beyond the value of tangible assets. Organizational capital creates a situation in which the value of the assets as part of an ongoing organization exceeds the value of the assets in isolation. The added value accrues directly to the owners of the business. Indirect benefits accrue to the customers, suppliers, employees, and community neighbors that interact with the business. Key components of organizational capital include:

- Long-term relationships among managers and employees that enable them to work together effectively and efficiently. For example, over the years, people develop the ability to communicate intuitively and learn how to take on tasks without lengthy instructions.
- The reputation of a company with its customers and suppliers. Reputation, including brand names, makes it easier to sell products and negotiate terms. For instance, people pay a premium for Campbell's Soup because the brand name has come to signify quality.
- The opportunities for a company to realize profitable investments that grow out of the specialized skills of its managers and employees and their relationships with customers and suppliers. These opportunities, sometimes referred to as investment options or growth options, can come to account for a significant portion of a company's revenues over time.[7]

Valuation Terminology

Valuation experts use several pieces of terminology to express different types of value: intrinsic value, investment value, fair market value, and fair value. Valuators and users of valuations should be aware that courts in different states, building on specific cases in each state, may use definitions and terminology that vary from state to state. Courts in California, Texas, Florida, New York, and Illinois, in conjunction with the Federal Tax Court and the IRS, have been at the forefront of developing new concepts and opinions in business valuation. In general, the terminology described below is widely accepted in the United States. In any valuation, it is important to state the purpose of the valuation and the definition of value being used. This type of clarity can reduce confusion when the valuation is reviewed at a later date, or if the valuation is read or challenged by an outside party.

Intrinsic value is the amount an investor considers, on the basis of an evaluation of available facts, to be the true or real worth of an item, usually an equity security. Intrinsic value is the value that would become the market value when other investors reach the same conclusions.[8]

The *investment value* of a business is relevant to a specific investor. It can and will differ among individual investors, because each person or business entity has different expectations regarding the expected earnings and riskiness of the business.

Fair market value refers to the price to which a willing seller and a willing buyer will hypothetically agree, if both parties have access to full information about the business, and neither party is compelled to act. Valuators and Internal Revenue Service Revenue Ruling 59–60[9] place substantial weight on actual market transactions between willing sellers and buyers (often referred to as compelling evidence). This negotiated result assumes, of course, that all parties were aware of all the relevant facts underlying the transaction and that neither participant was forced to accept the terms. Fair market value is the term used for gift and estate tax valuations.

Fair value[10] refers, like fair market value, to the price that would be agreed to between well informed buyers and sellers. An important difference is that there is typically no discount for lack of control under a fair value valuation. This term is typically used in valuations involving minority shareholder disputes and corporate divorce and dissolution.

Marital value is a term used with increasing frequency in valuations associated with marital divorce. Although not yet a well-developed concept, it concerns the value in a business that involves an in-spouse and an out-spouse.[11] Definitions can vary from state to state, so it is imperative to review court decisions, case law, and state statutes in the specific state in which the valuation is to occur.

Two other frequently used terms, *going-concern value* and *liquidation value*, focus on the assumptions that underlie the definitions of value above. Going-concern value means that the business is being valued under the assumption that it will continue to operate on a regular basis in the future. Liquidation value means the value of a business if it were broken apart and the business assets were sold individually.

Underestimates and Overestimates of Value

A valuator has the responsibility to present a sophisticated estimate of value of the business through the science and art of valuation. The analysis will often lead to an estimate of value that differs substantially from what an overly optimistic seller desires to achieve. An independent valuation can place a value on a business that can be quantified and estimated with a reasonable degree of certainty, provided all players are using the same valuation assumptions and methodology. The result should enable the parties involved to make a wise investment decision and move on to other issues without spending excessive time arguing over price. Negotiating strategy can be improved by being ready and by having the best estimate of value, instead of wishful thinking.

In addition, if a business is overvalued, the owner may lose valuable time and perhaps miss a qualified buyer who believes the company is too expensive and pursues other opportunities. Overreaching—setting an extreme asking price—can easily have this effect. Remember, the real buyer will probably be one of the first to surface and is generally sophisticated enough to evaluate the risk of wasting time negotiating with someone who is not being realistic about the price of the company.

Undervaluing a business is just as troublesome. If a business is undervalued because of a lack of awareness of trends in the market or an alternative method of valuation, such as investment value, the business may sell very quickly and never give the owners or their estates the chance to achieve the best price.

Extremes of undervaluation or overvaluation often arise when the seller or buyer relies on hearsay that grows out of industry rules of thumb. Rules of thumb often get transmitted imprecisely between friends who have lunch twice a month or from the person in the adjacent seat at the last industry conference. People mean well by passing on what is assumed to be reliable information about a multiple of earnings from a best friend's cousin. However, do they mean earnings from operations, earnings before tax, earnings after tax, adjusted earnings, or unadjusted earnings? Is it before or after depreciation? Was the price paid in cash, or was part of the price contingent upon meeting future sales and profit goals?

Most businesspeople are familiar with the price-to-earnings (P/E) ratio from publicly traded companies. This valuation ratio, if properly applied, can be used to value a closely held company. However, one cannot simply blindly apply a median P/E ratio from publicly traded companies to a closely held company's earnings to arrive at the company's value. For example, for eating places (SIC Code 5812) the median P/E ratio is 19.59, but the 25th percentile P/E ratio is 12.59, and the 75th percentile is P/E ratio is 59.35.[12] This is a wide valuation range. Furthermore, 50 percent of the companies had a P/E ratio outside this range (25 percent had a P/E ratio < 12.5 and 25 percent had a P/E ratio > 59.35). It takes a trained and experienced valuation analyst to determine where the subject company lies within this range.

Consider the case of an emerging technology company. The company had a clear position in its industry and had spent millions of dollars in research and development to emerge as the leader in its niche. The consultant working on the project valued the company at approximately $5 million. From experience, legal counsel recognized that this value appeared to be low for a company with its type of niche profile.

Unaware of the value determined by the consultant and of the expectations of the client, a limited-scope[13] valuation by a professional valuation firm produced a range of values for the company. The engagement results were quite gratifying for the client; research on the industry and competitive companies, along with the subject's business study and analysis, confirmed much of management's thinking.

The low end of the range of values from the valuator turned out to be much higher than the consultant's $5 million. It turned out that the other consultant may have been lowballing the value of the company to make a quick sale and earn a commission or may have neglected to consider many of the complex issues associated with the company, its industry, and the competition. The end result was that the business owner ended up selling his business for a price within the range of values given by the independent valuation firm, a price that was more than double the $5 million recommended by the original consultant. One lesson to be learned from this example is that clients should generally engage disinterested, independent valuation professionals who work on an hourly basis and who do not stand to gain from a particular valuation estimate. If this business owner had not done so, he may have left literally millions of dollars on the table.

SUMMARY

As this chapter has shown, valuations are needed for many reasons. In addition to the two broad rationales (the lack of an efficient market for private companies and the need for owners of private companies to have an exit strategy), such varied business endeavors as creating strategic partnerships, merging or acquiring a business, forming an estate plan, and setting up an ESOP all demand valuations. These and other scenarios all benefit from a valuation as a baseline to help establish value. Once the value of the business has been estimated, the owners and the shareholders can move ahead confidently with their plans, knowing that they have a thorough valuation in hand. Chapters 3 and 4 will discuss in more detail the components of business valuations and the process underlying reliable and successful valuations.

NOTES

1. Bradford Cornell, *Corporate Valuation: Tools for Effective Appraisal and Decision Making*, Burr Ridge, IL: Irwin, 1993, pp. 23–24.
2. As a basic internal control, businesses should keep a backup set of records off premises in a safe place. This warning is rarely heeded, but records storage companies exist just for this purpose. (See "Business Records Storage and Management" in the Yellow Pages.) A valuator should document this advice in a letter to the client.
3. Internal Revenue Service Form 8283—Noncash Charitable Contributions. Income Tax Regulations, Chicago: CCH Inc., 1995. Reg.1.170A–13 (c)(3)(B). For the definition of a qualified appraiser, see Reg.1.170A–13(c)(5).
4. ESOP Association, *Valuing ESOP Shares*, 2nd ed. Washington, DC: ESOP Association, 1989, p. 8.
5. The in-spouse is the spouse operating the business, while the out-spouse is on the outside looking in. An out-spouse has little or nothing to do with the day-to-day operations of the business.
6. Henry Campbell Black, *Black's Law Dictionary*, 6th ed., St. Paul, MN: West Publishing Company, 1990, p. 342. Books like Michael Diamond and Julie L. Williams, *How to Incorporate*, New York, 2nd ed., Wiley, 1993, have more details about the rules surrounding the election of S corporation status.

7. Bradford Cornell, *Corporate Valuation: Tools for Effective Appraisal and Decision Making*, Burr Ridge, IL: Irwin, 1993, pp. 23–24.

8. Shannon P. Pratt, *Valuing Small Businesses and Professional Practices*, Homewood, IL: Irwin, 1986, p. 14.

9. Internal Revenue Service Revenue Ruling 59–60, Section 4.01(g)(h), 4.02(g)(h).

10. The following quotation is from an article by James Schilt called "Appraisal Under Corporations Code Section 2000" from the Summer 1985 *Business Law News:* "Section 2000 of the California Corporations Code calls for three court-appointed appraisers to determine the fair value of a corporation so a dissolution may be avoided by purchase of a plaintiff's shares. From an appraiser's standpoint, the wording of Section 2000 is disconcerting, as it calls for a valuation that 'shall be determined on the basis of the liquidation value but taking into account the possibility, if any, of sale of the entire business as a going concern in a liquidation.'" Read the entire article for further clarification.

11. Donald A. Glenn, *Advanced Family Law Topics*, California CPA Education Foundation Continuing Professional Education, Redwood City, CA: 1995, Chapter 3, p. 4.

12. *Cost of Capital Quarterly*, 1995 Yearbook, Chicago: Ibbotson Associates, located in Fishman et al., *Guide to Business Valuations*, Exhibit 5–12.

13. A proprietary term of ValueNomics®.

The Components of a Business Valuation

This chapter describes the general building blocks that valuators use and the principles that tend to guide current business valuations. Many of the rulings and regulations affecting valuation have been promulgated by the U.S. Treasury Department's Internal Revenue Service. The most noteworthy regulation, Internal Revenue Service Revenue Ruling 59–60, states that valuators should pay close attention to the following issues when valuing a business:

(a) The nature of the business and the history of the enterprise from its inception.

(b) The general economic outlook and the condition and outlook of the specific industry.

(c) The book value of the stock and the financial condition of the business.

(d) The earning capacity of the company.

(e) The dividend-paying capacity.

(f) Whether or not the enterprise has goodwill or other intangible value.

(g) Sales of the stock and the size of the block of stock to be valued.

(h) The market price of stocks of corporations engaged in the same or similar line of business having their stocks actively traded in a free and open market, either on an exchange or over the counter.[1]

A business valuation is based on factual information—a set of internal and external factors derived from a company's financial statements, performance, operations, products, and services, along with the influences of industry competition, government, and the economy. Once this information has been gathered, it is up to the valuator to use his or her education, training, experience, and professional judgment to arrive at an estimate of value.

The principal internal factors are historical performance; financial strength; profitability/earnings and cash flow; company management, structure, and ownership; size and condition of operations; business systems; protection of products and/or services; operations; forecast/projection/budget; and a written business plan.

The principal external factors are competition at local, regional, national, and international levels; size relative to similar operations; the industry; the environmental impact of the industry; government intervention; and economic conditions.

INTERNAL FACTORS

Historical Performance

The past and future earnings power of a business is often the single most significant factor in the valuation of a business. The historical performance of a business and its future prospects depend on the results of operations, the company's financial position, and its cashflow. This set of factors profiles how well a company has been performing and where it may be headed.

Detailed, concise financial statements are a critical component in determining the worth of a company and facilitating the tasks of a valuator. In fact, the quality of a company's financial records strongly influences how much work a valuation will demand. Audited financial statements, as described below, are especially useful. IRS Revenue Ruling 59–60 recommends that a business retain at least five years of financial information and tax returns with supporting ledgers and documents. Of course, financial records are only one source of information about a company, and historical financials should not dictate value in isolation from other factors.

If management does not maintain thorough and accurate records, the results of the valuation may be based on outdated, incorrect, or even fraudulent information. The valuator will be handicapped (and will have more work to do) when charged with the responsibility of adjusting historical accounting for transactions at the valuation date in order to present a reasonably accurate picture of the economic and financial position of the company. These adjusted financial statements are commonly referred to as "normalized" financial statements. (See the sidebar later in this chapter for more detail about adjusting or normalizing financial statements.)

Historical data are also crucial in identifying trends about how well the company will do in the future. How management has operated the company in the past suggests future behavior and management quality. One point to keep in mind is that a well-informed buyer will question management's integrity if it appears that the company was cheating the government. If a company is taking overly generous deductions or using overly aggressive tax policies, it is likely to be equally dishonest with potential buyers.

An excellent example is the valuation in a minority shareholder buyout that uncovered management improprieties on certain tax deductions. In the course of business in the 1980s, the owner of this business elected to take excessive deductions. The majority shareholder was seriously compromised and forced to settle immediately with the minority shareholder.

Although statisticians suggest that, in general, more data lead to more reliable results, in some cases historical performance may not be a strong indicator of the health of a company. For example, for an emerging company with several years of operating losses, detailed financial statements may be of some help, but they will not necessarily control the estimate of value. It may be more informative to know that the company has a proprietary interest in a technology on which it has expended substantial research and development funds and that the revenue from this effort has yet to materialize. In this instance, the prospects for the future, and not historical data, will control the valuation.

Of the three types of financial statements prepared by certified public accountants—audited, reviewed, and compiled—that offer an historical perspective on a business, audited statements represent the highest standard of reliability to a valuator, whereas compiled statements are generally the least reliable. An audit from a qualified CPA enables the valuator to spend less time on due diligence, thereby providing a less expensive valuation. Audited and reviewed financial statements can also add value for the company. They signal that company management is astute in financial matters and recognizes the value added of having an audit or a review performed.

One representative example of the value of audited or reviewed statements is the analysis and report on internal controls that is conducted as part of the process. Less extensive financial statements, such as compiled or internal statements, do not generally include this type of review. This report and other parts of an audit or a review underlie the strength of the financial statements as the highest level of assurance to an outside user that assets are safeguarded and that results of operations are reasonably stated in accordance with Generally Accepted Accounting Principles.[2] This step alone may add value to the company.

Although the audit or review process is not meant to detect fraud, internal controls, if fully operational, will serve to deter some fraudulent and unethical behavior. Of course, fraud can still occur even if the company has a good system of internal controls; collusion and criminal intent are powerful forces, and even the best systems of internal controls are sometimes circumvented.

Another example of the value of an audit or a review is a legal representation letter obtained by the CPA that explains the contingent liabilities facing a company. When a company presents compiled or internally prepared statements, they probably will not include valuable information on contingent liabilities. A valuator could therefore be forced to increase the scope of the engagement to ensure that there are no material, off-balance-sheet liabilities such as pending litigation. A commonly overlooked contingent liability is unfunded retirement, which frequently arises in professional partnerships with old agreements when partners are approaching the date of eligibility to retire under the terms of the agreement. This unfunded liability can have a dramatic effect on the value of the remaining partners' equity interests.

Financial Strength

The balance sheet serves as an indicator of a company's financial position and its strengths and weaknesses. These vital statistics measuring a business's health include assets, liabilities, and owner's equity. The valuator looks for sound balance sheets with good ratios. Many of management's decisions and policy are reflected through the analysis of a balance sheet.

A balance sheet represents a snapshot at a given time, and a series of balance sheets from several successive years can form the basis of what is often an extremely valuable sequential statement analysis. It is not just earnings that drive a valuator's estimate of value; the balance sheet also tells a story of management's capabilities and serves as a permanent record. Many companies with average earnings gained value through a strong balance sheet.

Profitability/Earnings

An accrual-basis income statement reflects the results of operations and typically gives a reasonably accurate representation of earnings, whereas a company's cashflow statement provides insights into its cash position. However, in interpreting these data, the valuation analyst should also take into consideration how long a company has been in business; relations with and turnover of employees, customers, and vendors; return on investment; operating performance; and financial condition relative to other companies in the industry as factors affecting earnings and cash position.

The valuator should remember the importance of the accrual-basis financial statement. Do not underestimate the value of the proper accounting for simple transactions and the ability of management to match revenues and expenses properly. Pay attention to detail, for it is often in the detail that one will detect the "tail that wags the business dog," and that tail may indicate a misplaced priority, such as on tax considerations.

Company Management

How well a company is managed also affects value. Both the quality of management and the depth of management are critical. Is management savvy and knowledgeable? Is it able to develop a team spirit that thrives despite the pressures of day-to-day direction and disruptions? Are there effective, flexible accounting and reporting systems in place? Is the company run by a charismatic leader or a technological wizard who is chiefly responsible for the company's success? If that key person leaves, would the company be seriously affected? A key person discount may be necessary.

Company Ownership

Just as the profile of management is important, so is the size of the block of ownership being valued. If the interest being considered for transfer is a minority interest, an adjustment for a lack of control may be appropriate. In addition, some contend that in certain circumstances a control premium is relevant when a controlling interest is being transferred. It is very important to know the base value of the company before any discounts or premiums for control are applied. Certain valuation methodologies yield a control value for a company, while others arrive at the minority value. For a more complete discussion of this issue, see Chapter 14 of Pratt's *Valuing a Business.*

The valuator must consider these issues carefully. For instance, in the transfer of a controlling general partnership interest in a private, closely held partnership, there may actually be a discount adjustment in many situations. Consider that in many states a general partner has fiduciary responsibilities to the limited partners. How can the general partner sell his or her interest for a premium when he or she might well have been able to sell the whole company and achieve liquidity for all investors? If the general partner did something like this in California, it is quite likely that the limited partners would not just stand by and watch; they would sue.

The IRS contends that there is even a premium associated with such concepts as a swing vote[3] for a minority interest, for example, in a company with three shareholders. The IRS believes that the minority interest has a premium by being in a position to align itself with another equity interest in the company and swing the control in one direction or another. This situation assumes, of course, that the two other minority interests who require this person's vote never figure out they have the swing vote power as well! In any case, the valuation analyst should analyze the specific factors affecting the amount of control inherent in the equity interest being valued.

Although family-owned businesses have traditionally thrived on the close bonds of family ties, the trust and dependence inherent in these companies can also serve as a business risk. For instance, a family relationship can disintegrate, adversely affecting the health and future of the company. Many family partnerships and operating companies, however, work very well; the continuity of ownership and policy can greatly assist the family business to accumulate substantial wealth for family members.

Company Structure

In addition, the legal structure of a business—corporation, partnership, or sole proprietorship—may affect its worth. A good example is the contingent tax liability on highly appreciated assets held by a C corporation. Trapping appreciating assets in a C corporation is not a good business practice. Prior to the repeal of the General Utilities Doctrine in the 1986 Tax Reform Act, a taxpayer could adopt a plan of liquidation for the corporation and avoid taxes on the sale of appreciated corporate assets at the entity level. The taxes were paid only once as a capital gains tax on the distribution of proceeds subsequent to a plan of liquidation. This approach was a particularly good strategy even earlier when there was a more favorable capital gains tax rate at the individual level.

After the repeal of the General Utilities Doctrine, the seller of a company must either sell the assets of the company or sell the shares at a price to reflect the contingent tax liability trapped in the corporation. In an actual transaction, a well-informed buyer will certainly decrease the purchase price to reflect the trapped taxes and the lower basis in the assets. A complex issue like this one requires lots of attention from a valuator.[4]

Size of Operations and Barriers to Entry

Size serves as both an internal and external factor. Size often acts as a guarantor of financial strength and market share. On the other hand, despite its size, a small company in a capital-intensive industry may thrive because of high barriers to entry into the marketplace. However, if it is easy to enter the market, competition will be more intense, and the value of a company is reduced.

A good example of the impact of low barriers to entry was the initial rush of computer retail stores selling hardware and software in the beginning of the personal computer era. The first IBM computer store that we visited offered only hardware and operating system software. The machine with a printer cost over $6000 and had a single floppy disk drive and 64K of RAM. Within months, there were stores sprouting up like wildfire because of the low barriers to entry. As competition flourished, only the strong and strategically balanced stores survived. Then discount stores with acres of inventory in warehouses entered the market, and margins dropped to a level supportable only by high volume. Today, only a few specialty stores with niche positions survive.

Condition of Operations

The physical condition of a business has a lot to say about how it is run. A company with state-of-the-art systems and equipment will dictate a higher value than a company with substantial deferred maintenance and an obvious lack of reinvestment. This situation frequently occurs when it is management's policy to remove earnings from the company year after year. A value consultant who sees this pattern may want to recommend that a client build equity and reinvest in the future so that the next generation or next owner will not take over the shell of a going concern and so that the current owner will have something of greater value to sell.

Business Systems

To maintain value, it is necessary to protect those physical and intangible assets which are unique to a company. Trademarks and patents are examples of assets that are directly protected. Most other assets are not directly protected, but they may receive limited protection through company policies, procedures, and protocols. Examples of these other assets include accounting systems, operations and policy manuals, documentation, procedures, company records, retention plan, trade secrets, customer lists, and vendor lists. Something as simple as a well-maintained vendor list can have value if management knows how to use it. For example, if management has a regular system to compare the prices from regular vendors with prices quoted by competing providers, then this company is likely to have a higher value than a company that has no such policy of keeping costs down.

As the valuator assesses these various elements, the well-managed company will command a higher valuation for having systems and policies that are well defined, documented, and protected. These polices reduce the risk of business failure and make it easier to pass on the value of the entity to the next generation of owners without material disruption or a reduction in value.

Legal Protection of Products and/or Services

A company's products and services obviously contribute to value. Their quality, pricing, and unique attributes relative to the industry are key in determining future earnings power. The ability to safeguard these proprietary assets through patents, copyrights, trademarks, and intellectual property protection adds to value.

Operations

Measurement of a company's results of operations relies on more than historical reporting in the form of financial statements. As an example, there was a company in the high-tech business that had unsightly losses for many years in the early 1980s and yet was commanding a substantial business value in the marketplace. Accounting principles[5] had dictated that this company deduct as an expense the substantial research and development costs for an emerging product that would require still more investment; however, the prospects for this product were extremely positive. When the valuator's industry and competitive research were concluded, it was clear that this company held the largest share of the market, and the market was on the verge of booming. In fact, the company was building substantial equity in a product that had significant potential for market share against little competition.

The market did boom, and in our last contact with the president, we heard about the numerous suitors making bids for acquisition. This company was not in a position to go public, but it filled the niche of supplying a key ingredient—an electronic component in large computer hardware systems—to many companies vying for control of a bigger market in which this product played a key role.

The president of this company and key management knew there was value but could not articulate it, and the historical results of operations were telling an opposite story. The lessons to be learned are that historical earnings are not always the sole source of value and that opportunities or threats often require research and analysis before the valuator is able to determine the estimate of value.

Forecast/Projection/Budget

A forecast presents "to the best of the responsible party's knowledge and belief, an entity's expected financial position, results of operations, and changes in financial position."[6] A forecast is the most likely future pattern of activity for a business. A projection, on the other hand, represents an entity's expected financial position based on hypothetical assumptions. A projection reflects one or more what-if assumptions that differ from the existing situation. A projection might be based on one of the following hypothetical assumptions: What if the price of a barrel of imported oil doubles? What if chicken is found to be carcinogenic? What if a giant national bookstore chain opens up across the street from a local bookstore?

A budget is primarily a management tool used to specify financial and operating objectives for a given perod of time (i.e., a month, a quarter, or a year). Often a consultant prepares or assists in the preparation of forecasts or projections. A budget is usually created by members of the financial staff inside the company with input and direction from management.

Forecasts or projections are essential to the discounted earnings/cashflow method of valuation, a common method used to value companies. The resulting estimate of value is the present value of an earnings stream or a cashflow stream extended into the future for a reasonable period of time, plus the present value of the terminal value.[7] The assumptions used in forecasts or projections of the earnings or cashflow streams and the assumptions used in the discount rate drive the result.

If the company does prepare budgets and the company's historical performance consistently meets or exceeds management's goals, a valuator can maintain a higher level of confidence in management's ability to estimate the future, which is a benefit to the valuation process. Surprisingly, many businesses do not compare actual results against annual budgets. Failure to have budgets and a comparison policy is a serious weakness and reflects negatively on management and its abilities to operate a business.

Written Business Plan

A valuator should consider the underlying assumptions, logic, and numbers in a company's written business plan. A written business plan serves as a map not just for management but also for people unfamiliar with the company who require a concise document to understand management's intent and

CPAs who prepare forecasts or projections are held to particular reporting standards and presentation guidelines promulgated by the American Institute of Certified Public Accountants (AICPA).[8] CPAs are well advised to have two separate engagement letters if they are preparing a forecast as well as a business valuation. These are two separate engagements that are generally held to different sets of reporting standards. In particular, the reporting standards for business valuation may be issued either by a governmental authority or by an association other than the AICPA.

However, a valuator must be careful when taking an engagement that requires substantial adjustment to financial statements other than those that are normalization. A licensed CPA may be held to higher standards than a valuator who is not licensed. The CPA's engagement letter should clearly communicate the scope of the assignment and any limitations, including clarification of his or her role. This area has significant potential for misunderstanding.

direction. Many small business owners and entrepreneurs bypass the benefits of a written business plan because they fear that it will cost time and resources that could be better allocated or because they lack the skills to develop a plan.

A coherent written business plan suggests to the valuator that management understands its business. A plan is also a reference point when a valuator projects future earnings as part of the estimate of value. Too many owners and managers consider the written business plan to be something that is placed in a file drawer and never looked at again. The savvy entrepreneur will have a plan and will receive a higher valuation from a valuator.

EXTERNAL FACTORS

The valuator is required to consider factors external to the day-to-day operations of the business.[9] In many situations, these factors may actually influence the final results of value more than the internal factors. Examples of external factors include competition, industry, environment, government intervention, and the economy.

Competition and Size Relative to Similar Operations

A company's performance in the competitive marketplace—locally, regionally, nationally, and internationally—has a strong influence on the value of the business. Many of the internal factors, such as proprietary content of business systems, protection of products and/or services, size relative to other companies in the industry, market strength, and market share, affect a company's ability to maintain a competitive edge. But it is not only important to judge the company's performance internally; it is critical to weigh how well it holds out against its competition.

When we talk about industry, we refer to a group of business interests with a common goal making and/or selling similar products or services. Competition, on the other hand, is the subset of the industry that is in direct or close contention for sales with the business being valued, or it is reasonably similar and can be used as market-comparable evidence.

When a valuator reviews a company, he or she is looking for issues such as stability and growth potential of the business and then relates these factors to how the competition is performing. This process can be termed a *microanalysis*. The bigger picture, the *macro-*

analysis, is how the industry as a group of common interests performs. It is important to look at both the micro- and macrolevels, because they show how the company and its industry are each performing.

Truly market-guideline companies are good baselines for comparison; however, it is up to the valuator to make sure that variances among the market-guideline companies are adjusted to reconcile substantive differences between the company being valued and the guideline companies. For example, a search may locate companies that are profitable and well funded with little leverage, have a good dividend-paying capacity, and invest heavily in research and development. Are these companies comparable to a business that is highly leveraged, has erratic profits, and pays out any semblance of profit to the owner in the form of above-market compensation and perks? Probably not, so this situation requires the valuator to adjust the company's financial position and results of operations. However, if the potential guideline companies are very different from the subject company, a market-based valuation approach may not be applicable.

Industry

Another important external factor is the general vitality of the industry in which a company participates. Consider the success of a neighborhood video store in the late 1980s and its struggle just to stay alive today. Analysis of only the short-term prospects of the video rental industry and not the longer-term threats to profitability (DirecTV, cable-on-demand, large Blockbuster-type stores) would be incomplete.

Another example of the impact of industry trends is a management that retains product lines that have become simple commodities with significantly reduced profit margins. Savvy managers spot these trends and adjust the course of the business to compensate for market evolutions. A worthy example of this situation was a valuation consulting engagement for a hospitality client. The valuation consultant recommended a simple pricing restructure to meet consumer expectations about lodging. Sales skyrocketed, as did the value of the company. This type of recommendation by a valuator can dramatically improve satisfaction among the client's customers and can lead to referrals for new business for the valuator.

The industry analysis can yield valuable information that will enhance the value of a business beyond the valuation report. A well-written industry section of the report will almost always have information regarding the industry that is helpful to management. (See Chapter 4 for more detail about industry analysis.)

Impact of Environmental Factors

Both a business owner and the valuator need to consider how business is affected by environmental issues. For instance, if the business is a chemical plant, does it meet regulations or is it subject to expensive renovations in order to pass inspection? Is that the reason the business is for sale? Also, the valuator must consider natural environmental impacts such as earthquakes, storms, fire, flooding, drought, and infestation. The 1989 Loma Prieta earthquake in northern California, for example, caused material damage not just to real estate but also to business activity in the local area as well.

Government Regulation

For a business in an industry subject to government regulation, national or state legislation can increase the cost of operations and affect the value of a business. The increased costs may take the form of cash or resources diverted from other uses.

Santa Cruz County experienced the most severe damage from the Loma Prieta earthquake in 1989. Fifteen percent of the county's housing stock was damaged, and over one-fourth of the commercial and industrial buildings located in the county were either damaged or destroyed.[10] "The city of Santa Cruz was in something of a state of shock after the earthquake....[In fact] one year later, nothing had been rebuilt."[11] In the fourth quarter of 1989, sales of general merchandise were 63% less than in the fourth quarter of 1988.[12] The number of home sales in Santa Cruz County dropped over 40% from the Fall of 1988 to the Fall of 1989.[13] Median home prices for the Monterey–Santa Cruz area dropped 7.0% compared with the California median from October 1989 to November 1989, and prices did not begin recovering until March 1990.[14] The Santa Cruz County Housing Authority determined that "housing demand actually deteriorated and rental prices fell 7–10% in the two years following the earthquake."[15]

Since the value of apartments is driven by rental income, a conservative adjustment for the effects of the earthquake on the price of income-producing apartments in Santa Cruz County might be in the 7% range. This adjustment would be necessary to reflect a material change in economic conditions due to the Loma Prieta earthquake, if the real estate appraisals did not incorporate the effect of the earthquake.

Consider as an example a small health care practice that now has to comply with the impact of protective control measures to shield its employees and patients from the AIDS virus. Although such a change has benefits for society by helping to prevent the spread of a terrible disease, this use of resources does not produce direct revenue for the practice. On the other hand, if management does not take measures to prevent the spread of AIDS, there is the potential for a liability. The overall theoretical result would be for all such health care practices to decline in value because of the additional costs for AIDS prevention measures. In order to value the practice accurately, the valuator must be aware of this type of trend and factor it into the analysis of a practice that has not yet complied with the necessary preventive measures.

Economic Conditions

Few businesses can claim to be immune from regional, national, and international economic events. Strategies and financial reserves to meet the demands of a slow economy can raise the value of a business. In a valuation, an analyst studies and interprets the economic outlook for a business and its industry and then relates these to the external factors of the general economy that most influence a company's financial position and results of operations.

Consider the case of a car dealer in the late 1970s who thought he was immune to increasing interest rates and inflation. As gas prices soared, demand for his vehicles plummeted, and rising interest rates ate away at his company's very small working-capital reserve. In a matter of months, the reserve was gone, and bankruptcy loomed. When times were good, he simply had not addressed the need to have capital to survive an unexpected downturn in business. He felt his management and selling skills were more powerful than the forces of the economy and external factors over which he had no control. Unfortunately, he was mistaken.

SUMMARY

A business valuation is based on a combination of internal and external factors affecting the business, its industry, and the economy. The primary internal considerations are historical performance, financial strength/balance sheet, profitability/earnings, company management and ownership, company structure, size and condition of the operation, proprietary content, protection of products and/or services, operations, forecast/projection/budget, and a written business plan.

On the external side, the valuation depends on such areas as local, national, and international competition; size relative to similar operations; environmental impact of the industry; type of industry; government intervention; and economic conditions on a regional, national, and international scale.

Whether it is internal or external factors affecting the business being researched and analyzed, the valuator should take an independent, investigative approach that can identify issues and solve problems to arrive at the most probable estimate of value. Then the valuator must be able to communicate and defend that finding in a clear and concise way to those who will rely on it.

NOTES

1. Internal Revenue Service Revenue Ruling 59–60, Section 4.01.
2. Jan R. Williams, *Miller GAAP Guide,* San Diego, CA: Harcourt Brace & Co., 1994.
3. Internal Revenue Service Technical Advice Memorandum, Code Sec. 2512.
4. Gary Jones and Dirk Van Dyke, "The Case of Contingent Tax Liability: To Discount or Not?," *The Valuation Examiner,* 1st quarter, 1994.
5. Financial Accounting Standards Board, *Current Text Accounting Standards, General Standards,* Norwalk, CT: Financial Accounting Standards Board, 1994, p. 38837.
6. Don Pallais and Stephen D. Holton, *Guide to Forecasts and Projections,* Fort Worth, TX: Practitioners Publishing Company, 1990, Vol. 1, 115.16.
7. Terminal value is not a stand-alone valuation methodology. Terminal value is part of the calculations that are necessary to arrive at a final estimate of value using the discounted cashflow/earnings valuation method. The discounted cashflow/earnings valuation method is explained in almost any valuation or finance text.
8. American Institute of Certified Public Accountants, *Codification of Statements on Auditing Standards,* Chicago: CCH Inc., 1995, p. 761. Bailey, Larry P., *Miller GAAS 1995 Guide,* San Diego, CA: Harcourt Brace Professional Publishing, 1995, Part V, Section 17.
9. Internal Revenue Service Ruling 59–60, Section 4.

10. Cynthia Kroll et al., "Economic Impact of the Loma Prieta Quake: The Impact on Small Business," Working Paper No 91–187, Center for Real Estate and Urban Economics, University of California, Berkeley, pp. 3–5.

11. Mary Comerio et al., "Post Disaster Residential Building," Working Paper 608, Institute of Urban and Regional Development, University of California, Berkeley, February 1994, p. 46.

12. Kroll, "Economic Impact," p. 15.

13. Ibid., p. 23.

14. Ibid., p. 21.

15. Comerio, p. 46.

CHAPTER 4

The Process of Conducting a Business Valuation

KEY PHASES OF A VALUATION

Without an understanding of the business valuation process, it may almost seem as simple as one, two, three. There are, however, many complex issues which must be identified, researched, and analyzed before an estimate of value can be reached.

A comprehensive business valuation begins with the engagement process and is followed by three major phases: research and data gathering, analysis, and estimation of value and reporting. (See the Valuation Process Chart on the next page.) Specific segments of the process are defined in Internal Revenue Service Revenue Ruling 59–60. The steps explained in this chapter have evolved over the course of more than 25 years of experience.

Prior to starting the process, however, it is necessary to determine what standard of value the valuation is based upon: fair market value, fair value, investment value, liquidation value, or intrinsic value. The purpose of the valuation will determine the appropriate standard of value to use.

THE VALUATION METHODOLOGY

In a *fair market value* valuation, the valuator estimates the hypothetical estimated price at which a business would change hands between a willing buyer and a willing seller when neither party is under any obligation to make the deal and when both parties are fully aware of

BUSINESS VALUATION PROCESS CHART

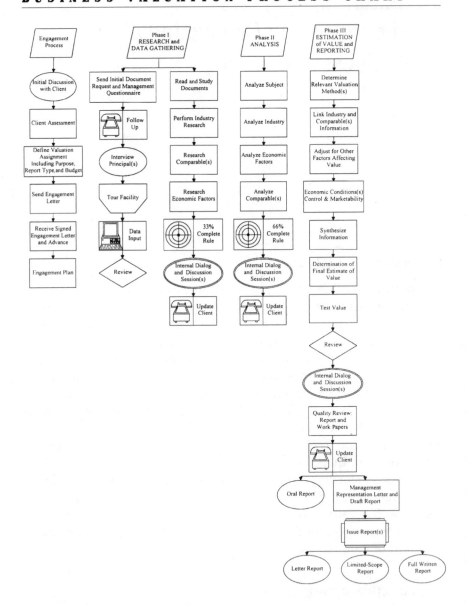

all the relevant facts. Fair market value is the standard of value for gift and estate tax valuations and for many other purposes.

Fair value, guided by common law and/or state government agencies, is considered primarily in disputes with minority shareholders. "Appraisal Under Corporations Code Section 2000" is a good article on this type of value for the state of California.[1] The California Corporations Code states that fair value "shall be determined on the basis of the liquidation value but taking into account the possibility, if any, of sale of the entire business as a going concern in a liquidation.[2] Typically, the goal of fair value is to provide minority shareholders with an equitable result. This definition has confused many people, and it takes some time to grasp. It says that if one can reasonably assume that the business can be valued as a "going concern" and sold to a theoretical buyer who is not purchasing it in a fire sale, then that hypothetical transaction has more weight than a liquidation of physical assets. In addition, the assumption is that there will be no specific adjustments for lack of control. Remember, the business is assumed to be sold as a whole entity (if possible) and as a going concern.

Investment value is the value of a business to a specific buyer. Value in this case depends upon the specific buyer's skill set and any potential synergies with the buyer's existing business or businesses that may occur as a result of the purchase. *Strategic value,* another term for investment value, is the price a buyer is willing to pay to strengthen "a company's competitive position in a segmented market.[3]

Liquidation value is based solely on the value of assets and liabilities rather than on earnings. It presumes that a business stops operating as a going concern, sells off its assets, pays off its debts, and includes the costs of liquidation. Under this premise, the proceeds that remain constitute the value of the equity interest for the owner(s) of the company.

Intrinsic value "represents an analytical judgment of value based on the perceived characteristics inherent in the investment.[4] This definition assumes that the market value will eventually come to equal the "true" or "real" or "intrinsic" value when other investors arrive at the same views.

THE VALUATION PROCESS CHART

The Valuation Process Chart can be used as a tool in aiding a valuator with the major steps of a business valuation. The chart separates the valuation process into four distinct parts that are discussed in this chapter: (1) the engagement process, (2) research and data gathering, (3) analysis, and (4) estimation of value and reporting. The chart is an overview that highlights the major issues to address in a business valuation engagement. However, the business valuation chart is not a detailed step-by-step approach that is universally applicable. Every engagement is unique and may require additional research or additional factors to consider.

THE ENGAGEMENT PROCESS

During the engagement process, a valuator (1) reviews information about the business to be valued, (2) determines the scope of the project and whether it can be undertaken realistically, and (3) decides whether to accept the prospective engagement. Clients and their advisers are often anxious to find the estimated cost of the process and usually are eager to provide the necessary information to assist in determining a reasonable fee. This section describes some of the questions that need to be considered to ensure the right fit between a valuator and a client.

An engagement acceptance form can serve as a tool for a valuator to understand more clearly the target company and to help the valuator decide whether to accept an engagement. Practitioners Publishing Company (PPC) publishes a useful sample.[5] Besides eliciting basic data such as the type of business and the people with whom the valuator will be working, the engagement acceptance form helps define the scope of the project and outlines important issues that a valuator should consider prior to accepting a project.

When we talk about the scope of the valuation, we mean what the engagement entails: What definition of value we are looking for—fair market value, fair value, and so on—what equity interest is to be valued, whether sufficient historical financial information is available, which valuation methods are appropriate, what kind of report will be used to communicate the valuation conclusions, who will receive the final report, and the role of the valuator.

The valuator should present a letter of understanding in the form of an engagement letter, outlining the scope of the project, its estimated cost, and expected out-of-pocket expenses. The engagement letter should have a provision for fee adjustment in the event of unforeseen or changed circumstances that substantially affect the scope of service or content of the final report. (See the sample engagement letters in the Appendix.)

It is advisable not to establish a fixed-fee form of compensation that is too low or that could consciously or unconsciously prevent a valuator from doing a thorough analysis. A valuator should expect to receive an advance (we recommend 50 percent of the estimated fee), and should limit the period for client acceptance of the conditions of the engagement to 15 business days.

California Accountants Mutual Insurance Company (CAMI-CO) publishes a loss prevention binder that serves as a valuable tool in crafting engagement letters that protect the interests of the client and the valuator.[6] The other outstanding source for sample engagement letters is the AICPA.[7] A book like *Guide to Business Valuations* (see the Bibliography) has many helpful standardized forms and questionnaires, including an assessment form (Volume 3), to assist the valuator. This binder reference guide is one of the best tools in the library of a valuator. Practitioners Publishing Company (PPC) also offers *Guideware*, a software tool designed to make the job easier. This software contains templates of forms that can be customized to fit specific valuation situations.

Ensuring the Right Fit

During the engagement assessment stage, valuators should carefully consider the following five questions based on input from the prospective client in order to ensure that the valuator/client relationship is optimal.

• **Are you aware of any conflicts of interest or problems about independence?** In our view and the view of many in the valuation field, a valuator should not perform a company's business valuation if he or she is also a close adviser to the company or performs services in accounting, tax, or policy consulting for it. The valuator should seek the right estimate of the worth of a business, not serve as an advocate for the client. Government agencies are paying closer attention to valuators who are perceived as having a conflict of interest.

Consider the CPA who performs the audit of an ESOP-owned (employee stock ownership plan) company as well as a valuation of the company's stock, or consider the accountant who prepares the federal estate tax return (Form 706) and a valuation for an estate. The appearance of a lack of independence stems from the possibility that the preparer, either consciously or unconsciously, may furnish an estimate of value that favors the client.

Usually, a company will save money in the long run by having the most accurate estimate of value, instead of an advocacy opinion. An advocacy opinion of business value is often apparent and can actually trigger an audit or lead to an unfavorable result.

For example, a drastic undervaluation for tax purposes can result in an undervaluation penalty payable by the valuation analyst, under Section 6701 of the Internal Revenue Code.

There are, however, specific situations in which a valuator can become involved as the advocate for a client,[8] offer valuable assistance, and assist in obtaining the best negotiated price for the business. A typical example of this role occurs when a client comes to a valuator and expresses his or her desire to sell or buy. This valuation would be an investment value valuation. The example, of course, assumes that the valuator follows the valuation standards of an accredited association and expresses an estimate of value in accordance with the canons of ethics related to the process.[9]

One of our peers was recently discussing conflicts of interest, an area about which little has been published. Although his list of questions and situations was complex, he knew the answers just on the basis of common sense and on his ethics as a CPA. He was receiving a great deal of pressure from his partners to produce hours and billings and needed some reassurance that his position not to do certain valuations was appropriate. Incidentally, as a result of the conversation, our firm picked up a new engagement through his referral, and we consult for him occasionally on those engagements where he feels confident that no conflict exists. This kind of professional cooperation and cross-referral is essential to the development of a business and should be encouraged, not feared.

A respected attorney with a large law firm put it succinctly: "I do not recommend analysts who perform valuations for their ongoing accounting and tax clients." This issue is driven by the marketplace, plain and simple. It doesn't matter what the valuator thinks; it's the consumer of valuation services who is thinking and reacting. A valuator should remember the phrase *the appearance of lack of independence* (the operative word is *appearance*) the next time he or she is considering performing a valuation for a regular client.

• **Is the expertise to perform the engagement within the valuator's capabilities?** At its core, it is a question of whether the valuator has sufficient experience and training to handle a specific valuation or has the ability to obtain the knowledge necessary for the valuation.

It is not necessary to have years of experience in a particular industry to perform valuations of a business within that industry,[10] but the valuator should become familiar with the industry prior to undertaking the engagement.

• **Is there sufficient staffing both to perform and to oversee the valuation?** Although a valuator's staff may have the capabilities to manage the engagement, the question is whether the firm has the time and resources to accept the engagement in the context of the existing workload.

In professions like accounting and law, one of the most difficult management tasks is to plan for the workload that grows out of various projects. Because professional service firms often have problems of this type, it is useful to share the following experience as a point of relevance and comparison.

Our office generally takes assignments in the 100- to 250-hour range. We keep an ongoing analysis of our work in progress and evaluate it against the scope of any additional projects that we are considering. For example, as this chapter was being written, we had a backlog of over 2000 hours with a capacity of 150 hours per week at reasonable efficiency. On the surface, we seem to have a backlog of about 13 weeks, but we will accept additional projects. In reality, we don't have as much of a backlog as it appears, because there is little certainty about when or if certain projects will be completed. Some projects, in fact, settle early; others require smaller increments of time over longer periods. Such issues are often influenced by the dates when cases goes to trial. Workload management is a continuing challenge for any valuation firm.

The normal turnaround time for a project is anywhere from four to eight weeks; however, projects sometimes become stalled while a valuator waits for information from other professionals involved in the project, such as a real estate appraiser who must complete his or her assignment prior to a certain phase of the valuation. Of course, valuators can also work overtime to complete projects that become squeezed by a backlog; such backlogs are often caused by valuations held up by litigation scheduling.

Being on time is one of the issues most critical to client satisfaction. A valuator may be asked to get an assignment completed by a certain date because of a court deadline or to complete a valuation by year end so that the taxpayer can take advantage of gift-giving opportunities. The critical question is: Can the normal high-quality and comprehensive valuation work be performed within a tight time frame?

• **Do the terms of the proposed engagement, including fee arrangements, violate applicable professional standards?** A valuator must consider whether anything about the engagement subjects him or her to undue legal risk or makes the valuator uncomfortable about accepting the engagement. For instance, a company may have been involved in an environmental accident or may sell a product morally distasteful to the valuator. These concerns may affect a valuator's ability to be an independent arbiter of value.

A decision has to come from both the head and the heart. The logic can be straightforward, but the moral questions are often more complex. We were asked by a government agency to value a business that many might consider distasteful—the conversion of a pub to a topless bar. Normally, if a buyer or seller of this business were to ask us to value it for sale, we would decline the engagement. However, we accepted the project because the government had decided that the easiest way to deal with the problem was not to litigate with the business owner but instead to pay the owner a fair price for the most profitable use and close the operation—probably a less expensive proposition for the taxpayers. The opposing valuator in this matter accepted the assignment for the same reason.

- **Are you aware of any potential fee collection problems?** A valuator has to be sure that the client is able to pay for the valuation. If not, this inability to pay may have the appearance of a contingent fee arrangement. A valuator has the opportunity to inspect the prospective client's financial statements and/or tax returns in the assessment phase, so they should be reviewed as carefully as a bank credit analyst would review them.

Even if there are some doubts about the client's ability to pay, the valuator may want to ask for certain things in his or her engagement letter to reduce the risk of nonpayment or the appearance of a contingent fee arrangement. Although market conditions may dictate modified billing and collection policies, certain procedures work well in most markets. The most basic procedure is to agree in advance on what the fee is going to be and how it is going to be paid.[11]

First, the valuator should estimate and disclose the specific amount he or she expects the fee to be and build in flexibility for unforeseen changes or circumstances that might arise during the engagement. The valuator should also require an advance in the amount of the minimum fee, progress payments if the engagement is protracted, and payment in full of any outstanding invoices prior to the release of the final estimate of value or the final report. These steps are fairly standard among most consulting service professionals.

The Engagement Letter

At this point, if the two parties have agreed to work together, the valuator will present an engagement letter that clearly and objectively states the scope, limiting conditions, terms, objectives, and estimated cost of the project. This letter should eliminate any surprises later unless unforeseen circumstances arise after the engagement has begun. As noted above, the fee arrangement should make clear to the client the necessity to increase fees for unforeseen work. (See the Appendix for an example of a limited-scope engagement letter.)

THE THREE PHASES OF A VALUATION

PHASE I: RESEARCH AND DATA GATHERING

The research and information-gathering phase provides the valuator with hard data that serve as the foundation for a business valuation. This phase is extremely important for a reliable, robust valuation. Examples in this section demonstrate the importance of three things: information that suggests critical factors of value, relevant and up-to-date market-comparable data, and site visits.

Internal Data

During the research and data-gathering phase, the valuator collects as much data as necessary for the assignment. The usual sources include internal company data, such as annual financial statements and federal tax returns typically for the last five years; interim financial statements for the year to date; copies of sales and financial projections; cash accounts; accounts receivable and accounts payable classified by age; an inventory list; analyses of significant accrued liabilities; operating budgets; legal documents, such as leases, loans, and buy/sell agreements; details of employee benefit plans; collective bargaining agreements; board meeting minutes; lists of patents, copyrights, and trademarks; and business plans.

The extent and depth of the research is driven by the type of engagement. Practitioners Publishing Company publishes useful guides for gathering data, including a document request list and a list of questions for management. Forensic engagements require much more depth and detail than nonforensic engagements. A valuator in a forensic engagement requests, for instance, the detailed accounts receivable behind audited financial statements.

External Data

The other principal areas of information are industry, economic, and market data. These sources, if available, include economic trends, regional and local demographics and economic conditions, industry data, competitor-specific data, comparative financial data, industry reports, initial public offering documents, and data on market rates of return.

Internal company information does not provide all the evidence of value; external research is also vital to the process. External research is more than pulling out an old copy of the *U.S. Industrial Outlook* and copying a short description by a government economist into a valuation report. It takes a focused, concerted effort to find the external information that is useful in developing the estimate of value.

Interviews of industry experts can be very useful. One phone call with the right expert can provide the valuation analyst with an abundance of information on the industry. There may be certain pieces of information that only an industry expert would have: the latest market transactions, trends, government regulations, and so on. We have learned a lot by interviewing industry experts. We may also, depending on the engagement, interview acquisition directors for companies in the subject company's industry as part of our research.

Industry data are even more abundant than information on the competition. Governments, universities, and private associations generally have more data than can be assimilated in a reasonable amount of time. The key is learning to find the data and filter out the issues that are irrelevant to the business interest being valued.

> Outlook: The economic outlook in general and the condition and outlook of the specific industry in particular.[12]

IRS Revenue Ruling 59–60 states that all relevant factors affecting the fair market value of a business should be analyzed, including the economic outlook in general and the condition and outlook of the specific industry. Of course, the outlooks for the business, the industry, and the competition need to be examined to develop an accurate estimate of value. If a valuator simply runs a formula or uses a multiple of revenue to estimate value without adequately considering the outlook for the future, then he or she has omitted a critical ingredient.

The economists' reports in the *U.S. Industrial Outlook*[13] have been a good starting point in the past. Although the government discontinued the *U.S. Industrial Outlook* after the 1994 edition, older issues still provide an excellent initial source. At the end of each segment of analysis is a bibliography of the primary sources of the information used to form an outlook. Most of these information sources are available by telephone, on-line, or at the local library. A telephone call to the head economist in charge of that segment of the *U.S. Industrial Outlook* may yield current information.

We recall a valuator who was valuing a business that manufactured a product in high demand from the construction industry. It was the early 1980s, and real estate development was booming. Subdivisions, development of raw land, and high-rises were sprouting like wildflowers. The owner of the business was negotiating to buy back a minority shareholder's small equity interest in the company. The owner was extremely enthusiastic about the prospect of once again owning the entire company and very optimistic about the future. The valuator examined the historical performance of the company and recent industry trends. To say the least, they were rosy.

Unfortunately, the valuator neglected to research what experts in the field of real estate economics were predicting for the future of the industry. They foresaw trouble arising from a host of tax law changes and from overcapacity in real estate markets. Had the valuator done his or her job correctly, this prediction would easily have been discovered, and the price for the minority equity interest would have been adjusted accordingly. As it turned out, the majority owner of the company overpaid for the minority interest, and the company soon failed because of the downturn in the real estate industry in the late 1980s. A valuator does not necessarily have to be an industry expert to reach complex forecast conclusions; there are many sources of information that will provide the assistance.

Market Comparables

For those who are lucky enough to have businesses in a niche that has comparable public companies, there is an abundance of publicly available data. These sources on competition are bulging with good information, and they are accessible through easy-to-use, relatively inexpensive data outlets, such as CompuServe®, America Online®, Prodigy®, Lexis/Nexis®, Dun & Bradstreet®, Standard & Poor's®, or sites on the World Wide Web.[14] Also, NACVA, ASA, and

Shannon Pratt's Business Valuation Update publish directories of vendors to industry.

Take, for instance, a search for a company that has the primary portion of its revenues in the same Standard Industrial Classification Code (SIC Code)[15] as the business being valued. A company's largest line of business is given the company's primary SIC code. A company with other lines of business will also have several secondary SIC codes. After the relevant SIC codes are identified, one can search for the appropriate material on-line, or one can call investor relations departments of each company and request copies of annual reports, 10-Ks, and proxy statements.

In the process of searching for material, it is important to filter the data to companies in the same general location and with other similar characteristics. It is best to have comparable companies whose attributes are similar to the subject company; however, this is not always possible. A company may not be a market comparable if all its manufacturing is done in a different country or if the manufacturing for the business under valuation occurs in a state with a noncompetitive business climate.

Developing Market Comparables

An adjustment for lack of control is a good example of the benefits of external evidence. Internal evidence demonstrating lack of control for the specific equity interest may be obvious, but external evidence to quantify the amount of the adjustment to be applied to a minority equity interest is not as easy to find. In other words, no one is going to dispute the existence of a lack of control, but the percentage adjustment is supported by evidence that is external to the business.

For instance, it may not be relevant to compare a group of real estate investment trusts (REITs) with properties around the country and varied asset profiles, including high-rise office buildings, a racetrack, and agricultural land, to a family limited partnership (FLP) equity interest in an apartment building located in Palo Alto, California. Add in that the REIT properties are leveraged and have a mixed history of distribution, whereas the FLP has no debt or distribution history and has a capacity to distribute cash to investors. Such an example is not the profile of market comparability.[16]

Sometimes, alleged market-comparable studies are used that are over a decade old. However, adjustments that are related to REITs for lack of control vary with the volatility of the real estate market. These relatively old studies are valid only to prove the existence of an adjustment for lack of control; the percentage adjustments themselves are relevant only to partnerships with assets similar in character to a basket of REITs at a specific point in time.[17]

The IRS and courts are particularly sensitive to the market-comparable issue.[18] Too many tax return practitioners have been using discounts from old court cases and studies rather than engaging a specialist to develop the estimate of value for the particular situation. This is done primarily to save clients money, but it is not a smart decision, because the IRS will most likely reject the result and the client could be faced with additional costs.

In this type of situation, a valuator usually needs to perform his or her own studies and to find evidence relevant to the current situation. Ideally, one finds REITs with over 50 percent of their portfolio in the same type of real estate as the FLP and with published appraisal results as close to the valuation date as possible. Then one adjusts the REIT study result to factor the differences in leverage, profitability, distribution-paying capacity, and other economic conditions. Finally, one must also adjust for the amount of control a limited partner has in the FLP as compared to an investor in a REIT.

This first phase of research and data gathering comprises much more than just getting the documents to fulfill a checklist. Too often, checklists are not tailored to a particular situation. It may be a waste of client and staff time to request documents that are not going to be needed; it is up to the valuator to target the document collection to the specific valuation situation.

For example, as part of valuing a restaurant, it is important to review copies of the chef's food cost analysis. Food cost control is a vital aspect of the value of any food service operation, and it should be tested against more than just an industry standard. Instead, it should be investigated carefully. Although a food cost analysis is a rather detailed document to request from a business, this type of targeted information can provide the insight for the core components of a valuation.

Information on Competitors

It is difficult, time-consuming, and expensive for a small company to perform regular and detailed analyses of its competition. Therefore, it is important for the small company to belong to an industry association that tracks relevant data, trends, and results of operations of other businesses in the industry.[19] Well-managed companies have association memberships and pay regular attention to their study results, government regulations, current events, and forecasts of the future. Valuators should obtain written consent from their clients for associations to release information to the valuator as an approved consultant to the client/member.

Better-managed companies with adequate resources are also those that are always tracking their competition and are aware of changes that may affect the operations of their own business. This type of intelligence leads to informed knowledge of product, market share, and key employee movement, as well as increased value.

This information is not gained covertly, although it is tempting to think of an individual wearing a trenchcoat stooped over a desk in the office of a competitor snapping away with a minicamera. More likely, the individual is a researcher hovering in front of a computer screen, using a telephone, or digging through periodicals and newspapers for a flash of those key words or phrases that will spark an interest. Gaining an advantage from data is hard work and full of dead-end searches and fatigue, but it often enables the researcher to locate that special article or tidbit that fills a gap in knowledge.

Research Techniques

A valuator must develop good interview skills and an investigative mind and must read constantly. The information that is vital to the best estimate of value may lie deep in the text of an article, a brokerage house research paper, an industry analyst's report, or an obscure study by a university professor. It may even be a small clue that one stumbles across while reading the gossip column of the local newspaper or an editorial in an industry association newsletter. The best work is done by those valuators who can discover the relevant evidence to support their hypothesis and then effectively communicate their findings orally or in writing.

Consider the following example while pondering the balance between the art of business valuation and the science of business valuation. A valuator collected boxes of financial and market information from the target company in the outdoor sign printing industry, interviewed all relevant parties, and visited the business location for a tour of the facilities and a meeting with some of the key operating personnel. During the tour, the valuator noticed a piece of equipment that looked new: an elaborate computerized plotter/printer. The recently installed high-tech equipment was dramatically changing how this business operated and was improving profit margins substantially. The future earnings of the company were going to change and, thus, the estimate of value. If the valuator had just sent out a document request list and had not toured the facility, the importance of the new equipment would have been missed. One thing is certain. No one in the company had brought this change in operations to the attention of the valuator.

Touring the facilities of any operating business to be valued (when permitted) is a crucial part of the information-gathering stage of Phase I. The moral of the story: Keep your eyes open and learn to interpret what is and what is not actually there.

PHASE II: ANALYSIS

Once a valuator has collected the relevant information, he or she must analyze the data quantitatively and objectively, looking for trends and indicators, both positive and negative, that offer clues about the value of the company with respect to the environment in which it operates. By weaving together the external and internal factors, the valuator can analyze the company's business performance and determine how it stacks up against its competition. The components of this phase are described in Chapter 3.

The industry analysis can yield information that will enhance the value of a business beyond the valuation report. A well-written industry section of the report will almost always have information regarding the industry that is helpful to management. Many individuals attempting to gain certification in the valuation specialty fail miserably in this area of their written reports submitted for peer review. Almost anyone can run a formula by dropping in numbers on a template, but few are capable of finding, analyzing, and synthesizing the information in an industry analysis back to the business valuation at hand and communicating their findings in writing. How good are your reports in this area? Remember that IRS Revenue Ruling 59–60, Section 4.02(b), "Factors to Consider," requires the consideration of this issue.

The value of a business as a going concern is directly reflected by its earnings history, trends, and future earnings capacity. The price that a buyer is willing to pay is then related to the period of time it will take to receive back his or her invested capital and a reasonable return on investment; generally, a period of seven years or less for a normal, private, closely held business enterprise is reasonable. In the case of a less normal situation, such as a high-risk business or one in which the "tax tail" has been wagging the "business dog," the period is closer to five years or less. Buyers are generally unwilling to assume the risks of the seller unless appropriately compensated. On the other hand, a company with a strategic advantage may be worth a substantial multiple of historic earnings or may merit a low discount factor in calculating discounted earnings or cashflow—it depends on the facts and evidence in each case.

PHASE III: ESTIMATION OF VALUE AND REPORTING

The final phase of the valuation is to select and apply appropriate methodologies and to articulate the estimation of value. This estimation is then presented in a report form, of which there are four types as dictated by the purpose of the engagement and needs of the intended users of the report: a full report, a letter, an oral report, and a limited-scope report. This phase is often the most difficult and challenging of the three phases of conducting a business valuation.

During the estimation-of-value phase, the author of the valuation report must synthesize data, link industry and comparable information, and adjust for factors that may affect value to reach the best, or even perhaps the most probable, estimation of value. To conclude the estimation of value, the valuator must articulate the results in a form that is easily understood by those who have not spent time with company management, the data, and the analytical process.

Do you recall a class in college where the professor had only a final exam to determine your grade for the term, and the test posed only one question? You had spent the entire term reading, studying, attending lectures, and organizing notes; it all came down to a blank bluebook waiting to be filled in. That is not unlike the situation when Phases I and II are completed.

What might a hypothetical seller or buyer who has all the relevant evidence in hand do under a given set of circumstances? That is the one question that lies in front of a valuator. You cannot answer this question and get an "A" from the trier-of-fact without having attended the lecture, taken notes, collected the evidence, and performed the analysis and studies—in short, done your homework. It is only then that your estimate of value will be respected and followed.

There is a school of thought out there that contends it is acceptable to take the easy way out by averaging the results of various methods of value calculated before the estimation-of-value phase, but we do not agree. With extensive research and analysis of numerous court cases, we have yet to find any authoritative support for the method of averaging. In fact, IRS Revenue Ruling 59–60 specifically states under Section 7, "Average of Factors:"

> Because valuations cannot be made on the basis of a prescribed formula, there is no means whereby the various applicable factors in a particular case can be assigned mathematical weights in deriving the fair market value. For this reason, no useful purpose is served by taking an average of several factors (for example, book value, capitalized earnings, and capitalized dividends) and basing the valuation on the results. Such a process excludes active consideration of other pertinent factors, and the end result cannot be supported by a realistic application of the significant facts in the case except by mere chance.[20]

A valuator should be prepared to take a position using his or her judgment: One of the valuation methods is probably close to the value a real seller and a real buyer would agree upon. If the results of the methods are averaged, the valuator has only taken an estimate that is close and mixed it with answers that are further from the truth, thus moving even further away from the best estimate of value.

It is judgment that lets the valuator be 95 percent certain of the result—an acceptable margin of error, given all the relevant evidence and the scope of the engagement. A team of analysts gets to this point of completion through hard work, and many discussions and debates about the evidence, and by having a bit of chutzpah. Once again, the art form of business valuation shows through.

The Valuation Report

At least four different kinds of reports may be used to communicate the results of the valuation. They range from highly technical, fully documented reports to more informal oral reports. The nature and purpose of the engagement, the client's intended use of the information, and the client's budget all determine the form and extent of the valuation report. All reports, however, should outline the relationship among factual information, quantitative analysis, and the intangible, more subjective parts of the analysis.

The National Association of Certified Valuation Analysts (NACVA)[21] has established member standards for three of these reports that provide direction to the valuator and ensure quality for the client and, in many cases, the trier-of-fact. Other association member standards may differ from those of NACVA. We have chosen NACVA standards for demonstration purposes. The fourth type of report, often used at our firm, is the proprietary *limited-scope valuation*. This type of report should not be confused with USPAP's summary report, which is based on the same data as a full report but has less detail presented.[22]

It is the task of the valuator to identify and report on the value so that the uninformed parties can understand the result, even in light of historical reporting of operations that seems to point in a different direction. This ability to communicate is vital. It is crucial to report findings in an easily understood written report so that employees and others unfamiliar with financial matters can grasp what lies behind the valuation.

Full (Formal) Written Report

The general format of a full written report includes an identification or cover page, a table of contents, an estimate-of-value letter, the body, and an appendix containing financial statement summaries, common size analysis, independent appraisals on tangible assets, and other relevant documents and schedules to support the valuator's findings of value.

The cover page should include the name of the enterprise that is the subject of the report, the type of report, the effective valuation conclusion date, the name of the valuator and/or his or her firm, and the date the report is issued.

Although the term *opinion letter* is accepted by some valuators, we believe it should be reserved for use with the attestation function by CPAs, and we question its applicability to the valuation process. This phrase may lead a reader to believe, if the valuator is a CPA, that a different level or mix of service has been rendered by the valuator than actually performed. Instead, we recommend the phrase *estimate of value.*

The estimate-of-value letter serves as a synopsis of the results of the valuation, including its purpose, the valuation date, identification of the standard and premise of value, description of the equity interest being valued, estimate of value, reference to the limiting conditions, and an executive summary. The table of contents following the letter provides easy access to the comprehensive material included in the report.

The body of the report contains the meat of the valuation: an explanation of the reasoning and methodology behind the estimate of value. This major section of the report expands on the purpose of the valuation and discusses the approach to the valuation. It includes the following: a statement of limiting conditions, such as basing the valuation on historical and prospective financial information provided by the client rather than on data elicited by an audit; an adequate description of the business background, industry, markets, competition, management, ownership, and structure; a financial review; the nature of the security interest being valued; identification of the security and the percentage of ownership it represents; and the valuation methodology.

Letter (Informal) Report

A less formal written report is used when the valuator has been engaged only to issue a letter report even though the valuation performed could be appropriate for the more in-depth, formal report. This report contains an estimate-of-value letter and body, similar to the ones included in the longer report, but the major difference is a shorter valuation description and a shorter discussion of the reasoning behind it.

Oral Report

When a report is presented orally, it is often accompanied by a written outline to ensure good communication. A precise oral report should identify the purpose of the valuation, the valuation date, the standard and premise of value, the valuation methodology, the equity interest being valued, the limitations on the use of the oral report, the conclusions about the estimate of value, and any limitations on the scope of the engagement.

Limited-Scope Valuation Report

The limited-scope valuation is the most common type of report in our firm, although perhaps it is not the most profitable for a valuation firm. This engagement is market-driven—clients want inexpensive analyses, so the report contains a very frank engagement letter and significant limitations on the scope of the assignment. (See the sample engagement letter in the Appendix.)

Since the client has placed a limitation on time and money, a valuator must prepare a report to fit the assignment. The valuator needs to perform enough work to be reasonably sure that the limited-scope estimate of value is close to the estimate of value from a full-scope valuation. However, one can never be 100 percent sure how closely a limited-scope valuation relates to a full-scope valuation until a full-scope estimate of value is performed.

It is not an easy task to balance resources under a limited-scope engagement. A valuator must investigate the industry, look for market comparables, analyze the company financial statements, and calculate an estimate of value in the context of limited data. This process requires a great deal of experience and a skilled hand to guide the investigation through to a confident finish.

This type of limited-scope valuation is similar to the direction taken in many audit engagements today. In the past, accountants worried about whether or not cash reconciled; today, they need to be able to stand back from the situation and recognize potential problems at a higher level, not necessarily the exacting detail. The detail, if necessary, can come after the issues are identified. Similarly, in the limited-scope engagement, the valuator is charged with determining an estimate of value on the basis of limited research and analysis. An experienced valuator should be able to determine this value as a result of years of experience and continued knowledge combined with limited research and analysis. Then, if a reason develops to expand the process (e.g., an unfavorable determination from an IRS audit), the valuator can do so without having to start from a blank slate.

Representation Letter

As a final note, the management of the company should be asked to sign a representation letter. This letter (see the example in the Appendix) confirms the representation of the reliability of the information that management provided, and it will be requested at the end of the engagement and will accompany the reviewed copy of the final draft of the valuator's report. The final draft of the report is reviewed by the client only for factual accuracy, not for the size of the estimate of value. The report can be issued once a final payment on account has been remitted, the draft report has been initialed on every page by the client, and the signed management representation letter has been returned to the valuator.

SUMMARY

As you become initially more familiar with valuations, you may feel overwhelmed by the magnitude of the process, but with more experience you will gain an increased level of comfort. It may not be as simple as one, two, three, but this description of the process and methodologies should begin to paint a clearer picture of what the process should entail.

There are five different concepts upon which value is based: fair market value, fair value, investment value, intrinsic value, and liquidation value. In fair market value, the analyst determines the hypothetical estimated price at which property would change hands between a willing buyer and seller, neither of whom are under any obligation to make the deal and both of whom are fully aware of all relevant facts. Fair value is used primarily in disputes with minority shareholders; investment value is the value of a business to a specific buyer; intrinsic value is the "true" value of the business; and liquidation value is based solely on assets and liabilities rather than on earnings.

The comprehensive business valuation process consists of the engagement assessment and three major phases: research and data gathering, analysis, and estimation and report of value. During the engagement assessment, valuators determine the scope of the project, whether they can accept the assignment, whether the client is appropriate, and what the valuation entails. An engagement acceptance form can serve as a tool for helping a valuator understand the project and the people he or she will be working with.

To ensure an optimal relationship between valuator and client, valuators should be aware of the following: Are there any problems concerning conflicts of interest? Do any potential fee collection problems exist? Is the engagement within the valuator's capabilities? Does the valuator have sufficient staffing to perform and oversee the valuation? Do the terms of the proposed engagement meet the ethics and standards of the valuator's professional association?

Phase I provides the valuator with hard data. Key information includes both internal sources—financial statements, off-balance-sheet and contingent liabilities, operating budgets, legal documents, accounts receivable and payable, business plans, and business projections—and external sources such as economic trends, regional and local demographics, competitor data, comparative financial data, and industry reports.

In Phase II, the valuator analyzes the information about the company, its industry, economic trends, and market comparables. Phase III presents the estimation of value on the basis of information and analysis gleaned during the first two phases. To reach the estimate of value, the valuator links industry and comparable information and adjusts for any factors that may affect value. Results of the valuation can be presented in full written reports, letters, oral reports, or limited-scope valuation reports; the most appropriate type of report is based on the kind of engagement and the client's intended use of the report.

NOTES

1. James Schilt, "Appraisal under Corporations Code Section 2000," *Business Law News*, 8:4, Summer 1985.
2. California Corporation Code § 2000, Subdivision (a).
3. Bruce R. Robinson, *Strategic Acquisitions: A Guide to Growing and Enhancing the Value of Your Business*, Burr Ridge, IL: Irwin, 1995, p. xiii.
4. Shannon Pratt, *Valuing a Business*, 3rd ed., Homewood, IL: Irwin, 1996, p. 26.
5. Jay E. Fishman et al., *Guide to Business Valuations*, Fort Worth, TX: Practitioners Publishing Company, March 1994, Vol. 3, VAL-2.
6. CAMICO, *Loss Prevention: A Manual for an Accounting Practice*, Redwood City, CA: California Accountants Mutual Insurance Company, 1996. (800) 652-1772.
7. AICPA, *Communicating Understandings in Litigation Services: Engagement Letters*, New York: American Institute of Certified Public Accountants, 1995.
8. Generally Accepted Auditing Standards (GAAS), Rule ET §191.54.107–108.
9. The Appraisal Standards Board of the Appraisal Foundation develops and publishes the Uniform Standards of Professional Appraisal Practice. Appraisal Standards Board, *Uniform Standards of Professional Appraisal Practice*, Washington, DC: The Appraisal Foundation, 1995. Also, some states are regulating this area through statute, so check with the relevant state CPA society for the regulations and ethics.
10. "Specific Industry Experience Not Needed to Qualify as an Expert," *Shannon Pratt's Business Valuation Update*, September 1996, p. 10, referencing *Blinderman v. Reib*, No. 1–94–2557, 1996 WL 454954, (Ill. App. 1 Dist. August 13, 1996).

11. Charles B. Larson and Joseph W. Larson, *Innovative Billing and Collection Methods That Work*, Burr Ridge, IL: Irwin, 1995.

12. Internal Revenue Service Revenue Ruling 59–60, Section 4(b).

13. U.S. Department of Commerce, International Trade Administration, *U.S. Industrial Outlook*, Washington, DC: Government Printing Office, 1984–94.

14. The Securities and Exchange Commission's EDGAR Web site, which accesses electronic versions of public submissions to the commission, is particularly valuable: http://www.sec.gov/edgarhp.html.

15. U.S. Office of Management and Budget, *Standard Industrial Classification Manual*, Springfield, VA: National Technical Information Service, 1987.

16. Internal Revenue Service Revenue Ruling 59–60 (1959–1 C.B. 237), Section 4.01, (g) & (h), Section 4.02 (g) & (h).

17. Tax Court Memo, 1991–279, *Estate of Berg v. Commissioner*. See *Estate of Berg* for additional comments on this issue. Lance S. Hall and Timothy C. Pollack, "Strategies for Obtaining the Largest Valuation Discounts," *Estate Planning*, January–February 1994, pp. 38–44.

18. Tax Court Memo, 1994–539, *Luton v. Commissioner*.

19. Valuators should be sure that management is aware of the benefits of association membership.

20. Internal Revenue Service Revenue Ruling 59–60, Section 7.

21. NACVA, *1995 Membership Directory*, Salt Lake City, UT: NACVA, 1995, pp. 1–5 to 1–12.

22. Appraisal Standards Board, *Uniform Standards of Professional Appraisal Practice*, Washington, DC: The Appraisal Foundation, 1995, p. 19.

CHAPTER 5

The Power of Valuation Consulting

The process of providing business valuation services to a business owner should not end with delivering a report, placing a dollar value on the business, and receiving the fee. Instead, these steps can often be the beginning of an ongoing consulting relationship. Together, the business owner and the valuator can develop worthwhile strategies for improving the value of the business. The consulting assistance of a valuator complements the work of a traditional management consultant because a valuator focuses on the broad strategic drivers of the firm's value instead of specific functional tactics.

Although business valuations may sometimes appear as a necessary evil forced upon business owners by divorce or litigation, the valuation process can serve as an integral management tool for increasing the worth of a business. By focusing on the specifics of a business and its industry, a business valuation draws attention to areas of a business that may enhance or diminish value. And in situations that involve the death of a business owner, the business may be the most important yet least liquid asset of an estate.

This chapter discusses the power of valuation consulting. We describe a specific example of how it has been useful, we highlight the importance of the engagement phase, and we discuss nine other-than-ordinary practical strategies for managing and increasing value. Toward the end of the chapter, we pinpoint six potential pitfalls in valuation of which valuators and their clients should be aware: from working with incomplete data or insufficient third-party information to using a formula approach for a valuation.

THE ESSENCE OF VALUATION CONSULTING

Valuation consulting calls upon the science and art of business valuation to assist a business owner in improving the value of his or her company. To complement management consulting, which often focuses on improving strategies and tactics through particular functions (e.g., marketing, operations), valuation consulting focuses on how strategies and tactics create value for business owners. This type of higher-level analysis is not often provided by typical management consulting firms, although the top-tier strategy firms are increasingly aware of its importance. It is an approach that might be more commonly applied by investment banks, but because investment banks are so transaction-oriented, they are less likely to have the expertise and time to work through the information with which a business valuator is accustomed.

An Example of Valuation Consulting

The following story illustrates the importance of creating a strategic team approach to valuation and suggests many of the themes that will be raised in this chapter.

An attorney called a valuator to discuss a potential business valuation assignment. The attorney quickly outlined the situation: Negotiations were going on to sell a high-tech company, and management was eager to know what a reasonable estimate of value would be. The attorney said that he would send over a package with some relevant information to conduct a "first blush"[1] determination of value that would require only an oral report.

Since it was not the valuator's practice to accept rush engagements, even when business was slow, the valuator hesitated and advised the attorney of the inherent disadvantages of performing a rushed analysis. The attorney said he would take the points under advisement and consult with his client. The valuator agreed to read and study the documents being sent over and to consider accepting the engagement on the basis of "agreed-upon procedures" and with the provision that he could interview the client and tour the facilities. The attorney approved the valuator's requests.

Because of the short time frame, the valuator toured the business facilities and interviewed management that weekend. During the course of the tour, he was able to discuss the valuation process with management. The president of the company was an astute businessperson who understood the value of a more in-depth analysis of the industry, the competition, and the business. He agreed to slow down the negotiations and to allow the valuator to proceed with a full valuation while providing an interim oral report in two to three weeks.

During the first and second phases of the engagement, the valuator and the client discussed numerous aspects of the business. As the valuator expended his scope, conducted his industry research, searched for market comparables, and analyzed the competition, he shared his findings with the president. These discussions led to more open communications and eventually to substantial trust in the valuator's work. The president began to ask probing questions and authorized an expansion of the scope of the engagement.

The president learned from the valuator's research and interviews of key people in the industry that his company's services and products were of interest to larger companies attempting to enter his geographic area. The acquisition of his company would allow the larger companies to gain market share and some value-added features for less than the cost of developing them. In addition, purchase of his company added some channels of distribution, allowed the bigger company to enter his market earlier than planned, and provided some engineering expertise that the acquiring company lacked. These were definite strategic advantages that the valuator was able to pinpoint and communicate to management, which was too deeply involved in day-to-day operations to focus on. That in itself is a big advantage of engaging a consultant: to do the things management does not have the time or energy to accomplish. In many cases management is bright enough but just too tired at the end of the day or just too pressed for time.

Today, the president would explain that, during the valuation process, he did learn many valuable things about his own operations, the industry, and the market for his company's products. In fact, the knowledge that he gained led him to take the company off the market and to make some changes in management that have clearly improved the value of his company. In addition, he occasionally calls his valuation consultant just to touch base and to stay current. There is also the potential for a new engagement for the valuator: an update of the old report as management develops a stock ownership plan for key employees.

In the end, the company was sold for a price that was three times what had been originally offered. By staying in close contact with the client during and after the valuation, the valuator was able to build rapport and to continue the relationship after the completion of the engagement. The value-added benefit for the client was information that the company neither had the time nor the inclination to pursue on its own. This information led to a fresh look at the company's strategies and enabled the president to increase the value of the company substantially.

The Value-Added Engagement Phase

As described in Chapter 4, the engagement phase provides an opportunity for valuators to add significant value for their clients. By highlighting the scope of the project and fees, the engagement phase solidifies the basis of the relationship with a client and helps set mutually agreeable expectations.

By using an engagement acceptance form, a valuator can understand the target company more clearly and thereby decide whether to accept an engagement. Practitioners Publishing Company provides a useful sample.[2] In addition to basic data about a potential client, the engagement acceptance form helps define the scope of the project and outlines important issues a valuator should consider prior to accepting a project. Once a valuator decides to take on an engagement, he or she outlines the scope of the project, estimates its cost and the out-of-pocket expenses, and provides for any necessary fee adjustments in an engagement letter.

Ongoing Relationships and Feedback

As the previous section suggests, much of the valuator's effectiveness depends on developing strong ongoing relationships with clients that permit both the valuator and the client to be honest and forthright.

Once the valuation is completed, the valuator should sit down with his or her client and discuss how and why the conclusions were reached and the implications of the findings. The written report should be used as a springboard for discussing which factors enhance or distract from value at the time of the valuation and which factors can improve value in the future through careful management.

It is the independent analyst who becomes the reporter of valuable information regarding the business interest, the one who can objectively analyze a business internally and externally and assist in focusing on how to increase value through smart management and policy. The company might be confronting something as basic as paying too much for insurance, easily remedied by referral to an insurance company more familiar with the industry. Or perhaps the company is overcompensating its owner/manager and key executives, leaving insufficient funds to capitalize a profitable business future with adequate funding for working-capital needs for operations and capital expenditure for growth. The consultant will provide a reality check. With that knowledge, management can improve earnings, free cashflow, and reduce the controllable risks associated with running the business. Although management may not be capable of controlling industry or economic risk, it certainly has control over much of the risk within its own operations and those decisions and strategies over which that risk shadows.

Establishing a partnership with the client is crucial in preparing for the future. The valuator's guidance can help the client perform a valuation before an opportunity arises to realize the worth of the business or before a crisis situation forces the client into getting a valuation under severe time pressure and higher costs. By working closely with a consultant, management should be able to get more out of the business than just its liquidation value. Management can build equity to bolster a going concern by developing the company's ability to attract customers, maintain good vendor relationships, develop and keep systems operating, and foster a happy workforce eager to continue the operations without disruption.

Once the owner/manager of the closely held business understands how the value has been determined, he or she can focus on developing a strategic plan for increasing value on the basis of overall personal, family, and employee goals.

MANAGING VALUE

Several elements of the valuation process are so important that they merit reemphasis. At a more general level than the specifics described in Chapter 3, this section describes the importance of knowing the industry and looking to the future. A valuator should not wait to react to situations affecting value; instead, a valuator should be proactive and assist a client in following his or her plan's guidelines. Although a client usually has not considered it, managing value is just as important as managing sales, production, human resources, and earnings. After all, don't most officers, directors, employees, and shareholders of public companies do that? They check the value of their investment almost every day through the World Wide Web, radio, television, and the newspaper. How often do the owners of a private, closely held business check the value of their business? Usually when it's too late: After they've been served with a subpoena.

Knowing the Industry

One of the ways in which a valuator helps clients is to ensure that clients do not operate in a vacuum about what an industry is doing. Industry and economic trends may have a strong impact on a company's operations. Good valuation analysts have expertise in locating the right sources of data, evaluating them, and enabling the business owner to use the information to his or her greatest advantage.

As we progress in the information age, an unbelievable amount of data has become available on specific industries. Whereas we once relied on being close to a well-stocked university library, today we can tap into computer networks, use the fax, or make phone calls. Articles, books, studies, reports, and charts about the past, present, and future abound, and it takes only legwork and some directed research to find lots of useful information. The competitive analysis section of Chapter 4 provides more detail.

Once the relevant data are collected, the valuator must read, study, and interpret the information and then write a comprehensive report of his or her findings. This work provides a valuable service to owners of private, closely held businesses, who may have only a limited understanding of their industry. In the case of most companies with less than $5 million in sales, they and their staffs have only so many hours in a day. Midsize businesses with more than $5 million in sales usually have sufficient staff to keep abreast of industry trends.

We are always amazed by the mountain of trade journals, association newsletters, and junk mail that piles up on the desks of business owners and never gets read. In our industry overview section of the valuation report, we put this diverse information into perspective so that the owner can grasp the overall industry picture and how it relates to his or her business. For example, a business that is flourishing in a weak industry may not be maximizing the return on the time and resources of the business owner. Perhaps diversification is the key to a higher return on the owner's capital in the future. Or consider the business that is doing poorly in a flourishing industry. The owner has to then ask: "What am I doing wrong?" and make the necessary changes.

Throughout the valuation report, footnoted information and sources help clients build their own research and provide them with evidence to support the findings of the report. A critical element of managing value is to keep information about the industry current. After all, "knowledge is power."[3]

In a study of the local restaurant market, one valuator discovered that within a 15-mile radius of the heart of his valuation subject, there were over 2000 new restaurant seats opened or opening in a six-month period of the valuation date. The owner of the restaurant in question was aware that some development of new restaurants was occurring, but had no idea of the scope. Together, the valuator and the owner were able to determine that this was going to substantially impact the business in the future. With this knowledge the owner quickly developed a strategic plan to refurbish his restaurant and put a marketing plan in place to counter the effects of so many new seats in the market area. Restaurant patrons can be very disloyal and move to the next hot concept when they are not being satisfied. When over 2000 new seats open, the market does not get larger. Rather, the pieces of the pie get smaller and smaller until yet another restaurant goes out of business and the market returns to an equilibrium. This is not rocket science but can be managed if owners are aware of and savvy to protecting the value of what it is they have: customer goodwill.

STRATEGIES FOR IMPROVING VALUE

After considering the industry, the competition, and the outlook for the company, it may be important for the valuator and client to work together to enhance value. In this section, we discuss nine practical strategies for enhancing the value of a company other than the ordinary. These strategies complement the initial reasons for business valuation discussed in Chapter 2. Although some writers would focus on the traditional in this regard, we believe our readers are out of the ordinary and already have knowledge of the importance of such issues as a need for working capital, management of overhead, and maximization of profits. We have discovered, that even though some of the following nine points appear simple and obvious, private, closely held business owners and their advisers need to reconsider them carefully.

Strategy 1

Maintain or adjust client financial records on an accrual basis. Accrual-basis accounting matches revenues with expenses for business cycles; cash-basis accounting is often subject to mismatching. A particular example comes to mind in which a service business was seriously misguided by keeping its financial records on a modified accrual basis. The firm served as a subcontractor to a manufacturing company that did not recognize income until the product was shipped from the manufacturing facility. In fact, the contract for the subcontracting stipulated withholding payment for the subcontracted work until the sale was final (i.e., until shipment to the ultimate customer). The subcontractor became eager to enjoy the benefits of its labor and concocted a non-GAAP method to recognize income many months prior to actually receiving it. The consequence of this accounting policy was to seriously mismatch revenue and expense by recognizing income too soon and deferring the expenses until paid.

The situation had an unfortunate ending. The principals of the business began to borrow money from this mismatching of revenue and expense to pay themselves before the funds were available. As might have been guessed, the need escalated to recognize more potential revenue sooner and to borrow more and more. Then, the principals lost an account through dispute, decreasing expected revenue. Instead of dealing with the problem and correcting their error, they accelerated the recognition of income from other customer accounts through an aggressive change in estimate assumptions, took these statements to the bank to increase their line of credit, and borrowed more.

This scheme caught up to them when a lawsuit arose through a business dispute that required the valuation of their business. The valuator engaged by the opposing side discovered this accounting issue and restated the firm's financial statements to reflect GAAP with respect to the correct timing of revenue recognition. The value of the business was seriously impaired, and the credibility of management became suspect. This is a classic example of an impatient management team that could not wait for its reward. It happens all too often and will negatively affect the value of a business.

Strategy 2

Be sure owners and managers are providing for the future. One responsibility for business owners and management is to consider their own needs and the needs of their employees during retirement. A valuator should investigate to see if it makes sense to develop a profit-sharing plan and/or a retirement plan for owners and employees. If one already exists, is it sufficiently well funded and well managed?

Although the funding of these plans generally appears as an expense on the financial statement, the valuator should be aware that benefits are accruing to the owners of the business and its employees. Advance planning of this type is a positive sign of management's intent and concern about the welfare and longevity of the business. An action by management to drain cash from the business only for short-term self-gratification will be reflected negatively in any later negotiations to sell the business.

Similarly, and more directly focused on the business owner, the valuator should discern whether the appropriate wealth planning has been done. It is critical for a business owner to make preparations for the period in life when the business has been sold and funds are no longer being generated. By anticipating what a business is worth, a valuator can help a client's wealth-planning efforts to ensure that there will be sufficient capital during the retirement years.

Strategy 3

As mentioned in Chapter 3, it is important to be aware of how environmental issues may affect a business. A business that has addressed environmental issues will be worth more than a business in the same industry that has not addressed environmental issues. More and more is known about these kinds of issues and their impact on even small companies. Considerations from pollution to proper land use can affect ownership value. These variations in value can be substantial and need to be considered as a factor in the valuation process. To help improve value, a valuator can highlight the importance of these issues to management, demonstrate how other companies in the industry are handling similar problems, and offer suggestions about how management can investigate environmental issues to manage potential liabilities.

Strategy 4

Make careful decisions about the location of the business. Being situated on an earthquake fault can discourage investors and detract from value. Valuators performing business valuations in California have become more sensitive to this issue following the Loma Prieta and Northridge earthquakes. Obviously, some location decisions made in the past limit the range of options for a business owner. However, future location decisions can be made so as to increase value or at least not diminish value. For instance, the owner of a marine supply store in Louisiana might choose to expand in another coastal state (e.g., North Carolina) that has different weather patterns and different economic conditions.

After analyzing the effects of the 1989 Loma Prieta earthquake on an estate's ownership interests in a real estate business located near the epicenter of the quake, we found evidence suggesting that an economic conditions adjustment of 7 to 10 percent was appropriate. How do those floods, fires, volcanic eruptions, or other natural disasters affect a business interest when the valuation is performed near the date of the event? The analysis indicated that the amount of the adjustment declined as time passed. As a planning tip, a business owner might want to consider taking advantage of a disaster by making gift transfers immediately after these types of events in order to avail himself or herself of an adjustment to value. At this point, the adjustment will be at its maximum.

Strategy 5

As noted in Chapter 4, factor in the effects of the economy, whether good or bad. The Reagan administration in 1981 inherited from the Carter administration what it referred to as the "Misery Index,"[4] an index that is the sum of the inflation rate plus the unemployment rate. By the end of the 1980s, it loomed much less large. The Misery Index was as high as 22.5 percent during 1981, and at year end 1996 it was only 8.4 percent.

Strategy 6

Consider both historical data and projections (see Chapter 3), even though the emphasis on the past compared with the future will depend on the individual situation for each business. For an emerging company, there will be less attention paid to its past performance and more to its future planning and financial projections. Why? Because an emerging company most likely does not have much of a past record, and the basis of information to determine its value is highly dependent upon its future prospects.

Strategy 7

Don't let the "tax tail" wag the "business dog." That is, do not make business decisions solely on the basis of minimizing business and personal income taxes. Lowering taxes often goes hand in hand with a decrease in business income and/or cashflow, and thus runs counter to a business owner's long-term objective of increasing the value of a business. It is common in private, closely held businesses to make decisions on the basis of tax ramifications. Of course, we would all like to pay less taxes, but taxes are a cost of doing business.

In the eyes of a potential buyer and his or her valuator, financial records reflecting a decision to minimize earnings for tax reasons may serve as a deterrent and perhaps even give the buyer leverage to drive down the price. Instead, use the valuation as a starting point for increasing value through the right balance of tax strategies and remember to keep in mind how tax strategies fit in with overall business goals. For example, a profit-sharing plan and/or pension plan can be used to keep taxes down and can actually add to business value. A valuator will generally add back to earnings the contributions to qualified plans in which the majority of the benefit from continuation in the plan will inure to the buyer after acquisition.

Another example is depreciation policy. The seller may have used accelerated depreciation methods, including Section 179 deductions, to reduce tax liability.[5] A valuator will catch this choice and will normalize the financial statements accordingly. Most legal tax policy is apparent to a valuator and can be adjusted for, thus normalizing earnings and increasing the estimated value.

Strategy 8

Make sure that clients' records reflect the current business value. It is easy to become complacent and let an estimate of value become stale. We recommend that clients update their valuation as often as the end of every business operating cycle, or at least every three years. A valuation is not just a question of putting a price tag on a business. It becomes a report card for measuring the character and progress of a business. It can serve as a strategic management tool for increasing business value by uncovering strengths, weaknesses, opportunities, and threats, and thus provide opportunities to build upon or improve value.

Knowing the current value of the business can also prevent potential problems from developing. The initial valuation may appear to be costly in relationship to the perceived benefit, but one of the advantages is the ability to update the valuation annually at a reduced cost. It will come in handy in the event of a sudden divorce, death, or unexpected disaster such as a fire.

After all, a client does not hesitate to buy insurance in case something untoward happens; however, the client seems to ignore the question "What is the value of the business lost?" Suppose that the business has taken a substantial upswing and is worth far more than the coverage under the terms of the interruption/loss policy, and that a flood damages all computer disks and paper records. Having a current written estimate-of-value report in the hands of the valuator for safekeeping is going to benefit a client immediately.

Another example is the spouse who believes the business is worth a fortune and files for divorce thinking that he or she will get the equity in the house while the spouse who runs the company—the in-spouse—can have the business. If the in-spouse has engaged a valuator to value the business at the end of each business cycle, then the evidence is difficult for opposing counsel to dispute. If this value has been represented by management to employees, investors, lenders, and independent board members, then it will carry substantial weight, and the marital estate can move on to other matters.

This example brings up an interesting point. If an out-spouse (the spouse who does not run the business, who is typically *out*-side the business, as opposed to the spouse who actively manages the business, who is *in*side the business) handles his or her own affairs separately from the in-spouse, a financial adviser may want to consider recommending that a valuation of the in-spouse's business be performed annually. This valuation can be used for wealth planning, dividing equity between marital partners, and determining insurance requirements. People check on the value of their residence with the arrival of each newsletter or bulletin from the local real estate brokerage agent, but how often do they evaluate the worth of what is often their largest asset, one that produces the most cashflow—the family business? In addition, although both spouses watch with interest the value of their residence, it is generally only the in-spouse who has even a general idea of business worth.

Strategy 9

Develop an exit strategy so that family members and partners are not left at loose ends after a critical owner or manager leaves the company. An exit strategy depends heavily on knowledge of the value of the business. As described in Chapter 2, an exit strategy is one of the key reasons for a business valuation. Especially in private, closely held businesses, it is important to establish succession plans and associated changes in ownership control as much as possible.

AVOIDING VALUATION PITFALLS

From over 25 years of experience, we have learned about a wide variety of problems and issues that can handicap the process of business consulting. Some of these mistakes we have seen for ourselves; others we have heard about from colleagues and peers. If ignored, these critical areas can undermine the valuation process. These six pitfalls, often mundane in retrospect, range from missing data and incomplete records to insufficient time for a thorough valuation.

Potential Pitfall 1

Working from incomplete or untimely data. This pitfall seems to be more the rule than the exception. It is extremely annoying not to have all the information that is needed to perform the evaluation analysis. For a valuator working on a fixed-fee engagement, it could mean a loss of income. The way to avoid waiting for client documents is to put a clause in the engagement letter which states that the valuator can reasonably be expected to complete the report within X to Y weeks *after* the receipt of all necessary information. Make it clear that not producing documents will delay the completion of the report.

Let's take a hypothetical situation, one that may be encountered frequently, especially with private, closely held businesses. The business is a small manufacturing company that is only three years old. The trends were fairly flat for the first two years, but then the company secured a very large 15-month contract from a Fortune 500 company, a contract that proved to be very profitable. There is a tendency to discount the contract because of its unusual size in relationship to prior business. Sometimes referred to as the "large-client syndrome," this kind of contract may cause a valuator either to remove it from operations in performing the estimate of value or to discount it.

Here again, investigative skills are valuable to balance the science and art of valuation. The valuator needs to make some inquiries: Was the contract terminated, or is there any reasonable prospect of termination by the customer? The valuator needs to interview the client and possibly the client's new customer. Let's assume the contract is not in danger of being terminated, and it is likely that the contract will run its normal course and provide profitability to the company being valued. In addition, the customer is very happy and intends to give the client more contracts in the near future because of excellent performance.

The next question is: If this contract had not been in place, could other customer prospects in the pipeline have taken its place during the same time period? In fact, there were other prospects that had to be turned down because of this large contract. In addition, because of the satisfaction of the Fortune 500 customer, more opportunities from other Fortune 500 companies have arisen. These contracts will not only fill the void left after the completion of the current contract but will also provide a good reason to expand.

Without carrying this example too far, we can start to get the picture. Taking a situation at face value could cause substantial harm to the value of the company. Adjusting the trends of this company for a "large-client syndrome" would be the wrong thing to do. If anything, the profile of this business is one of an emerging operation with a strategic advantage that has caught the eye of larger public companies.

The lesson here is to perform interviews, follow through on document requests, and carefully read the information to ensure that client data are complete. Too many valuators accept financial statements and tax returns and are too inexperienced to analyze additional information. Those valuators are not pursuing the appropriate scope of the engagement and are falling short of the best estimate of value.

Potential Pitfall 2

Allowing a lack of time to interfere with the valuation process. The primary reason for this pitfall is client procrastination, which is often tied to worry about how much the engagement is going to cost. To minimize this pitfall, valuators must educate the client and other consultants who may be involved in planning for the valuation by presenting the range of available valuation options. The client should know that it is not always necessary to jump into an engagement seeking a full written report; instead, it may be better if the engagement begins with a limited-scope valuation and an oral or letter report. This option gives clients and their advisers an opportunity to get an early assessment of the range of value, the projected time constraints, and a more informed cost estimate of a full-scope estimate of value.

Unfortunately, it is often difficult to square the value-added services with additional costs to the client, and it may be necessary to turn down an engagement. For valuators, the challenge is to educate clients about the value of valuation services so that it is not necessary to compromise by lowering standards. Marketing materials can assist in presenting this message; communications can emphasize value-added services and their ability to bolster the valuation process.

Potential Pitfall 3

Lacking relevant third-party information. This pitfall can be overcome with time and research skills. Although theories of value often deal with hypothetical transactions, there is a need to support analysis of a hypothetical transaction with proxy data in the form of available market evidence.

This is an area in which the government is currently attaching valuation adjustments with respect to estate and gift tax matters. According to the IRS, real estate investment trusts (REITs) are not always relevant comparables for the control adjustment, even when it appears there is a good match through underlying assets and the region of the country. Suppose that the underlying asset is farmland valued at $10,000 per acre and that the subject of the limited partnership equity gift is farmland worth $40,000 per acre. Or consider that the REITs have in excess of 500 equity owners and the limited partnership has only five, IRS logic says this is not market-comparable evidence. This argument in itself will not eliminate the use of the comparable; however, it will burden the business owner with the added cost of having the valuator expand the scope of the research, analysis, and report to document the evidence necessary to support the estimate of value.

A good approach to developing third-party evidence is to talk with the source of the proxy (conduct an interview). It is as simple as picking up the phone and asking; usually, there will be no difficulty in eliciting information. Start with the company's investor relations officer. This person's name and telephone number can usually be found in the annual report of a public company. State exactly why you are calling and explain your need for information. If the officer on duty does not have the information, he or she will generally refer you to someone within the company who can help.

Potential Pitfall 4

Using a set formula approach to valuing an equity interest or letting a software program do the work. Formulas and computers are only one part of a valuator's tool kit. It is the valuator who, in the end, must construct the estimate of value by combining the science and the art of valuation. For this reason, we have not written chapter after chapter about discounted future earnings, excess earnings, net adjusted assets, betas, discount rates, present value, or regression analysis. Many of the books in the Bibliography do a good job of discussing these important topics in detail.

To avoid reliance on a formula approach, we brainstorm and hold discussions with colleagues at the end of each phase of the valuation process. We share viewpoints and knowledge on topics relevant to the outcome. It is this process rather than the application of a formula that leads us to an estimate of value that makes sense under specific circumstances. In fact, we do not generally run formulas until Phase III, the estimate of value.

Potential Pitfall 5

Working with inadequate or poorly kept business records and accounting policies. A valuator needs to understand the books and records of the company to determine their quality. If it appears that the records require substantial adjustment beyond the scope of a normal valuation engagement, the valuator may insist upon a revised engagement letter and assignment prior to continuing the valuation process.

However, a valuator must be careful when taking an engagement that requires substantial adjustment to financial statements other than those that are normalization. A licensed CPA may be held to higher standards than a valuator who is not licensed. The CPA valuator's engagement letter should clearly communicate the scope of the assignment and any limitations, including clarification of his or her role, since this area has potential for conflict of interest and professional liability for a CPA who is performing a business valuation.

Potential Pitfall 6

Accepting at face value financial statements that are not prepared in accordance with Generally Accepted Accounting Principals (GAAP). A valuation consultant will not always be working with audited, reviewed, or compiled financial statements. For some engagements, the only financial information available may be the client's tax returns or internally prepared financial statements that may not follow GAAP. If a valuator comes across an obvious departure from GAAP when analyzing the company's financial statements, the valuator should rectify the problem in most circumstances. However, it is not the valuator's responsibility to restate completely the company's financial statements in accordance with GAAP. See Chapter 4 of Fishman's *Guide to Business Valuations* for an excellent discussion of this topic. For example:

> Financial statements in a valuation engagement may be adjusted for different reasons and in a different manner than in a normal financial statement preparation engagement. The adjustments:
>
> (a) provide the consultant with a consistent, reasonable starting point for the valuation decision [GAAP adjustments]
>
> (b) give the consultant an insight into:
>
> > (1) what prior operations might have looked like under normal conditions (and on a consistent basis with comparable companies), or
> >
> > (2) what a prospective buyer might reasonably be expected to obtain from the company in the future, using history as a guide.
>
> The adjustments described in point (a) are GAAP adjustments. The adjustments described in point (b) are referred to as normalization adjustments.[6]

SUMMARY

Just because the estimated valuation number has been reported, the report has been delivered, and the fee has been paid, that doesn't mean the valuation process is over. Instead, this is the time to look ahead to increasing the worth of a client's business. The valuation can serve as an integral management vehicle for achieving this objective. As a consultant, a valuator can offer an objective analysis of the future of the business and its industry, giving his or her client an opportunity to turn things around if problems exist. Developing a value is often only the beginning of an ongoing relationship with a client. At the same time, valuators should be aware of certain pitfalls which could adversely affect the value of a client's business.

The written report serves as an ideal springboard for evaluating what factors have contributed to or distracted from adding value to the business. With this knowledge, a client can determine strategies and design a plan for addressing business and personal goals. Some primary factors to consider are knowing the industry, keeping abreast of the competition, and looking toward the future.

While working with a client to enhance value, a valuator should keep these practical strategies in mind:

1. Maintain or adjust client financial records on an accrual rather than on a cash basis.

2. Provide for the future by developing a profit-sharing and/or retirement plan for management and employees and evaluate wealth planning for the business owner.

3. Be aware of how industry and environmental issues may affect the business.

4. Carefully analyze the location of the business.

5. Factor in the effects of the economy, whether positive or negative.

6. Consider both historical data and projections.

7. Don't let the "tax tail" wag the "business dog"—in other words, don't make business decisions solely on the basis of minimizing business and personal income taxes.

8. Make sure that client records reflect the current business value through regular valuation updates.

9. Develop an exit strategy so that family members and partners are not left hanging when a critical owner/manager passes away.

With so much attention being paid to improving value, it would be counterproductive to fall into some common traps when preparing a business valuation. Try to avoid the following pitfalls: (1) working with incomplete and untimely data; (2) not allowing enough time for the valuation process; (3) lacking third-party information; (4) accepting a formula approach to valuing an equity interest; (5) working with inadequate or poorly kept business records and accounting policies; and (6) accepting financial statements that are not prepared according to GAAP.

NOTES

1. First Blush Valuation® is a registered trademark of ValueNomics Research, Inc.

2. Jay E. Fishman et al., *Guide to Business Valuations*, Fort Worth, TX: Practitioners Publishing Company, March 1994, Vol. 3, VAL–2.

3. Francis Bacon, *Meditations Sacrae*, 1597.

4. Nicholas Comfort, *Brewer's Politics*, London: Cassell, 1993, p 386.

5. Internal Revenue Code Section 179, §1208.

6. Fishman, p. 420.07.

CHAPTER 6

The Role of the Valuation Expert

Although the Yellow Pages may serve as a good source for finding a house painter or a dry cleaner, it is not the ideal source for locating a business valuator. Reputation is what is important for survival and longevity in the valuation business; in most cases, the marketplace will weed out those who are unethical or incompetent.

Clients do not need a "hired gun" who has been trained through advocacy work. In the past, it was common for the legal community to engage a valuator merely to support a particular position, not to search for the best estimate of value. Although this practice still exists, it occurs less frequently. In the long run, the advocacy bias creates disharmony between parties trying to reach a good-faith agreement on the value of a business. Choosing an advocacy position adds nothing to the negotiation process; in fact, it can only slow it down or even end it.

Although legal counsel is ethically obligated to be the client's advocate, a valuator does not have the same role. It may be easy to fall into the trap of trying to look like a hero, but it is the valuator's responsibility to defend his or her estimate of value. A valuator should not put his or her reputation at stake and risk potential legal liability by issuing a biased estimate of value.

The valuator's work should be in the pursuit of the best estimate of value. The assumption is that the other side's valuator is equally intelligent, and with time and hard work, he or she will uncover the truth and the best estimate of value. A valuator is most likely to impress a client, as well as the opposing expert, if the estimate of value is reasonably close to the number reached by the opposing expert.

Take a hypothetical divorce engagement in which both sides secure their own valuators who are paid to support their clients' positions. The results are apt to be so polarized that the chance of resolution is even more unlikely than it was in the beginning. The advocacy valuator in this example will serve to further increase the parties' ill-will toward each other.

THE ADVOCACY POSITION

Advocates are generally consultants who favor the position of their client. This role is acceptable in some circumstances, such as when clients hire a valuator for assistance in positioning a business for a merger or an acquisition. This valuator advocate's position, however, should be disclosed to all concerned parties, particularly if the value is to be represented to a third party. Other situations may not be as clear-cut; a problem may arise if an accountant prepares both a valuation and the financial statements and/or tax returns.[1]

Although a certain valuator may appear to be the logical person to assist a client on a particular engagement, participation should be considered very carefully. A primary concern is how government agencies, such as the IRS, the Department of Labor, and the Securities and Exchange Commission (SEC), perceive the situation. There may be doubt as to whether the consultant is really trying to represent an independent estimate of value for the business fairly and objectively or instead is trying only to please the client.

> With regard to this independence requirement the Department [of Labor] notes that new section 401(a)(28) of the Code [added by section 1175(a) of the Tax Reform Act of 1986] requires that, in the case of an employee stock ownership plan, employer securities which are not readily tradable on established securities markets must be valued by an independent appraiser. New section 401(a)(28)(C) states that the term "independent appraiser" means an appraiser meeting requirements similar to the requirements of regulations under section 170 (a)(1) of the Code (relating to IRS verification of the value assigned for deduction purposes to assets donated to charitable organizations). The Department notes that the requirements of proposed regulation §2510.3–18(b)(3)(iii) are not the same as the requirements of the regulations issued by the IRS under section 170 (a)(1) of the Code. The IRS has not yet promulgated rules under Code section 401(a)(28).[2]

In determining whether an accountant or accounting firm is not, in fact, independent with respect to a particular plan, the Department of Labor will give appropriate consideration to all relevant circumstances, including evidence bearing on all relationships between the accountant or accounting firm and that of the plan sponsor or any affiliate thereof, and will not confine itself to the relationships existing in connection with the filing of annual reports with the Department of Labor.

Further interpretive bulletins may be issued by the Department of Labor concerning the question of independence of an accountant retained by an employee benefit plan.[3]

Although the IRS prefers not to accept a value determined through an advocacy position, this position may vary according to local rule. If a valuator is not perceived as being disinterested, the result could be a costly second valuation while under audit or while preparing to defend the value in Federal Tax Court. This preference for independence is also maintained by the Department of Labor and the SEC. We have had discussions with CPAs around the country who have done a business valuation for companies for which their CPA firm does the audit or tax work. A number of these CPA firms have reported difficulties with the IRS regarding the issue of independence. There is one thing that can be said unequivocally: Valuator independence will continue to be an important issue with the IRS.

The moral is: A client should engage a valuator who is independent and objective, has integrity, and, most important, maintains respect within the industry. If clients shop for a valuator as they would for a doctor—a person with high-quality credentials and a good reputation—they should find a valuator who will provide sound, empirical evidence supporting an objective estimate of value.

THE VALUATOR: ASSUMING THE ROLE OF THE EXPERT WITNESS

Since a business owner never knows when a dispute may lead to litigation and the need to know the value of the enterprise, it makes sense to engage a valuator who has substantial experience as an expert witness, someone whose opinion the court and the legal community respect. This aspect of an engagement requires yet another skill set in a valuator: testimony. Not only should a client confirm the valuator's education, training, and experience, but a client's attorney should also confirm that the valuator's credentials will hold up in court to the rules of an expert witness and the intense scrutiny of opposing counsel.

The law governing testifying and submitting evidence in federal court by an expert is defined by Federal Rule 26. The rule requires that a written report to support any testimony be available 90 days before trial or within 30 days if it is a rebuttal.

Disclosure of Expert Testimony

(A) . . . a party shall disclose to other parties the identity of any person who may be used at trial to present evidence under Rules 702, 703, or 705 of the Federal Rules of Evidence.

(B) Except as otherwise stipulated or directed by the court, this disclosure shall, with respect to a witness who is retained or specially employed to provide expert testimony in the case or whose duties as an employee of the party regularly involve giving expert testimony, be accompanied by a written report prepared and signed by the witness. The report shall contain a complete statement of all opinions to be expressed and the basis and reasons therefore; the data or other information considered by the witness in forming the opinions; any exhibits to be used as a summary of or support for the opinions; the qualifications of the witness, including a list of all publications authored by the witness within the preceding 10 years; the compensation to be paid for the study and testimony; and a listing of any other cases in which the witness has testified as an expert at trial or by deposition within the preceding four years.

These disclosures shall be made at the times and in the sequence directed by the court. In the absence of other directions from the court or stipulation by the parties, the disclosures shall be made at least 90 days before the trial date or the date the case is to be ready for trial or, if the evidence is intended solely to contradict or rebut evidence on the same subject matter identified by another party under paragraph (2)(B), within 30 days after the disclosure made by the other party. The parties shall supplement these disclosures when required under subdivision (e)(1).[4]

In an effort to impeach a valuator's testimony in court, opposing counsel may suggest that the valuator is a "hired gun" because many of his or her engagements are litigation-related. If a valuator has stuck to his or her association's ethics and standards and has not been an advocate, this charge should be difficult for counsel to prove. Testimony for hire is a short-term strategy and will catch up to those valuators who embrace it.

A valuator should seek out a good book[5] on being an expert witness and read it as part of his or her training. Anyone performing business valuations is likely to end up testifying in the not-too-distant future. There is also a highly recommended videotape series, *The CPA as an Expert Witness* by Brian P. Brinig, J.D., CPA, and James McCafferty, J.D.[6], available from ValueNomics Research, Inc.

As an expert witness, a valuator will be called upon to render an opinion for the trier-of-fact. The judge and/or jury may have little or no experience in a complicated arena of business valuation; it is up to the valuator to explain competently the estimate of value in short, simple, and easy-to-understand terms.

When a valuation matter does go to court, experts who try to impress the jury with verbosity and braggadocio, complicated theory, and mathematical formulas or who attack the opposition find that their opinions are not often followed. An experienced valuator will teach the jury and judge, assist them in understanding the discipline in lay terms, and present the case for the estimate of value simply and to the point without stooping to an attack of the opposing valuator.

The courts are demanding quantifiable results with clear and relevant evidence to support a valuator's conclusion. A valuator presenting an estimate of value in a federal court may also have to comply with the new Federal Rules for Civil Procedure and Evidence. The valuator may further need to consider any local rules adopted by the local district court, such as the Ninth District Tax Court Rule 143.

> Expert Witness Reports: (1) Unless otherwise permitted by the Court upon timely request, any party who calls an expert witness shall cause that witness to prepare a written report for submission to the Court and to the opposing party. The report shall set forth the qualifications of the expert witness and shall state the witness' opinion and the facts or data on which that opinion is based. The report shall set forth in detail the reasons for the conclusion, and it will be marked as an exhibit, identified by the witness, and received in evidence as the direct testimony of the expert witness, unless the Court determines that the witness is not qualified as an expert. Additional direct testimony with respect to the report may be allowed to clarify or emphasize matters in the report, to cover matters arising after the preparation of the report, or otherwise at the discretion of the Court.[7]

In general, this rule also means that a valuator will have to present a substantial curriculum vitae in conjunction with a detailed written report setting forth his or her qualifications.

Even with all this attention to detail, the government may decide to audit. In addition, it may still choose not to accept the proposed value if it appears too low; instead, the IRS may engage its own expert to estimate value, which may be significantly higher, thereby leading to a proposed increase in the tax liability for the transfer.

WHEN A VALUATOR NEEDS OTHER SPECIALISTS

In certain circumstances, valuators need to call upon other specialists to assist in their ongoing valuation practices. Valuators require help in these situations because they do not have the expertise themselves or within their organizations. These experts range from technical specialists in engineering or finance to colleagues in the valuation industry. Such experts are usually hired as subcontractors, and depending on the specific engagement and what can be negotiated, they are paid either at an hourly rate or by a fixed fee.

As an example of how technical specialists could be used, a valuator might call upon an environmental engineering firm for perspective on environmental issues, a health care equipment specialist for knowledge of portable MRI (magnetic resonance imaging) equipment, or a crop specialist for understanding agricultural issues. The environmental specialist can share expertise about the severity, riskiness, and potential liability of groundwater contamination at a client's facilities. For the valuation of a medical practice, a health care equipment specialist can provide insight about portable MRI machines: the cost of software upgrades, the frequency and cost of maintenance, and likely patterns of obsolescence. These types of equipment issues loom especially large in a valuation if a medical practice has lots of resources invested in capital equipment.

It is important, as well, to find just the right specialist. An agricultural specialist can be useful in conjunction with a valuation of a farm's output. An important issue may revolve around the fact that table grapes in the Central Valley of California yield a very different value per acre than wine grapes in Napa Valley. Even from one end of the Central Valley to the other, crop values for the same commodity differ according to the specifics of the consumer market, the weather, and the time of year the commodity is harvested. A specialist in crops needs to appreciate these subtle differences so that a valuator can develop the best estimate of value.

Real estate appraisal and some of the intricacies of finance, accounting, tax, and economics are all significant specialty areas where valuators occasionally need assistance. Each of these fields is usually understood by valuators at a broad level, but for components of a valuation engagement, valuators may not have the required, up-to-date expertise in house. An appropriate division of labor suggests that valuators may wish to call upon external experts rather than develop or maintain the expertise themselves.

Valuators may also call upon valuation colleagues for feedback and advice and to avoid conflicts of interest. On a day-to-day basis, valuators contact professional colleagues to use their peers as sounding boards, to run ideas past them, and to discuss refinements and intricacies of underlying valuation issues. Other valuators are also useful in situations of conflicts of interest; another valuator can perform a valuation which would be inappropriate for one valuator to do. Lastly, on large valuation engagements where the risk and exposure for the valuation firm are significant, a valuator may call upon another valuator for a quality review: Do the valuation process and the estimate of value make sense?

THE QUEST FOR THE "RIGHT" VALUATOR—A CLIENT'S PERSPECTIVE

This section is written for those who are choosing a valuation firm; it is also useful for valuators who want to understand what potential clients will be considering as they select a valuator.

When it comes time to hire a valuator, company managers, owners, and their advisers—a business valuator's prospective clients—often look for guidelines to assist in the search and selection process. In this section, we suggest several tips about how to find an appropriate valuator.

• *Identify the new guard of valuators.* These people are governed by association standards of their peers, are independent, and operate with a style that does not create polarization among participants. Clients should begin by consulting with several professionals associations for referrals. The National Association of Certified Valuation Analysts (NACVA)[8] and the American Society of Appraisers (ASA)[9] are but two examples. These organizations have detailed directories of their members.

Anyone can put an ad in the Yellow Pages, but to be listed in a professional association directory, a valuator needs to meet certain requirements. These organizations develop standards and codes of ethics and provide quality review and continuing education. The AICPA, as of the end of 1996, has begun to create an accreditation program in business valuation.[10] It is critical, however, that clients interview professional valuators to determine if they have the proper fit.

A recurrent theme in this book is the importance of engaging an independent valuator. It is worth repeating the point. Hiring a valuator who appears to have even a slight conflict of interest may compromise the client. We believe that it is generally not advisable to use a valuator with whom the client has an established, substantial business relationship. Doing so can taint the appearance of independence and possibly even subject an expert to impeachment as a witness.

When the government is the party requiring the valuation, a particularly skewed value may cause suspicion. The result may cause more than just a blemish on a valuator's reputation; the IRS has the authority to punish the valuator with a civil penalty under Section 6701 for aiding and abetting an understatement of tax liability.

Consider a hypothetical situation involving an estate valuation for tax purposes. Both the taxpayer and his or her legal counsel decide to use the family CPA as the valuator under the assumption that this accountant is most familiar with the business. Unfortunately, the family CPA performs only one or two valuations a year, is too close to the business owner to maintain objectivity, is unable to quantify appropriately certain assumptions made about the industry and market comparables because of a lack of resources, and has been trained to produce the lowest legal tax for the taxpayer, not necessarily the best estimate of value. The value will undoubtedly be understated, and it will likely lead to an IRS audit and challenge, and perhaps even to a civil penalty. This result will only cost the estate valuable time and money. The family CPA who accepts this kind of assignment takes the chance of ruining the long-term relationship with the client and possibly the CPA's reputation. News travels quickly and an unfavorable resolution could do serious damage.

• *Check out the valuator's credentials.* Get a copy of his or her curriculum vitae and verify it. Call the professional organization listed to verify his or her certification, go to the library and read an article the valuator has written, and call references. What valuators have written and how they have conducted themselves in previous relationships are often more informative than a brief meeting.

A qualified valuator is likely to have at least a BS degree in finance, economics, or accounting, because the math and science requirements for the discipline are substantial. A graduate of a top university or college will most likely have completed upper-division classes in calculus, computer science, and research techniques, in addition to the classes in an academic major. The valuator should also have completed at least two upper-division or graduate-level classes in finance, accounting, and economics. Finally, the well-rounded valuator must be familiar with tax law and the rules of accounting, such as Generally Accepted Accounting Principles.

• *Visit the valuator's office and evaluate his or her professional demeanor.* Whether the valuator has an office in a glass-and-marble high-rise or at home, it is important that there is a professional learning environment with an emphasis on results, not on office location.

Here are some things to look for. Is the valuator's office well organized? Does he or she own a well-stocked library? Has he or she kept current with information and trends? Does the valuator subscribe to the important valuation publications? Does the staff have the right mix to support the valuation functions of research, analysis, and report writing? Is the valuator an active participant in a professional association within the discipline? Has he or she won any peer awards or recognition for contributions to the profession? How many hours a year does the valuator devote to valuation? Does he or she teach on a consistent basis or conduct workshops? What is the result of his or her reports with the courts or the IRS? Is the valuator working with respected professionals in the community? Has he or she been appointed by a court? In the end, valuators' writings and their conduct in previous relationships are often more informative than a brief meeting.

• *Make sure the valuator is credentialed.* Valuators should have credentials in business valuation from a professional association, such as the NACVA or the ASA. These credentials indicate that they have taken the time to receive certification or accreditation, have reached a certain level of accomplishment, and are following the standards and code of ethics developed by the organization. The AICPA and NACVA restrict memberships to CPAs; the ASA is an open forum with membership depending on individual qualifications.

How can you be confident that the potential valuator has kept current and is following the organization's standards? Qualified associations are implementing quality review programs designed to review policy and written reports of their members. The association will prepare a report indicating that the member passed the review on an unqualified (requiring no changes) basis. Ask the professional if he or she has undergone such a review and what the result was. You might even ask to see the letter from the association.

Professionals should also be active in professional associations and participate in continuing education courses to increase their breadth of knowledge. It is not inappropriate to ask to see continuing education logs. Ask how frequently the valuator attends seminars and what the course content is.

• *Seek out a valuator with experience in the valuation industry.* We recommend at least two years of service in the degree discipline prior to entering the specialty candidacy of a valuation analyst/appraiser. General requirements for the candidacy are a two-year, full-time internship as a valuation analyst/appraiser under a professional valuator. In addition, the candidate should have taken a variety of educational courses, passed certain exams, and submitted reports as prescribed by a professional association.

Suppose the candidate has not had an opportunity to work the recommended two years in his or her degree discipline, but instead began the candidacy directly out of college. In that case, the internship should be much longer, perhaps five years, under the direct guidance of a senior professional. It is not only a degree that makes a person qualified; also important are experience, achievement, results, and recognition by peers who deserve the designation.

• *Investigate the valuator's base of knowledge about many different types of businesses.* It is a resource that will constantly be drawn on as new engagements develop, and it is one of the elements required by the courts to testify as an expert witness.

(a) A person is qualified to testify as an expert if he has special knowledge, skill, experience, training, or education sufficient to qualify him as an expert on the subject to which his testimony relates. Against the objection of a party, such special knowledge, skill, experience, training, or education must be shown before the witness may testify as an expert.

(b) A witness' special knowledge, skill, experience, training, or education may be shown by any otherwise admissible evidence, including his own testimony.[11]

Specialization in a particular industry will generally come after a candidate for certification has had experience with many different businesses and has made the appropriate investment of time.

• *Check out the valuator's investigative skills.* In almost every engagement, a valuator has to identify red flags and make adjustments to normalize financial statements. A simple example is the adjustment from tax-basis depreciation. Many small businesses keep their books on a tax basis, and a valuation generally requires an adjustment from a tax to a GAAP basis of financial accounting. A more complex example involves the company that has made a change in an accounting estimate during one of the years under analysis and has compiled only financial statements with no footnote disclosure. A valuator will probably notice this change during the investigative phase of an engagement. However, some non-CPAs may not know how to normalize the financial statements in this case.

A valuator should take the research phase far beyond a simple glance at the *U.S. Industrial Outlook*. This aspect of the valuation process is the one that is most often skipped or underanalyzed. If this section of a valuator's work papers doesn't contain references to relevant articles, reports, or studies, then he or she probably has not done the job adequately.

• *Qualify potential valuators as people with whom a working relationship can be established.* Is there a positive chemistry? Are potential candidates inquisitive, analytical, and dynamic? Do they ask intelligent, pertinent questions? Are they respected by the business and professional community in which they serve? Do they have access to current information technology, such as on-line computer services? Do they have access to an updated, comprehensive library, either in house or in affiliation with a reputable academic institution?

• *Avoid valuators who prefer a formula approach.* Beware of using a valuator who follows rules of thumb. Consider two small, nearly identical group medical practices, charging the same fees and exhibiting similar financial statements. One is headed by a physician nearing retirement with an unfunded retirement plan; the other is run by two young physicians far from retirement. By digging, the valuator who deals with each case individually will find the difference and determine the best estimates of value. The formula appraiser will generally apply the same rules across both situations and incorrectly reach identical results for both practices.

• *Make sure the valuator is a good communicator.* Read copies of articles published by potential valuators. Do they have a marketing brochure which reflects a well-educated, knowledgeable, and experienced professional? Are they good writers? Ask valuators for a written proposal to determine if they understand the scope of the valuation assignment. Writing is important, because there are many situations in which the written report may have to stand alone.

Can they adequately represent their findings in deposition or negotiation? It is very important that valuators defend the value they have determined. Are the potential valuators good teachers and salespeople? After all, valuators must be able to educate their intended audience and to sell their findings. If they can't sell or teach, then they probably can't sell their valuation results.

- *Look at sample reports developed by valuators.* Are the reports worth the client's investment? Are they original or are they poured from a mold? What did they cost? Are they comprehensive with footnotes and exhibits? Did they successfully size up the situation and reflect the industry, market-comparable evidence, the business itself, the competition, and the effects of regional, state, national, and global economic conditions relevant to the valuation?

SUMMARY

With so much to consider before engaging a valuator, it is easy to see why letting "your fingers do the walking" is not an adequate resource. Choosing a valuator is far too important to leave to chance.

We recommend considering the following suggestions when seeking and engaging a valuation professional:

1. Choose an independent valuator who is governed by fair play and is free of any conflicts of interest. Don't select someone with whom you have an established business relationship. It doesn't make sense to make a CPA friend happy and then incur thousands of dollars in fees, taxes, penalties, and interest because your "amateur hour" buddy was wrong or was perceived to have a conflict of interest.

2. Check out a valuator's credentials by obtaining a copy of his or her curriculum vitae and verifying the facts.

3. Select a valuator with a BS degree (or perhaps an MBA) in finance, economics, or accounting and one with real-world experience.

4. Seek out a candidate with a knowledge base of many different businesses.

5. Check out the valuator's investigative, research, and analytical skills.

6. Make sure the valuator is credentialed by a professional organization in the education and advancement of the valuation process.

7. Determine if the professional is active in professional associations and participates in continuing education courses.

8. Be sure you feel comfortable with the valuator and are able to establish a positive working relationship.

9. Avoid selecting a valuator who follows only a rule-of-thumb approach to valuation.

10. Make sure the valuator is a good salesperson and communicator who can sell his or her value successfully. Ask the valuator for a written proposal that displays his or her ability as a writer and communicator and ensure that it covers all the important aspects of the valuation assignment.

11. Look at sample reports by the valuator to determine if they successfully capture the issues relevant to the valuation.

Since many engagements revolve around litigation, it makes sense to hire a valuator who has experience as an expert witness. A valuation professional should make sure that he or she works in the interest of the best estimate of value and is not swayed by counsel or by the client. As described at the beginning of the chapter, advocacy positions must be approached cautiously. The challenge is to make the explanation of value easy to understand and acceptable.

NOTES

1. Independence is not impaired when a CPA firm provides appraisal, valuation, or actuarial services that affect the client's financial statements, provided that all significant matters of judgment involved are determined or approved by the client and the client is in a position to have an informed judgment on the results. GAAS Rule 101, interpretation number 54, regarding independence.

2. ESOP Association, *Valuing ESOP Shares*, Washington D.C.: The ESOP Association, 1989, pp. 40–41, footnote 4.

3. Labor Regulations, §2509.75–9, interpretive bulletin relating to guidelines on independence of accountants retained by employee benefit plan.

4. Federal Rules Booklet: *Federal Rules of Civil Procedure, Federal Rules of Evidence*, Boston: Dahlstrom Legal Publishing, 1994, Rule 26, pp. 36–7.

5. Joe Zier, *The Expert Accountant in Civil Litigation*, Toronto: Butterworths Canada Ltd., 1993.

6. Brian Brinig and James McCafferty, *The CPA as an Expert Witness*, San Diego, CA: Litigation Services Institute, 1992.

7. Federal Tax Court Rule 143 (7/1/90), 1f.

8. National Association of Certified Valuation Analysts, Brickyard Towers, Ste. 110, P.O. Box 17265, Salt Lake City, UT 84106, (800) 277–2009.

9. American Society of Appraisers, P.O. Box 17265, Washington, DC 20041, (800) ASA-VALU.

10. "AICPA Council Passes Accreditation Program in Business Valuation," *Shannon Pratt's Business Valuation Update,* November 1996, p. 9.

11. Edward J. Imwinkelried and Tim Hallahan, *California Evidence Code Annotated 1995,* Colorado Springs, CO: Shepard's/McGraw-Hill, 1995, p. 81.

CHAPTER 7

The Client/Valuator Relationship

$\mathbf{A}$ valuation does not have to give a client indigestion or heart palpitations. That's not to say that swimming at the beach wouldn't be a more enjoyable way to spend the day, but the valuation process does not have to be dreaded. If a client is cooperative and forthcoming with accurate and timely information, the valuation process can prove to be a cost-effective proposition. The key to a successful valuation is establishing a relationship of mutual trust among the valuator, the client, and the client's key employees and trusted advisers, such as bank lenders, legal counsel, CPAs, and insurance agents.

As described in this chapter, both the client and the valuator have certain roles to fulfill, and there is a pattern of interaction between them that is to be expected. Also, over time, valuators should begin to move closer in their estimates of value.

THE ROLE OF THE CLIENT: WHAT IS EXPECTED?

If there is agreement and follow-through based on a relationship of trust, the client's particular engagement goals and an estimate of value will be achieved expeditiously for a reasonable fee. Adopting a positive attitude at the outset paves the way for a straightforward, communicative relationship that enables the valuator to elicit relevant facts and information.

To do this, the clients needs to be open and forthcoming during a valuation. Otherwise, serious consequences can result: errors in estimates of value, a longer and more costly valuation process, and possible legal and insurance ramifications. A valuator expects the client to provide access to all necessary relevant information and to be complete about the details of the business.

Unfortunately, too often clients hide the truth and mistakenly assume that they can influence the estimate of value in their favor by withholding information. Such behavior is not in the client's best interest. As the client comes to understand the benefits of the process, he or she will be more willing to share the information that is needed.

Consider the following example. A valuator is rendering an estimate of value related to the buyout of a minority shareholder. The majority shareholder plays coy and fails to provide all the requested information, thinking he or she can hide the obvious. A few red flags enable the valuator to establish enough reasonable doubt that counsel is willing to file a motion to compel management to come forth with the appropriate documents.

What an embarrassment it is when a warehouse supervisor locates a pallet of boxes containing the evidence that had previously been "unavailable." To say the least, management appears suspicious because of its behavior. In response, the valuator will most likely expand the scope of the search, looking more aggressively for abusive tax practices, improper revenue recognition, and other dubious methods of misrepresentation of business profits.

Equally important, when a valuator is less than fully informed, an error in determining value can result. For example, not informing the valuator of protective provisions contained in a venture capital agreement could lead to overstating the value of the stock held by the nonventure capital owners. This is because the protective provisions contained in a venture capital agreement are there to protect the value of the venture capitalists' investment. This information, if not disclosed or discovered, could be used to discredit the valuator's report by other parties that do their homework and later discover the provisions which management has not disclosed.

Another example is the majority shareholder in a shareholder action who fails to inform the valuation expert of all the personal expenses he or she is deducting through the company. Then there is the plaintiff who tries to conceal his personal trips overseas and cash sales that end up in his personal bank account. In one such case, the insurance company for the defense was able to settle that matter quietly and to its advantage, since the plaintiff was seriously compromised by his selfish indiscretions.

Finally, there is the case of a fire that supposedly caused the failure of a client's business. In reality, the business failed because of the owner's negligent management, which was unrelated to the fire. There was a preponderance of evidence that the business was in serious financial trouble prior to the fire, and if not but-for[1] the fire, the business would have failed under its own mismanagement. If the client had been honest and given the valuator the correct information, the claim might have been partially paid, and everyone would have been happy. Instead, the truth was hidden, and it made the business owner, her legal counsel, and the valuator all look foolish.

Since hiding information will inevitably extend the duration of the valuation and drive up costs as more time is devoted to investigative work, a valuator must insist that the clients divulge all necessary and relevant information as early as possible. Like a detective, a valuator spots clues and searches through sometimes conflicting data for a conclusion that makes sense. In some situations, failure to disclose information at the right time may disqualify the use of the information later. An excellent example is the failure to disclose information in the written valuation report to federal courts as required by Federal Rule 26. Such failure could prevent the valuator from using the undisclosed evidence in his or her testimony (see Chapter 6).

THE ROLE OF THE VALUATOR: LIVING UP TO EXPECTATIONS

A substantial part of the relationship between a valuator and a client rests on the client's confidence that the valuator will follow general valuation concepts developed over time by professional valuation organizations, other valuators, case law, statutes, government regulations and rulings, and common business practice.

The valuator has an important role to fulfill: educating the client that the valuation is an investment, not a financial burden. The client and his or her management team should regard the valuator as someone who can provide a fresh perspective on the business enterprise and can provide information to assist them in increasing the value of the company. As described in more detail in Chapter 5, a valuator can assist a client in taking advantage of hidden opportunities that can increase value.

However, because valuation is still an art as well as a science, differences of opinion will still arise among valuators. The most common reason for these differences are variations in assumptions—for example, the expected growth of the market and the company, and the amount of risk involved in an investment in the company. Anything less than the best estimate of value will serve to mislead the client and counsel and will cost more than money; it can put a reputation at stake and/or provoke sanctions. The relationship between what the client wants the value to be and the valuation analyst's estimate of value is stated very clearly by the American Society of Appraisers' *Principles of Appraisal Practice and Code of Ethics*:

> The numerical result (of a valuation engagement) is objective and unrelated to the desires, wishes, or needs of the client who engages the appraiser to perform the work. The amount of this figure is as independent of what someone desires it to be as a physicist's measurement of the melting point of lead or an accountant's statement of the amount of net profits of a corporation. All the principles of appraisal ethics stem from this central fact.[2]

ESTIMATES OF VALUE BY DIFFERENT VALUATORS

Not only do the valuator and client need to develop a relationship of trust, but two valuators working on the same valuation also must play by similar rules. Consider a valuation where two "opposing" sides hire valuators. Given valuation professionals of the same caliber who have the same information and the adequate time and budgets to do their jobs, the results from both parties should be relatively similar.

We recall a situation when a mediator suggested that a second opinion be obtained after the in-spouse rejected the range of value determined by a valuator. It was gratifying when the second valuator virtually hit the midpoint of the first valuator's estimate-of-value range without any input from the first valuator or the mediator. This is a good example of two independent valuators working under common association standards and producing the same result—an outcome that should be the rule, not the exception.

The type of valuation that most commonly leads to variance in valuators' estimations is the divorce engagement. This is a dangerous place to take an advocacy position. Many early experts in the valuation profession cut their teeth on divorce engagements and, unfortunately, left a trail of inconsistent estimates of value that depended on which side they represented at the moment.

In one situation, a valuator made an adjustment for reasonable officer's compensation when valuing the in-spouse's business while engaged by the counsel for the out-spouse. This adjustment increased the value of the business, which benefited the out-spouse. Later, the same valuator did not make an adjustment for officer's compensation when engaged by counsel for the in-spouse. Because the value of the business was lower than if the adjustment had been made, the in-spouse benefited. This valuator was challenged on the witness stand and was destined to be penalized by the court, as well as the marketplace, since the individual would be considered less and less often for engagements. This pattern of behavior reflects badly on the valuation profession as a whole.

An outcome in which two valuators arrive at a reasonably similar estimate of value is happening more frequently than in the past, regardless of whether the original discipline of the valuator is accounting, finance, or economics. The association standards and theories of each of these professions are beginning to merge. In reality, the goal of each of these groups is the same: to produce the most probable estimate of value, given the same valuation assumptions and facts. Hopefully, readers of this book will forge the path to broader agreement on how to resolve the question of value. The best estimate of value is the single largest issue confronting the valuation industry, and such an estimate must come through what professionals deem to be logically defensible procedures.

We hope that valuators will come closer together in their estimates of value by minimizing their theoretical differences. We also hope that valuators will evolve toward differences that depend just on one or two assumptions that an arbitrator or a trier-of-facts can resolve. For example, we would be eager to see a difference that depends only on the appropriate discount rate, or solely on an assumption about the level of appropriate working capital for a business.

INTERACTION STEPS WITH THE CLIENT DURING VALUATION

During the course of a full valuation, there are a set of steps that the client and the valuator management must be sure to fulfill: the initial meeting, updates, and the distribution of a clear final report that can be easily read and understood by nonvaluators.

The initial meeting between the valuator and the client starts the ball rolling by offering a chance for the client to describe carefully his or her business and its strengths, weaknesses, opportunities, and threats. By building on this evaluation, the client and the valuator should be able to identify and analyze what benefits and risks are inherent in the business or industry. Furthermore, this comprehensive analysis often uncovers certain hidden opportunities that may be useful in a follow-on valuation consulting assignment.

The valuators should suggest that the client begin keeping a diary of thoughts and concerns as soon as he or she is aware that a valuation might be necessary. These notes and ideas help make the initial meeting between client and valuator much more productive. Because the client is usually very busy, the valuator needs to emphasize the added value that these thoughts can provide for the whole valuation process.

The client should be prepared to share his or her thoughts and concerns, no matter how ridiculous they may seem, along with the background papers documenting the business. Disclosure is a key to arriving at the appropriate value, and communication is critical to the process. Although most valuators are good interviewers and know what questions to ask, they cannot read minds. The smallest detail, which seems unimportant to the client, may be the fact that brings an important point to the surface.

During the valuation process, the valuator should touch base with the client at least once every few weeks either by telephone or in person to share ongoing thoughts and to provide updated information. The client has a need to know how the engagement is progressing. If the client is kept apprised of the progress of the valuation and the tasks that the valuator is performing, the client is likely to have a higher level of comfort about the valuation and a higher regard for the valuator, and the client should find the task of writing the final check for valuation fees more palatable.

It is important that the final valuation report be well written. In some instances, it must speak for itself, because the valuator is not present at a negotiation or at other situations in which the report's conclusions are utilized. If anything is misunderstood or not clearly articulated, users could misinterpret the report.

Make sure the client and counsel are comfortable with the facts in the final report before it is distributed—even if it needs to be read more than once. A client should take the time to read the document, perhaps let a few days pass, and then reread it. The client should ensure that the valuator has understood the business, the industry, market comparables, the competition, and all the assets, liabilities, and risks of the business.

Although multiple copies of the report are usually made available to both counsel and client, some restrictions should be placed on distribution, since the client does not want his or her competitors to see·it. Distribute copies on the basis of the recipient's need to know. Reports distributed to the IRS will remain confidential unless the case goes to court; at that point, copies will generally become discoverable and thereby may be made public.[3]

BALANCING THE WORKLOAD BETWEEN CLIENT AND VALUATOR

If the client is concerned about the cost of the valuation, there are tasks that a client can perform that will make the valuation less expensive. This depends on the sophistication of the client. In addition, the client or someone from within the company must have the time and the inclination to work with the valuator. He or she must also have the capability to perform the work to the satisfaction of the valuator.

The following steps should serve to decrease the cost of a valuation. A client can prepare an accurate projection of the firm's cashflow or fill out a detailed management questionnaire about the firm's operations. Or the client can furnish lots of useful industry research such as information about the competition and market trends as well as names of industry experts. Especially important, the client should review a draft of the final report for factual accuracy and potential misunderstanding *prior* to the issuance of the final report.

In one instance, one of the doctors in a medical practice provided much of the information. In another organization, the vice president of marketing drew upon his store of competitive information to give the valuator a broad overview of the firm's business—similar to a standard presentation given to the firm's prospective customers.

Yet, in other circumstances, assistance from a client can be excessive. One company owner sent as many as eight faxes a day to the valuator, and the cost of the valuation increased significantly because the valuator had to read and review each fax and test all the assumptions from the client. At the end, the valuator had to call the client to warn her not to redo the final report!

WHAT A VALUATION IS *NOT*

It is important for both the client and the valuator to remember what a valuation is not. A valuation is not a strategic plan for the company that sets the company's direction for the next three to five years. Neither is a valuation a long-term forecast of the company's revenues and expenses. Nor is a valuation a budget for the company's business for the coming year. Finally, a valuation is not a due diligence report as part of an acquisition or merger.

In some instances, clients rely too much on a valuation. It may be that a valuator is reviewing a strategic plan, a profit forecast, or a budget. However, the valuator is not taking executive or management responsibility for these documents, nor is the valuator assuming the validity of any of these results or reports of management.

The valuation field will always be a combination of art and science, and change is occurring at a rapid pace. In the near future, we predict that the Internet will be much better utilized, and prominent educational institutions will offer degree programs and certification programs in valuation. Appraisal and valuation organizations will resolve their minor differences. Some states will adopt licensing requirements for valuators, and the users of valuations will understand much more clearly the role of valuators.

SUMMARY

The valuation process is not designed to give ulcers, but it could cause a headache if the client's management is not prepared to cooperate with the valuator. After all, the client is working toward the same goal as the valuator: placing a reasonable value on the business. Consider the relationship to be one of mutual trust, in which the client is forthcoming with information that enables the valuator to accomplish his or her job according to ethical and association standards. Make sure both the valuator and the client are on a level playing field. A client should feel comfortable that the valuator is working in his or her best interest and following broadly accepted valuation methodology of the valuator's certifying or accrediting association. The result will be a more streamlined process taking less time, costing fewer dollars, and, most likely, arriving at a likely estimate of value. Withholding information can often lead to a longer and more expensive valuation process.

The client should be prepared to describe the business in full, explaining its strengths, weakness, opportunities, and threats. A client should record thoughts and concerns about the business and maintain background materials documenting them. It makes sense to put all the cards on the table instead of taking a chance that something unusual might surface.

Staying in touch with the client throughout the valuation process and keeping the client apprised of the progress of the valuation are crucial. This frequent communication is particularly important when the time comes for the final report—a document with which the client should be comfortable.

In addition, it is ideal for two opposing valuators to reach similar conclusions when they are working with the same information and using the same valuation concepts. Valuators must assume professional roles and establish the most probable estimate of value, not what the client would like it to be.

NOTES

1. "CPAs analyze what actually happened, develop assumptions about what would have happened but for certain circumstances, and explain these facts and assumptions in the form of an opinion." Peter B. Frank and Michael S. Wagner, *Providing Litigation Services*, New York, American Institute of Certified Public Accountants, 1993, p. 70/105.01.

2. American Society of Appraisers, *Principles of Appraisal Practice and Code of Ethics*, Washington, DC: American Society of Appraisers, 1994, Section 2.2.

3. Since the Internet is widening access to information that can be used as a competitive tool, such as a client's public disclosures, many firms are using alternative dispute resolution, when possible, to keep business affairs private.

CHAPTER 8

How to Price a Valuation

When people walk into a doctor's office, their first concern is often how much the visit is going to cost. Many consumers are preoccupied with the cost of professional services. A service has many intangible components, and most people buy services because they are not experts in the area. Therefore, they have trouble evaluating top-quality services for their money.

In the case of a valuation, clients are often already skeptical about what they are paying for. Without an understanding of benefits of a valuation and what it takes to accomplish these tasks, clients may reinforce their own negative biases regarding business valuations. This chapter discusses the issues behind the cost of a valuation so that both valuators and clients can develop a better understanding of the complex steps and benefits of a valuation.

CALCULATING COSTS: BREAKING DOWN THE VALUATION PROCESS

To assist clients, we have developed a proprietary valuation process, a simple step-by-step tool for outlining how to develop an estimate of value (see Chapter 4). This chart is an efficient road map for the valuator performing a valuation. It is also an educational tool for the client. It literally walks the user through the steps of a valuation: the engagement process; Phase I, research and data gathering; Phase II, analysis; and Phase III, estimation of value and reporting. The chart will explain to a prospective client how an estimate is reached and why it costs as much as it does.

For the client, a better understanding of the process should soften the resistance to the cost of the service. After all, it is the unknown that creates fear in people. Valuators as professionals must be willing to educate prospective clients.

WHY DOES A VALUATION COST WHAT IT DOES?

One of the major difficulties in justifying the cost of a valuation is the typical lack of understanding among business owners. For example, few owners realize how important it is to know the value of what is often their largest single asset and their primary source of income. (The major cost element for a standard full valuation pertain to the phases described in Chapter 4.)

Since many business owners are unaware of the importance of a valuation, they simply ignore details which could affect the cost of the valuation. Several recurring issues that often increase the cost of a valuation are poorly organized company records, lack of a business plan or a budget, and the wrong valuator.

Lack of Documentation and Organization

When a business fails to maintain proper records, such as financial statements, and fails to pay attention to the details of documentation, the onus to develop reliable data falls on the valuator. Because of the necessity of having to expand the scope of research and analysis with poor documentation and records, the price of the valuation will rise. After all, a valuator should not have to absorb the deferred cost of a client's sloppy record-keeping and business practices.

A business financial statement is a prime example of a record whose upkeep and level of preparation (audit, review, or compilation) can contribute to a less expensive valuation. The inadequacy of the financial statement often reflects a company's (especially a smaller company's) failure to hire a skilled accountant to maintain the records. Instead, the company may rely on a computer-based accounting software program to do the job. The software is certainly a suitable tool, but it should not replace the services of an accountant. Instead, it should complement the accountant. The result is a higher cost, because the valuator spends more time adjusting, restating, and/or normalizing the financial statement.

In terms of documentation, let's consider the minutes from the board of directors meeting. These minutes need to be current and relevant, especially for related-party transactions such as loans

made to shareholders, transfer pricing, and compensation for officer shareholders. Proper loan documents, tax returns, and personal
financial statements are necessary to validate the loan. If valuators
have to expand the scope because they lack good documentation,
the cost will rise.

Incomplete or nonexistent documentation of business operations is but one of the signals to a valuator that a significant level
of risk exists. These signs can decrease the value of the business as
well as increase the cost of the valuation.

Size of the Company

Unfortunately, a small business can find itself caught in a squeeze at
the time of valuation; a valuator cannot generally scale back services
or association standards just because of a company's size. A smaller
client becomes a victim of the diseconomies of small-scale operations.
Although it is typically more expensive to value a larger company, it
is not 50 times more expensive to value a company with annual revenues of $50 million than to value a company with annual revenues
of $1 million. Most of the activities that must be performed to value a
large company must also be performed for a smaller company.

This situation has led our firm to refine the limited-scope engagement in order to provide a low-cost introductory product (see
Chapter 4). A limited-scope engagement typically takes 60 to 70 percent of the time and cost of a full-scope valuation.

Reasons for Valuation

The variety of reasons for a valuation, as described in Chapter 2,
can dramatically influence cost. If the report is being prepared after
an IRS audit or for a federal trial, it is almost impossible to avoid
an expensive valuation. The federal rules for testimony and report
standards are higher in these areas and often differ from district to
district. Certain reports, therefore, require more detailed support,
especially since strong empirical evidence is required to convince
the authorities of the validity of the valuation conclusions.

Between state and federal courts, the rules and requirements
for family law, minority shareholder disputes, and eminent
domain valuation issues often vary. For ESOPs, the rules from the
U.S. Department of Labor, the IRS, and the AICPA can be difficult
to apply, and the government imposes so many different rules that
it forces a valuator to be knowledgeable in many areas. These

requirements indirectly add costs, because valuators need to be versed in a greater number of topics.

On the other side are the valuations undertaken simply to give a business owner an idea of the value of his or her company. Here the cost can be as little as half that of a valuation involving litigation or government regulation.

Lack of Business Plan or Budget

The existence of a budget is a clear sign that a business has considered the short-term future with respect to capital expenditures, sources of revenue, and overhead. This planning process is a signal that management is aware of the future and willing to invest for it. In addition, a well-written business plan can assist the valuator in quickly getting up to speed on many of the aspects of the valuation that would otherwise have to be created from scratch.

If a company is not well managed and lacks a business plan or even a simple budget, it is likely that some other critical information needed by a valuator may be missing. Something as basic as a budget makes the valuation process easier because it allows the valuator to check how the company is performing or has performed against a target.

With a good business plan to read and study, there will be a direct benefit for the client. It is much less expensive to value a business that is well organized with attention to detail and evidence of value. This type of business is generally worth more, because it is often well structured for a takeover by a new owner or management.

Choosing the Wrong Valuator

It is unnecessary to repeat the importance of the qualifications of the right valuator. Suffice it to say that the wrong valuator could cost a client more than just excessive billing; the higher cost could lie in the wrong estimate of value. In fact, it is possible that a valuation report could be ignored by an end user. According to Judge Halpern, the presiding judge in the *Estate of Freeman*, "We had difficulty with [petitioner's expert's] valuation....We accorded [petitioner's expert's] valuation report no weight." We refer the reader to this 1996 Tax Court memo for a detailed analysis of the factors that the Tax Court considered important for a business valuation.[1]

Let's take a look at a potential disaster. A business broker, serving as a valuator, undervalues a business in order to get a quick sale and commission. From the broker's perspective, if the business were valued more thoroughly, it might draw a higher sale price but it would not sell as quickly. The lack of a complete and relevant valuation skill set in this type of case can lead to a "guesstimate" of value or, in the worst case scenario, to an undervaluation of the company. As a result, the business owner may sell his or her business for much less than it is worth.

The above examples are but two of the problems that can occur when the wrong valuator is used.

THE VALUATION: HOW LONG DOES IT TAKE?

Although most valuations take approximately six to eight weeks, in some cases they may stretch out as long as six months or a year.[2] Sometimes a bit of crucial evidence holds up the valuation, and it may prove to be the deciding factor in a valuation or a negotiation. In one situation, a vital fact came to light only days before we completed our report. An academic research report was published that documented a significant economic conditions adjustment. Unforeseen delays had kept us from completing the report sooner; as it worked out, those delays allowed us the time to perform additional research that supported a multimillion-dollar adjustment.

In some instances, information from a third party may be needed, but that party's actions may be out of the control of the valuator. It may take time to track down the gemologist whose specialty is rare stones, but his or her appraisal may be critical to establishing the estimate of value for the business.[3]

A third party may also be asked to quantify a discount adjustment in matters such as gift giving and estate planning, and the empirical data necessary to substantiate the adjustment level are not always easily accessible. The valuator must find the necessary sources, convince the third party that divulging information will not be used against him or her, and elicit the market-comparable data. This could prolong the process, but in many cases it results in a tremendous difference in the amount of a adjustment—making it quite worth both the client's effort and money.

The typical report for an estate or gift tax audit is a more complex valuation and demands a full written report—another factor affecting the length of the process. (Check the local rules of Federal Tax Court as to expert witness report requirements and Federal Rule 26.) It is the content of a report that is important, not merely its weight. A judge or jury will appreciate the quality and quantity of the information to come to an informed decision, and the client will have a clear understanding of how the valuator came to an estimate of value.

Not all valuations need to be in the form of a full written report. On one end of the spectrum is the company that required a quick "first blush" letter report to be used internally by the board of directors prior to purchasing a very small engineering firm in San Francisco. The acquiring company was in the same line of business and needed only an independent third party to verify the estimate of value of the smaller company so it could be acquired from the widow of a friend who had died unexpectedly. If the firm was not acquired quickly, it would lose its value, and the estate of the deceased would be without an asset. Under these circumstances, the time frame was short, making the valuation less expensive. Why? The client signed an engagement letter agreeing to a limited-scope valuation with no disclosure of the value to third parties (i.e., for internal use only). In this instance, the valuation was less than a 5 percent variance from the CEO's, and the board closed the deal on time.

The type of industry, complexity of the business, and condition of documentation and financial records can also influence the length of the valuation and the degree of anxiety. Valuations revolving around unusual industries or falling prey to poor-quality financial reports, lack of cooperation, or failure to make a full disclosure of information may necessitate an extended valuation period.

KEEPING COSTS DOWN—TIPS FOR VALUATORS AND CLIENTS

Here are some tips on how to keep costs low for a valuation.

• *Practice preengagement due diligence.* A valuator should suggest that a potential client become familiar with a prospective valuator's education, training, and experience. The client should evaluate memberships in professional organizations, his or her testimony in depositions and trials, as well as any articles written by the valuator. Contacting professional organizations, universities, and the state licensing authority can provide some degree of verification.

A valuator should also suggest that the client contact at least three references to confirm a valuator's performance. Recommend that a potential client ask tough questions such as these: Was the value reasonable? Was the valuator's report followed? How much did it cost? Would you use the valuator again? A client can perform a credit check through a service like Dun & Bradstreet and can also request a certificate of insurance to ensure the valuator's liability coverage.

 • *Don't bite off more than you can chew.* One way for a valuator to lower costs is to break down the engagement into separate stages. A client can engage a valuator initially for an oral report, a letter report, or perhaps a limited-scope report. These reports can provide the client with a range of values for his or her business and allow the valuator to estimate the cost to complete the more complex steps of the engagement for a full-scope written report. The valuator's ability to gain a client's confidence can contribute to a better tolerance for additional costs. Also, clients can save money if they use their internal staff as much as possible to prepare documents and schedules for a valuation.

 • *Encourage communication between the valuator and the client.* Clients should continually monitor the valuation process through periodic meetings or phone conversations with a valuator, and they should request detailed invoices so that there are no surprises. It is important to be sure that client expectations about the time it takes to undergo a valuation are realistic so that there are no surprises when the client gets the bill.

For self-protection, a valuator should always use an engagement letter, which outlines the engagement's terms, the estimate of the fee, and under what circumstances the valuator may change the engagement. Although this point is only indirectly related to cost reduction, the letter can detail what is anticipated in the valuation and can indicate that the fee needs to be renegotiated if the engagement takes an unexpected turn. With this safeguard in place for the valuator, clients are more apt to accept a change in fees when they have a better understanding of the process.

 • *Do some comparative shopping.* A client should get more than one proposal for a valuation, just as for any professional service. Compare billing rates, the ability to deliver a finished report in a reasonable period of time, and sample reports. Be sure to consider the intended report's content, not just the façade. Last but not least, visit the valuator's place of work to achieve a suitable comfort level. This degree of comfort, not the cost, should be the driving force to determine which valuator is chosen.

 • *Encourage periodic valuations.* Although there is a limited amount the client can do to reduce the cost of a first-time analysis, one benefit of making the investment in the initial valuation is that subsequent valuations will generally cost less.

An ESOP valuation best illustrates this point. If a client engages a valuator for a period of three years, he or she can average the cost of the three valuations over the entire period. Say the first year costs $17,000 and subsequent ones $10,000 each. The valuator may be willing to accept a three-year commitment at a fixed fee of $12,000 a year. This would prove to be a win-win situation for both parties. The company can defer $5000 of the up-front cost and also save $1000 in fees ($17,000 + $10,000 + $10,000 = $37,000 vs. $12,000 × 3 = $36,000), and the valuator gains the benefits of locking up an engagement for three years.

IS THE VALUATION PROCESS WORTH IT?

Absolutely. Clients will want to know what benefits they will receive for their investment in a valuation. This is actually the first question a prospective client should ask. In basic terms, the valuation uncovers the worth of management. If the value turns out to be less than expected, it could serve as an opportunity for a business owner to work toward increasing the value of the company. On the other hand, if the company proves to be worth more than anticipated, it might be an opportune time to sell.

Often, a business owner is so close to operations that it is impossible to look at the company objectively. The corporate culture may all but overwhelm an owner and lock him or her into judging the business in a certain way. Thus, an outside party can be beneficial by providing a second opinion and offering a new perspective. A knowledgeable adviser is an asset to a client's existing management team. Furthermore, most business owners do not have the necessary skill set to value a business, even their own business. The ability to run a business successfully typically has little to do with the ability to value that same business accurately.

SUMMARY

Knowing why a valuation costs what it does makes it a much more palatable investment. The Valuation Process Chart in Chapter 4 is an important educational tool which illustrates how the valuation develops. When a client sees how complex a valuation can be, there is bound to be more acceptance and less fee resistance.

One of the major reasons potential clients balk at the cost of a valuation is that they do not understand how important it is to develop a value for their business—probably their single greatest asset and primary source of income. The following factors can influence cost:

1. Failure to maintain proper records—such as financial statements, board meeting minutes, and officer shareholder transactions—can mean additional work for the valuator, who has to expand the scope of research and analysis.
2. The cost of performing a business valuation is not directly proportional to the size of the subject company.
3. The reason for a valuation can greatly influence cost. At the high end are valuations performed after an IRS audit or for litigation. On the low end are valuations undertaken to place a value on a company for internal use only.
4. If a company lacks a business plan or budget, a valuator has to expand the scope of research to compensate for the missing information. A well-written business plan can apprise the analyst of many details which otherwise have to be developed from scratch.
5. Choosing the wrong valuator, someone who produces the wrong estimate of value, can be an expensive mistake.

There are many things that a client can do to help reduce the cost of a valuation:

- Break the engagement down into manageable pieces by starting with an oral report, which may be sufficient.
- Engage in frequent communication with the valuator—periodic meetings, phone calls, and detailed invoices—to prevent surprises. Delve into a prospective valuator's background and experience. This can eliminate the chance of hiring the wrong professional.
- Get proposals from more than one prospective valuator. The comfort level with a professional, not the cost, should be the driving force behind whomever the client chooses.
- Have periodic valuations performed. Although a client can do only so much to reduce the cost of the first-time analysis, subsequent ones will cost less.

If a valuation turns out to be lower than expected, this could serve as an opportunity for a business owner to try to increase value. On the other hand, if the company proves to be worth more than anticipated, this could notify the owner of a good time to sell.

Finally, a business owner who gets too close to his or her business often needs an objective third party to provide an opinion. Most business owners cannot value their own businesses, unless they are trained valuation practitioners. A knowledgeable adviser is an asset in providing a new perspective to a client's existing management team.

NOTES

1. Tax Court Memo 1996–372, *Estate of Ross H. Freeman v. Commissioner.*
2. See Chapter 4 for experience of the authors' firm for the duration and workload of valuation engagements.
3. The American Society of Appraisers is an excellent resource for locating appropriate specialists. The society publishes a directory of its membership with classification by specialty. *Directory of Professional Appraisal Services,* Washington, DC: American Society of Appraisers.

CHAPTER 9

Marketing Valuation Services

Marketing a service business takes a long time and lots of energy; marketing valuation services is no different. This chapter focuses on elements that are essential to marketing valuation services and developing a strong valuation practice: the marketing plan; marketing basics; setting marketing objectives; marketing strategies; advertising; other ways to publicize your firm; implementing the marketing plan; the World Wide Web; rewarding the team; and rejuvenating yourself.

THE MARKETING PLAN

First, let's define marketing. Simply stated, the cumulative objective of your marketing activities is to close an agreement for a valuation engagement. Marketing, then, is *everything* a business undertakes to get its goods or services to its end user, to market. This means that activities like advertising, sales, packaging, distribution, public relations, and contact management are all part of the marketing process.

Marketing covers a lot of ground and is absolutely critical to the success of your business. Since marketing encompasses so many diverse areas, the most tried-and-true way to organize marketing activities is with a marketing plan. Now, if you have already been involved in a business, or associated with a larger firm, you might be experiencing a little MEGO (my eyes glaze over) right now at the thought of putting together yet another of those fat three-ring binders that does nothing but sit on the bookshelf for the rest of the year. Not this time. We're in the lean-and-mean era right now, and the last thing we want you do is to create a new bookend.

A marketing plan is critical. Why? Let's use the analogy of a trip. You decide to take a trip. That's it—no plan, no nothing. You simply hop in the car and take off. Is the road you're on the right road? Yes. Since you have no destination, *any* road you are on is the right road! How about gas money? Well, you'd better have plenty, because this trip could take a while; there is no schedule. No schedule, no destination, and unlimited resources. Not bad—if you are a millionaire with no desire to achieve anything.

But if you are like most of us, your resources are limited. So, when we plan a trip together, we'd better figure out where we are going, how we are going to get there, and how much it is going to cost—before we hop in the car. Now, where do we start?

One of the first things to address is whether your market area needs the kinds of valuation services that you intend to provide. You'd be surprised at how many businesses start without taking a look at this most fundamental tenet. True, right now business valuation is one of the fastest-growing areas in niche consulting, but that doesn't necessarily mean it's high growth in all areas of the country. And, just as important, you might be in a particular area that has as many valuation firms as it can support for the foreseeable future. If you were a grocer and your little town of 5000 already had three megamarkets, odds are you wouldn't consider putting in another grocery store.

You need to do a little research first to see if there is sufficient potential to support your new valuation business. To find out if your area needs a valuation practice, let's take a look at why valuations are performed in the first place and who typically initiates them.

Valuations are primarily need-driven; that is, a situation arises for a business or an individual that *requires* a valuation to be performed. In some states and situations, valuations may even be required by law, as is the case in California, or anywhere in the United States for certain IRS-mandated valuations. In a community property state like California, a business owner involved in a divorce is required by the court to have the business valued by an independent valuator as part of the divorce process.

The need for a valuation can be driven by a number of different forces, such as:

The sale or purchase of a business

The evaluation of financing options for business expansions or acquisitions

Buy/sell or stock redemption agreements

The development of ongoing business plans and strategies

An employee stock ownership plan (ESOP)

Mergers or acquisitions

Marital dissolutions

Individual wealth planning, particularly with gifts and estate transfers

Gifts and estate taxes

Philanthropic planning, as would be the case with equity transfers by a business to charity

Other business transactions

Taking a close look at what initiates the need for a valuation will lead you right to excellent sources of both quantitative and qualitative information that you can use to help make the decision to proceed. For example, statistics are readily available regarding the sales and purchases of businesses in many areas. Mergers and acquisitions are typically announced in local papers or, for the larger mergers, can be tracked through appropriate government agencies. Local colleges, universities, associations, governments, and chambers of commerce are repositories for quantitative commerce information pertinent to valuation potential. Local libraries are good sources of business information, even more so now that they are interconnected electronically.

Of course, the World Wide Web is a terrific source of information. Using search engines, you can quickly detect any local firms that might already have established a presence via the Web. In the process of researching the Web for valuation topics, you will also be exposed to the many valuation and valuation-related businesses that are on-line. Some of these have been on the Web for a couple of years or more.

On the qualitative side, local attorneys, bankers, financial planners, CFOs, CEOs, controllers, and CPAs in general are good sources of information regarding valuations being performed in your area. We refer to these types of audiences as "influencers." Although they are not the actual initiators of valuations, influencers will either recommend or have a lot to say in the selection of those chosen to perform a valuation.

As you can see, there is more than enough high-quality information readily available on which to base your decision to do a complete marketing plan.

Here's another way to look at the marketing planning process. Right now, if you are just starting out, you may have determined through diligent and insightful marketing research that you have uncovered a gold mine. However, just discovering the gold doesn't get it out of the ground. Now you and your team need to think the whole process out, put it in writing, and *then* make the final decision. Integral to the final decision process is that you are to present your business and marketing plan to one of the most notoriously tough venture capitalists in your area—*you!* When you finish the plan, would you fund it?

MARKETING BASICS

To reiterate, the objective of *all* your marketing activities is to close an agreement for a valuation engagement. Marketing is the lifeblood of your business's success and should clearly be reflected in your business's mission. If you haven't previously done so, let's review what valuators do—our mission statement—to make sure everyone involved in the marketing process clearly understands the foundation on which all of our business activities, including marketing, will be built. Our sample mission statement affirms that we will:

- Perform high-quality valuations on the basis of proven valuation methods performed by the highest-caliber professionals
- Prosper as the first choice for professional valuations among clients and client advisers
- Produce profits through hard work, integrity, innovation, and continued education of our professionals
- Provide a challenging, diverse workplace that encourages professionalism and rewards results

Our mission statement gives us a clear idea of where we want to go—our goal. The next thing to do is describe where we are now—our present situation. If you have an existing business, your present situation could be expressed in these terms:

Strengths and weaknesses of your current business

Business skills that could transfer to your new valuation business

How well you are known in your present business community

Perceived strengths and weaknesses in particular valuation areas

Your physical assets, such as office space and equipment

Strengths and weaknesses of other members of your team

Your competitive situation: who your major competitors are or will be and how you stack up relative to them

Your present client base in terms of number of clients, client locations, types of services performed, and revenue generated for the different levels of service rendered

Benefits your new valuation business could provide to your clients

The goal of a situation analysis is to perform a very candid appraisal of where you are now, because it is from this point, this present situation, that you will be planning your road map to achieve your marketing objectives. Again using the trip analogy, if you don't know where you are, by definition you are lost and don't know how to get where you want to go.

SETTING MARKETING OBJECTIVES

Now that you have a very good idea of where you are, the next step is to determine where you want to go—your marketing objectives. To be realized, these objectives should be realistic and attainable, specific yet acceptable to all involved, challenging but flexible, and consistent. Another characteristic of lean-and-mean marketing these days is timeliness—not necessarily just speed, but timeliness. Once you hit the road toward your objectives, you can't dawdle.

Here's how we did it.

When Gary founded the company in 1993, his initial objective was simple: get one or two clients and get the job done for them in a timely and cost-effective manner. He wanted to impress the source of the referrals with a high-quality engagement that would be a win-win situation for all. His objective was not to bill $1 million in fees in the first year. Actually, his first-year objective was $120,000 in fees, and he comfortably exceeded it.

After achieving his objective for the first year, he began to build on it and we developed a one-year business plan for the year ahead. Our results for that year were good, and we exceeded the objectives for human resources, chargeable hours, and realization rate. A growth trend was developing, and we then planned the third year with the intent to develop a three-year plan during that time. At this writing, we are proud to say that the plan for the third year is on target, and our target for the fourth year is approaching $1 million in billings. Our solid 73 percent growth rate put us on the *San Jose and Silicon Valley Business Journal*'s list of the 100 fastest-growing companies in Silicon Valley.

All members of the firm clearly understand our objectives, because they helped determine them in the first place. We regularly report to everyone on the team our progress toward our objectives. This openness simultaneously encourages the team to work harder and to relax—that is, to attain balance through setting, and achieving, realistic objectives. Unrealistic objectives bring on burnout. Realistic objectives allow you and your coworkers the opportunity to experience success and to relax with minicelebrations as successes are realized.

Following are examples of other marketing objectives. Notice that they are specific, attainable, and clear:

- Introduce X number of valuation products or services by a specific date.
- Perform X number of valuations by a specific date.
- Achieve X percent return on investment for a specific time period.
- Introduce yourself or members of your team to at least X number of people who could use your services in your business community by a specific date.
- Meet the President of the United States and convince her that you are indeed the best choice for Ambassador to France by the year 20XX. (Actually, this has nothing to do with anything. We just don't want your eyes glazing over here.)
- Establish a presence on the World Wide Web by a certain date.
- Generate X number of high-quality leads through advertising by a specific date.

MARKETING STRATEGIES

With the starting point firmly in mind and the objectives clearly in sight, you're ready to map your route—strategies that define how you are going to achieve your objectives. Strategies are developed in the context of resource allocation. Similar to a road trip, limited resources must be properly managed in order to reach specific destinations. Keep in mind that a direct route may not always be the best way to reach a destination. A longer, more southerly route will avoid passes blocked by snow. An extra fueling stop on day 3 will ensure safely crossing the desert on day 4.

In other words, there are any of number of alternative strategies that will achieve your objectives. Your job is to evaluate the options and then come up with the most workable plans, given your resources. Here are some examples of strategy statements:

- Develop valuation products targeted to appeal to entry-level and middle-market businesses.
- Establish a market presence through targeted direct-mail advertising to CFOs and CEOs in your primary service area.
- Expand customer awareness of new valuation products through a newsletter and structured calling program.
- Increase interactive direct sales through greater use of the World Wide Web, augmented by heavy Web site awareness programs.

As you are developing your strategies, keep in mind something that we believe to be one of the most important tips in this book. We call it a strategy more than an objective, because it reflects something that might be defined as an attitude, a way of always doing business:

> Make it easy for your clients and prospective clients to do business with you. This attitude should permeate and be reflected in everything you do.

Making it easy for your clients to do business with you can be as simple as always having your phone number, address, e-mail, and Web address on everything you put in a client's hands. It includes printing a Rolodex® with this information on it and giving it to your clients and prospects even if you are not sure they still use such a system. It means being reached with no more than three menu choices on your voice mail system or, better yet, answering your own phone. It means putting a return, stamped envelope in something you want returned—for example, engagement letters or payments for your invoices. It means selecting a phone number that's easy to remember—you do have a choice in most cases. It means choosing a name for your business that someone can easily look up in the phone book. Did you ever try to look up a business that started with just a series of initials or, worse yet, just numbers? Try it sometime.

Write it on your wall 3000 times: "I will make it easy for my clients to do business with me." "I will make it easy for my clients to do business with me." Have your associates do the same. You can add this sentence if you want: "I need the money!"

Once you have developed alternative strategies, the next step is to evaluate the various strategies and narrow them down to the ones best suited to your situation, resources, and geographic location. Once chosen, different strategies can be hammered into how-to programs and procedures, complete with specific time schedules and resource allocations. Actual scheduling of activities will depend on your unique situation of course, but there is one tip in particular that is important to stress: consistency.

> Once implementation of the programs and procedures has begun, it is important to "stay the course." Giving up too soon on a strategy that hasn't had time to work or abandoning a working strategy prematurely are all too common occurrences.

We hope that you have been putting pen to paper or fingers to keyboard as you have gone through this process of identifying market strategies. Just in case you haven't, here is a checklist of where you should be right now.

	Completed	or	To be completed by
Mission statement	❑		_____
Description of present situation	❑		_____
Marketing goals established	❑		_____
Alternative strategies stated	❑		_____
Final strategies chosen	❑		_____
Programs and procedures established	❑		_____
Implementation schedule	❑		_____

ADVERTISING

One of the marketing tools you will use to help nail down that first valuation engagement is advertising. Often, advertising is confused with marketing, but marketing and advertising are not the same thing. Marketing is *everything* you do to move your goods and services from you, the producer, to your ultimate consumer. Advertising is just *one* of the things you do. Advertising, simply stated, is paid promotion—you pay to get the word out about your business. Magazine ads, newspaper ads, and direct mail are all different forms of paid promotion, different forms of advertising.

Why advertise? We'll put the reason to advertise in the form of a tip that any small businessperson should tattoo on the palm of his or her hand.

When your business or division is brand new, it is a well-kept secret. It will stay a secret unless you, or someone in your organization, makes the effort to inform the firms and individuals most likely to do business with you about who you are and what you can do for them.

It's a safe bet to say that few of us have the resources to be all things to all people. So, we have to let the important ones know—either the ones who do business with us directly or the ones who steer business to us indirectly. These people comprise our target audiences. The more narrowly we can define these audiences, the more efficient and effective we become in reaching them.

Advertising in some form is essential to building a business. Advertising is an investment. And as with *any* other investment, you have to be realistic about the return you can expect. A common problem is to expect too high a return from too little advertising. A one-inch ad run once in your local paper is not effective advertising; it is, however, an effective way to pour money into a hole.

Conversely, be careful not to overly "puff" yourself or your services. By this we mean advertising that pronounces with much pomp and circumstance that you are without peer, using a catch phrase like "Our name says it all" or "We have no competition." We are valuators and analysts for the most part. We recognize the need for professional assistance and we can normally expect the same of our target audiences.

At ValueNomics®, we use a marketing firm[1] to assist us in promoting ourselves and in making sure that our message is consistent with our goals. We have gone so far as to install our marketing consultant in adjacent office space. His advice is valuable, but it is probably his close monitoring and critical feedback that are most helpful. His feedback helps us to be realistic, and we know that he will make us reduce "puff" when we are tempted and help us create advertising that's meaningful.

So, what do we do, what do we advertise?

As mentioned earlier, one of the most fundamental and important tasks you can do to help maximize your advertising efforts is to clearly define your target markets. Target markets can be defined in a number of ways, such as:

- Characteristics of the ultimate end user, profiled in terms of (not in any order)

  Age/sex

  Geographic location

Education

Income

Type of business

Size of business

Typical position (CEO, CFO, CPA, etc.)

- Characteristics of typical "influencer" audiences, profiled in terms of (not in any order)

Typical position (banker, attorney, CPA, financial planner, etc.)

Type of business

Geographic location

In addition to these characteristics, keep in mind what we talked about earlier—the *reasons* that valuations are performed. Knowing the reasons for valuations will also help you identify important characteristics in narrowing your audiences. For example, divorce lawyers are good targets for valuations involving marital dissolutions; financial planners are good targets for valuations involving wealth planning; and CEOs or CFOs of growing businesses or businesses planning ESOPs are always good valuation targets.

Other audiences that we have targeted include local and state CPA society events, valuation association events, college alumni events, attorney-sponsored meetings and educational seminars, local community functions, insurance agent meetings, and seminars sponsored by bankers, investment bankers, and venture capitalists.

Some of the most valuable networking activities at ValueNomics® have been through professional society and association events. Many engagements come from general referrals from peers, such as other certified valuators and CPAs who understand the value of professional skills. In addition, many peers may be looking for a reliable valuator who can take on engagements that they cannot do themselves because of conflicts of interest, lack of objectivity, or time constraints. These individuals have an immediate interest in what you do, and a bond of friendship and professional respect exists from the start.

What should you advertise? One of the most important things you are trying to establish when you are just starting is credibility. As one of the steps to that objective, you need to make the buyer of the valuation service aware of your reputation as a valuator and of the credentials and experience that you have to offer. Three basic rules should be followed in this regard: (1) frequently remind your target audiences about what you do, (2) frequently remind your target audiences that you are available, and (3) consistently remind audiences that you are good at what you do.

Rule 1: Frequently Remind Your Target Audiences of What You Do

For certain professions, it is pretty easy for other people to know what their jobs are. For police officers, the uniforms, the sirens, and the flashing red lights send a clear message that these policemen and policewomen are fulfilling public duties. For valuation analysts, on the other hand, the outward appearance of clothing and activities does not communicate so clearly what valuators do. Thus, it is up to the valuators to let key audiences know what they do.

Often valuators—from partners to staff—assume that just because they have gotten a degree or passed an exam to become certified, the valuation work will fall into their laps. They sit by the telephone waiting for it to ring. This is just what you would expect. After all, until somebody gets the word out about this hot new business, it is, and will remain, a very well-kept secret. With the larger CPA and valuation firms in particular, most new work is typically passed to subordinates by the firms' "rainmakers." Rainmakers are the professionals, typically partners, who actively bring in new business to the firm. As the years pass, the junior executive's expectations for equity in the firm's practice grow, but he or she is continually overlooked for advancement into partnership. What is wrong? The telephone never rings. Why? Because they, the junior wannabes, do not take a proactive role in getting the word out—letting target audiences know what they do. You have to be your own rainmaker.

More often than not, it is a peer of one kind or another who recalls the work of a valuator and respects the quality of the work enough to place a call. Thus, a valuator's most likely assistant in practice development is another valuator, a CPA, an attorney, a banker, an insurance agent, or another business professional.

Practice development efforts and financial resources to support marketing should be focused on the audiences that will offer the highest returns on investment. With limited resources, the shots you take have to count.

On the other hand, sometimes it is the simplest and most innocent contact that leads to a ringing telephone. A person met in church, the local butcher, or the coach of a child's soccer team may all play a role in the process. However, the referral by a casual acquaintance or a chain of casual acquaintances is a matter of chance, and waiting for that type of referral is like waiting to win the lottery. Waiting for any referral is like waiting to win the lottery. So don't wait; be proactive.

Don't wait for referral business, ask for it.

Here's something to keep in mind about referrals. When you say, in your ads and through your literature, that you are the "best there is," there is often little reason for someone who does not know you to believe you. But when a potential new client hears from a trusted friend or business associate that "you are the best there is," you have just received as strong a recommendation as you are ever going to get. And that is why referrals are so important.

Rule 2: Frequently Remind Your Target Audiences That You Are Available

Think of the opportunities that occur on a day-to-day basis to tell someone how you are doing. A conversation opens with "Hey, John, how in the world are you?" "Oh, I don't know. I'm too busy to think about it." That type of comment is part of a lost opportunity; that glum declaration sets the tone for a relationship, and it is likely the other person might not call with a potential referral. Instead, think of the impact of the following conversation: "Hey, John, how in the world are you?" "Great! We're busy, but we're always looking for more. As a matter of fact, we just added…" John has set a positive tone for their professional contacts, and when appropriate, he should channel that tone to the topic of the excitement and success of his business.

People want to be associated with success. It makes them feel good too. Nothing attracts a crowd like a crowd. Take the chance to let contacts know that you have the capacity to handle more engagements and that you are hiring a few more people, that you have taken some additional space, and that you have expanded your computer system. These changes send a message of availability and confidence that you are good at what you do and that your business is growing. Put another way, ask for the business.

Rule 3: Consistently Remind Audiences That You Are Good at What You Do

Displaying and communicating the capabilities of a valuator must be done tastefully and with professional demeanor. It is inappropriate to place a red banner across the firm's next advertisement boasting of the firm's latest coup or most recent victory. A better chance for publicity and consumer awareness might be an article for a professional or trade publication that demonstrates intelligence and knowledge of a relevant subject matter. Many publications are eager for stories and will be interested in an additional perspective, especially if it stands to benefit their readers.

Potential venues for articles include forums as varied as insurance company newsletters, trade associations, and local newspapers. For instance, insurance companies disseminate "war stories" about bad outcomes as warnings for their insured and to inform their readers of potential dangers. Trade and professional associations try to assist their members with relevant information that serves the purposes of education and prevention. Local newspapers are always looking for articles of interest to their readers; the services of a valuator are likely to be a benefit to businesspeople in the local community. Consider writing an editorial or a letter to the editor. Readers will become familiar with what you do and will know that you are available, and that you are good at it.

There are other ways to let people know that you are good at what you do. Success can be part of an attitude. But it does not have to be an attitude with $1000 suits or luxury automobiles. Success can be presented with style and confidence that are not overbearing.

We are reminded of the managing partner of a consulting firm in our community. Everyone knows who he is, respects him, and knows that he is good at his profession. He is courteous to all, articulate and reserved, and stands straight. He is confident in his work and has more than once demonstrated his abilities. He has earned respect from others in the community.

We also have in the community the managing partner of another firm who has not been seen in a suit outside of court for many years. Although his dress is casual, his stature and confidence are excellent. He has demonstrated professionalism and quality so many times that his casual dress is not even noticed by most people who know him. It takes only a matter of minutes in a meeting for his prowess to come forth as he takes charge.

So, where should you advertise?

Valuators should advertise in many places, including trade publications, the local business journal, society and association journals, and directories. The objective is for the telephone to ring. If a valuator is not in front of key audiences consistently, he or she will be forgotten.

Our most recent advertising strategy centers around a profile similar to the one used by the financial community. We use tombstone advertisements[2] to profile the industries and valuation services that are the focus of our practice. These ads are short and to the point. The tombstone itself is a powerful image for consumers and readers of valuations to connote quality and professionalism. This approach works so well that we have reserved the rights to, and copyrighted, the concept. In addition to the understated message describing our specialties, we add our name, address, telephone and fax numbers, and e-mail and Internet home page addresses.

We also advertise in publications directed to specific audiences. These include monthly trade publications and annual professional directories. Another way we stay in front of key audiences is through direct mail, in the form of a bimonthly newsletter.

Another reason to advertise is this:

Wherever you don't go, your competition is sure to be.

This is yet another way of stressing the value of consistency. On-again, off-again attention to marketing is the most heinous of crimes against the success of your efforts to develop your practice. Valuators often analyze companies that are stagnating or beginning to go bankrupt because the owners were playing too much golf or were taking too many vacations. Laziness can be just as destructive. If you don't get "out there" consistently, your business won't grow or it will remain stagnant.

One final word about advertising. The purpose of advertising is to generate a contact—on the phone, through the Web, by e-mail, or in-person. That's all, just generate the contact. Once contact has been made, it isn't advertising any more; it's sales.

OTHER WAYS TO PUBLICIZE YOUR FIRM

Send Press Releases

Every time you add a new person, develop a new product, move to a new location, win an award, and so on, you gain a chance to put the name of your business in front of your audiences. We have developed a master publicity list for ValueNomics® that covers every relevant publication to which we would ever consider sending an article. It includes professional journals, local consumer and business newspapers, select electronic media, alumni publications, and trade newsletters—to name a handful. Then, when the opportunity arises, such as the hiring of a new analyst or the announcement of a new product, we write and send the release to the appropriate media audiences. Yes, it's a little work, but it all adds up.

Write Articles

We have found that writing articles frequently leads to calls from people who have read the articles and have copied them for colleagues and friends. If your goal is a successful valuation practice, we can't say enough to encourage you to write and be published. We still get calls as a result of articles written years ago. The act of publication makes you an authority and an expert in the eyes of both the referral source and the prospective client. If the editors of a journal or magazine chose to use your writing, it is assumed that you must be good.

Articles can also be used as direct-mail inserts in a firm's practice development newsletter. Such articles bolster the legitimacy of a newsletter and provide another item for recipients to pass around the office. A local business journal has a shelf life of several months and is typically passed to six other people for reading before it is filed or tossed. The "pass rate" can also be true for a well-written newsletter and any inserted articles.

Teach and/or Lecture

We lecture for the American Institute of Certified Public Accountants (AICPA), 10 state CPA societies, the National Association of Certified Valuation Analysts (NACVA), and the Practice Development Institute (PDI). You may wish to teach at the local junior college or adult school. Such experience helps keep you sharp, and it looks great on your résumé. Again, it is an issue of credibility. With higher levels of recognition, it is more likely that your telephone will ring with potential engagements.

IMPLEMENTING THE MARKETING PLAN

It is important to set realistic time lines to achieve your objectives. Put another way, "A goal is a dream with a deadline."[3]

We have a friend who clearly does not want a practice with $1 million in annual billings. His goal is a $500,000 practice, and that is how he manages it. Yet he has taken just about the same time to accomplish his objective as it has for us to achieve a revenue objective that will be twice as large. Each of us had a time line of three to five years to reach our objectives.

Of course, achievement is not merely measured by revenue. We may not be making more profit from higher revenues at this stage. It is in the long run that we want to make more profit, but we are also not convinced that more revenue at each step along the way will necessarily mean more profit.

We need to pay attention to our cashflow because of the need for investment in working capital, technology, human resources, education, office space, and marketing. We have to keep the pipeline of our marketing channel at a flow rate that fuels an appropriate level of growth. These multiple pressures demand a delicate balance of short-term and long-term planning with budgets, reporting, accountability, and a realistic time frame to achieve the goals for the company.

Keep in mind a range of error of three months in your planning horizons. If you are ahead of your plan by more than three months, it is time to reconsider plans and adjust. Or, if you are more than three months behind, you also need to reconsider. On the one hand, investments must be given time to work; on the other hand, adjustments should be made gradually. A quick change in plans may upset the equilibrium of your staff and referral sources. In addition, an original plan may actually have been working and you did not know it; perhaps all it needs is a little more time.

There is one absolutely critical element that you must have for the success of your marketing efforts and therefore the success your new valuation business. We think it's important to know this before you spend a lot of time on the implementation process, particularly if you are involved in a larger organization and are putting together a marketing plan for a new group or division.

> If top management doesn't understand the value of the marketing plan and embrace it fully, it is doomed. Go no farther. To succeed, the marketing plan must have top management's full and complete understanding and support. Without management's support, you are wasting your time.

There are a number of steps you can take to help ensure that all involved "sign on" to do their part with implementation of the plan. Here are a few guidelines:

1. Make sure that senior management has approved and embraced the plan.
2. Make the plan a living, working document. Keep the plan, or at a minimum a summary of the plan, readily available. At some point you are going to get a question along these

lines: "Shouldn't we consider advertising to so and so, or send some direct mail to thus and such?" With plan in hand, your answer should go something like this: "No, that's not our target market and it won't help us meet our objectives." Or "That's a great idea, but we'll either have to reallocate resources or find some extra money to spend on the effort."

3. Avoid the fat notebook syndrome by divvying up the plan into elements and handing out just elements to those responsible for implementing them. With a complete understanding of the overall mission of the firm—your mission statement—everyone should have a clear idea of where his or her element fits in.

4. Make sure broad, two-way communication is the rule for all who are involved in the implementation process. Good two-way communication will enable those responsible for implementation of elements to understand how the elements fit together.

5. Keep participants clearly apprised of progress and accomplishments as well as any areas that need more attention.

As with advertising, a key element of successful plan implementation is consistency. Put another way, you simply have to keep at it in order to make it work. Consistent effort will help level the hills and valleys of your revenue-generating activities. A typical situation for businesses, small businesses in particular, is to work real hard getting the business in, then stop trying to get business in and switch to getting the work done. The engagements get delivered and then, guess what—there is no work because everybody has been cranking the reports out! And so on. Be disciplined, and maintain the balance.

Reinvigorate the plan as time goes on. Revise the plan as the firm and the market environment inevitably change in unforeseen ways. Remember, the only constant in life is change. Depending on the size of a firm and its particular market niche, it is probably wise to review the marketing plan every six months.

Use a Contact Management System

One of the ways we help ensure consistency, particularly in farming the leads we worked so hard to generate with our marketing efforts, is with a contact management system. After a contact has been made with a person who may be a source of referrals, it is important to keep your name and your firm name in front of him or her. There are many ways to do it, but personal contact is likely to be the mechanism that works most effectively. We suggest that you employ a consistent method to manage your contacts. Systems vary from a Rolodex® to a software program like ACT!®. The sophistication of the system matters less than using and maintaining it regularly to achieve the consistency necessary for balanced and controlled growth.

Why spend so much effort on your contacts? Contacts are your gold. You will spend money generating them, and even more getting them to a point where they will be willing to do business with you. Did you know that on average it will take about five sales calls to close a sale? Do you know the most expensive kind of marketing activity you can undertake? Trying to win back a client you have lost. How about the easiest yet the most profitable marketing activity? Taking care of the clients you already have. Your existing clients already know who you are and what you do. You don't have to spend more money generating first-time credibility. Again, hard-earned clients and contacts are gold.

> Your existing client and contact/referral list is one of your most
> valuable assets. Guard it fiercely and use it wisely.

With Whom Should You Be in Contact?

Generally, peers in the valuation profession will send you the most work. Ironically, the people who might be perceived as your competition could turn out to be the most valuable source of engagements. Next in importance as sources of referrals are attorneys, then insurance agents, business brokers, investment advisers, bankers, investment bankers, venture capitalists, general business consultants, college classmates, and casual acquaintances. Other sources include various branches of government: the IRS, the courts, and even the local district attorney or the city attorney.

Farm the Contacts

A good lesson can be learned from the real estate brokerage community. After you have made a contact and entered into the contact system, "farm" the contact. We call it working the database. In short, there are three things that you must do: (1) lunch, (2) lunch, and (3) lunch. That's right—take a referral source or a prospective referral source to lunch. It is a great way to get to know someone, and always pick up the check.

However, we have over 2000 contacts in our database after only three years, and we cannot take them all to lunch. The next step is to stay in contact with some kind of mailing every two or three months. We distribute a newsletter specific to valuation services. There is a substantial cost in terms of time and money, but our readers—our target audiences—appreciate the useful information, and it serves to put us in front of current and potential clients and contacts on a *consistent* basis.

The next important step in staying in touch with referral sources is to send a "thank you" when they refer you business. We recommend a letter for small referrals and sometimes a basket of fresh fruit. Gifts in the range of $35 or less are appropriate. (Some people enjoy a bottle of wine, but be sure to know your referral sources, because not everyone drinks alcoholic beverages.) On occasion, we have given larger gifts of certificates to a local bed and breakfast or a local restaurant, but these types of gifts are reserved for consistent referral sources or for very large engagements. Actually, it is not the size of the gift but the act of saying "thank you" that is important.

How to Build Value in Your Firm Right from the Start

Here are a few other tips that could be included in your implementation process to help build the value of your firm.

If you haven't already come up with a name for your firm, here is a suggestion: Make it easy for potential clients to remember who or what your business is and what it does. This means steering away from acronym soup with catchy names like TDB Associates or AB&C Group, and not letting egos run amok with names like Shepardson & Associates, or Winkin', Blinkin & Nod. Every dollar you spend on stationery, signage, brochures, advertising, public relations, and the like is a chance to *build value in the name of your business*. For a quick exercise on how this works, look at the trucks hauling freight on your local highways. Notice the ones that tell you a complete story in one quick glance. Then notice how many trucks are pretty, but don't relate one iota of information about the firms that spent literally tens of thousands of dollars having them painted.

Another point on building your own firm's value, particularly through the use of collateral material like stationery, signage, and brochures, is to be consistent. Did you ever notice how companies like Hewlett-Packard, Microsoft, and American Express, to name a few, always have the same feel to their ads, brochures, and signage? This is no accident. These companies learned long ago the value of consistency in the way their audiences see them. Some firms have been consistent for so long that they now "own" a particular color or geometric shape. Think of a tall, skinny pyramid—Transamerica, of course. A rectangular real estate sign with blue on one half, white on the other—Coldwell Banker. An umbrella—TravelersGroup.

You can start building your firm's value right from the beginning.

Another way to reinforce your firm's value is through the presentation material you provide your customers. Even a cursory valuation report gives you the opportunity to reinforce your own position in that the information you provide not only is valuable from the standpoint of *what* you are presenting, but can also "look" like something of value. Marketers figured this out a long time ago.

THE WORLD WIDE WEB

How the Web Will Impact Your Business and How to Use It to Market Your Business

What is this thing called the World Wide Web (the Web) and why should you give a hoot, much less consider it a viable marketing tool?

By now you are aware of the Web and have some inkling that "change is afoot." But how will it impact your valuation business? How can it help your valuation business?

First, the impact. As a valuator, you will be affected by the Web and the reason has nothing to do with marketing. The Web will have an impact on you because somewhere along the line you are going to be asked to perform a valuation of a business that has been affected, positively or negatively, by the Web. For example, how are you going to value the new virtual businesses, the one-person operations with two computers, a Web link, and $1 million in annual sales? How about the manufacturer's representatives whose clients are going direct to the manufacturers for sales that the reps used to handle? Or how about printers? Are the printers going to follow the typesetters to near extinction? As we go to press, we are just starting to feel the impact of what some are calling a paradigm shift in the way business is conducted around the world. Quite frankly, this area is so new that we are just starting to get a handle on it as valuators. But change means opportunity too, especially for those of us with flexible, living marketing plans in place.

How can we use the Web as a marketing tool? First, a few basics. Notice we said that the Web can be used as *a* marketing tool, not *the* marketing tool. The simple act of putting your business site on the Web does not mean you should immediately contact your travel agent. As we go to press, some 90,000 Web addresses a month are being signed up in this country alone! Your presence on the Web is the same as when you start your business—your new Web site will be a well-kept secret.

The Web is an information junkie's paradise. It is a place where it costs more to develop the content than it does to place it on the medium. It is the exact opposite of paid advertising, where the medium—the time or space—costs more than the content. It will cost you more to develop the information to put on your Web site than it costs to make that information available to the entire world.

The Web is not just a market, but a conglomeration of all kinds of markets, from large to small—markets that can be targeted as narrowly as you want. Remember those target markets we defined earlier? They'rrre baaack!

Content—information—is the key to effective use of the Web for your marketing purposes. Just putting your company brochure on the Web is a waste of time. Why? Because the Web is not just an opportunity to provide in-depth, timely information about your business to your prospects, your target audiences. It also affords you the opportunity to develop a relationship with a potential prospect.

If we were to hazard a guess, you probably don't need hundreds and hundreds of valuation clients to make a real go of your business. So developing a close relationship with exactly the right kind of prospect would be well worth the time—it would be target marketing *par excellence.*

What makes the Web so different and so powerful is that it is interactive. When you hand out a brochure, the reader may read it, then put it aside to read later, or worse file it away. When you entice someone to your Web site, that person arrives sitting at the controls of an *active* communications device. The decision is made nearly immediately whether your site contains something of interest and is worth the time to explore further. You've probably been there. If a Web page is boring, takes too long to go from page to page, is trite or unclear, off you go.

But if you do it right, you establish credibility and get the e-mail or phone call that asks for more information or an appointment. Here are some additional tips to help you get the most benefit from your Web page.

- Hire an experienced Webmaster or firm to design your site for you. Unless you are already a programmer, even the best do-it-yourself Web site programs will be a big drain of time and energy. Go with someone else's experience—you'll be glad you did.

- A Web site is an ongoing commitment. If you aren't willing to keep content current, fresh, and appealing to the kinds of clients you want, wait until you are willing to make the commitment. Nothing will make you look worse than a "what's new" page on your Web site that list events from the summer before last (this example is based on actual observation).

- When working with your Webmaster, list your objectives and expectations explicitly. Include the specific target audiences you want to attract (you should know them by now), because it will be the content of your Web site that attracts and keeps them there.

- Always make it easy for your prospects to get back to you. This means automatic e-mail back to someone in your office, a clear listing of your postal address, and clear listings of phone and fax numbers.

- Promote your Web site. This means putting your Web site address on everything: business cards, brochures, letterhead, other ads, and so on. You may even want to consider a paid ad just to promote your Web site. You certainly want to send a press release out to announce your new site.

- Make sure your Webmaster knows how to announce your site to search engines and services. Also make sure he or she knows about keywords, metatags, and the like, particularly if your site is being developed with a site development software program that tries to avoid HTML coding.

- Search for, and become involved in, news groups in your areas of expertise. These are great sources of information and feedback.

There is no doubt that the Web is already having an incredible impact on the way all of us are doing business, and will be doing business in the future. It is a question not of whether you will become involved in the Web, but when.

REWARDING THE TEAM

A valuator is not an island. The employees of a firm and a firm's referral sources are a vital part of the success of a valuation practice. It can't be done without them. Earlier in this chapter, we discussed the importance of saying "thank you" to referral sources. To adopt a Hawaiian theme, thank your staff and share the coconut milk with them. Put in a goal-oriented incentive plan. Thus, when you win, they will win too. They are likely to show their appreciation by putting in long hours and hard work. Otherwise, it is just a job. A valuator can make it more than that: The practice can become an entrepreneurial challenge for all. Let them taste the sweetness of success.

REJUVENATING YOURSELF

Don't forget to take a vacation in between all the hard work. Obviously, it is important to fulfill obligations to clients. At the same time, your own energy level can get run down without a sufficient change of pace. Without renewed vigor, you might end up stranded on that island by yourself. And while you are on vacation, you are likely to dream up lots of new and exciting strategies to push forward the valuation practice.

Throughout all this, don't forget to listen to those around you. Lots of different people who know you are likely to have helpful and interesting things to say: your significant other, your employees, your peers, and your friends. Other people are a great source of information about what is working for them; listen to them carefully and then determine how their advice can be applied to your business. Some of the most valuable advice comes from those people who are closest to us, yet we often fail to hear what they are saying.

SUMMARY

Is marketing critical to the success of your business? You bet. By thinking it out, and putting pen to paper, you'll realize a significant return on your invested time. As you have made it this far in the book, we hope you have benefited from the sharing of our experiences and from the observations of those who have gone before. These shared experiences represent not just valuation businesses, but businesses in general. Taking a look at how somebody else has done it is almost always more cost-effective than learning it the hard way on your own.

Simple concepts like consistency, focus, resource allocation, objective setting, and the other areas we have covered in this chapter are valuable tools that can help ensure the success of any business—your business.

We encourage you to complete your marketing plan well before you click on the "open" sign. The process really doesn't have to be overly complicated. Keep the plan simple, workable, and flexible—no fat three-ring binder or bookends allowed!

Check our Web site at http://www.valuenomics.com for other marketing hints and valuation news, or to just watch as the site develops.

NOTES

1. CommCraft Marketing, Cupertino, CA.
2. Financial institutions use tombstone advertisements in newspapers and magazine to announce deals and financing that have been completed.
3. Leo B. Helzel and friends, *A Goal Is a Dream with a Deadline*, New York: McGraw-Hill, 1995.

CHAPTER 10

Considering a Career in Valuation

This chapter discusses several useful topics for people considering careers in valuation, including the skills and characteristics that valuators need—important skills they don't teach in school. It also covers the likely impact of industry trends on valuation jobs, and issues of ethics and advocacy.

SKILL PROFILE FOR VALUATORS

Valuators need to develop the skills that are described in this section through a combination of undergraduate and/or graduate course work, on-the-job training and learning from an experienced valuator, and continuing professional education. Some examples of paths to a job and a career in valuation are described below.

As the preceding chapters have made evident, the job of a valuator demands a diverse set of skills. These requirements include (1) the analytical skills of an economist, statistician, or mathematician; (2) an accountant's grasp of financial statements and accounting principles and professional skepticism; (3) the qualitative skills of a "big picture" strategist; (4) the research skills of an academic or librarian; (5) the knowledge of the relationship between risk and return and other important topics in finance; (6) the writing skills of an English major; and (7) the investigative prowess of a detective. The technical skills reflect the science of valuation; the qualitative skills reflect the art of valuation.

One potential career path for valuators is to major in business in college, work for an accounting firm after college, sit and pass the Certified Public Accountant exam after several years of work experience, and then specialize in valuation issues while building a career. Other paths lead people to develop many of the same skills but in a different order. For instance, a liberal arts major in college might work for several years in business and then return to school for an MBA before focusing on valuation. Undergraduate degrees in finance and economics are good preparation for an entry-level position in the valuation industry.

Valuators should master several important academic subjects and skill sets by the time they graduate from school:

Math and statistics

Accounting

Economics

Finance

Business and society—regulation, law, ethics

Research methods

Communications—writing, speaking

Information technology and computer systems

Computer skills—spreadsheets, on-line database research, word processing

To complement these skills, valuators need to have a mind-set and a group of personal characteristics that can help them provide a high level of service to their clients. Although the list below does not include all the characteristics of successful valuators, and it is unlikely that any one person has all these characteristics, it is useful to see the range of attributes.

Inquisitive

Thorough

Strong researcher, good at digging for information

Good interviewer

Results-oriented, persistent

Good listener

Articulate in speaking and writing

Able to move back and forth between detail and big picture

Reliable

Focused on the truth

Honest

Interested in business and business processes

Intelligent

Although the job of a valuator is similar to that of a CPA or financial analyst, it involves much more. Like a CPA or a financial analyst, a valuator has to be comfortable with numbers and adept at distilling stories and explanations from reams of data. Like a CPA, a valuator has to understand the logic and intricacies of developing and interpreting accounting and financial data to provide a picture of the organization's operations. Like a financial analyst, a valuator has to be able to formulate assumptions about the future and weigh the probability that various forecasts may or may not come true.

In addition to what CPAs and financial analysts traditionally do, valuators need to take on the view of a strategist to understand how a business stands up against its competitors and how industry and economic trends will affect the company's future performance. Another difference is that the rules and principles for valuation are much less agreed upon than Generally Accepted Accounting Principles (GAAP). There is no Valuation Standards Board that sets all the rules. Valuation is a field that is constantly developing and changing. Some CPAs who attempt to enter the business valuation field may feel uncomfortable with the lack of settled and mandated principles of valuation comparable to GAAP. For example, to obtain a discount rate, there is no simple mathematical formula to plug numbers into. Those who are considering entering the valuation field should be prepared for an intellectual challenge and be comfortable with ambiguity.

WHAT THEY DON'T TEACH YOU IN SCHOOL

Many of the skills that are important for valuators are not taught in any classroom—and some people might argue that they cannot be taught in a classroom. These areas include developing contacts, developing estimates from irregular sources, building a library, and sniffing out a rat.

Developing contacts in diverse areas is a skill that can be cultivated. To perform his or her job well, a valuator often has to find information that can't be gathered from easily available public sources. Contacts are people in a field or a business who have information that would be interesting to know for professional or personal reasons. These contacts can be useful in a variety of ways. For example, a contact may know a piece of information that is needed to push ahead on a valuation. A contact may understand an industry and its participants in a way that would take the valuator several weeks to develop. The contact may have information about business transactions within the industry. Or the contact may be able to share the names and phone numbers of other experts who themselves have some answers.

Another important skill for a valuator is the ability to develop estimates from irregular sources. Let's say that a valuator is trying to determine the production capacity of a client's competitor in order to benchmark a client's primary product. Even though this type of specific information usually is not available in an annual report or a 10-K, the valuator can develop a good estimate by linking several different pieces of information. From a service technician or industry knowledge, the valuator can find out that the plant in question has three production lines. From a trade publication ad or by contacting the manufacturer of the production equipment, the valuator can determine the designed production capacity of each line. From the client's workforce, the valuator may find a former employee of the competitor who can say that the three production lines run at efficiencies of 83 percent, 65 percent, and 74 percent. By combining these pieces of information and weighing their timeliness and reliability, the valuator can create a good estimate of the competitor's production capacity.

Yet another unsung skill for a valuator is understanding how to build a library in a thorough and cost-effective manner. Much of the work of a valuator and his or her staff involves using reference books and reports to develop the baselines and standards for a valuation. Most valuators will begin their libraries with the standard reference books and textbooks for the field. The tricky part is to figure out which specialized publications to buy and how to maintain an appropriate collection of trade journals and other sources of business valuation information so that the valuator has what's needed without renting a separate warehouse to store all the potentially valuable information! The advent of Web sites and the evolution of fee-based digitized information are providing new answers about how best to build a library. As more and more information becomes available on-line, it will be possible to have less of a physical library and more of an electronic library. However, we believe that it is beneficial to have certain key resources physically in our office, so that we can peruse these books and journals in our spare time to further hone our valuation skills.

Two potential solutions are to have a professional librarian offer advice about how to set up a collection or to develop a close relationship with the librarians at a local public or university library. Many librarians are eager to offer advice as consultants about how to structure a private business library. Nonetheless, given the unforeseeable ways that the Internet will develop, we must admit that even some lucky forecasting with a crystal ball won't prevent some of the incorrect choices about what to include in a library in a few years.

Last, but not least, is the skill of sniffing out the rat. From time to time, valuators confront situations in which the managers of a company to be valued have been using accounting principles or tax policy loosely. At first glance, the company may look clean, but good valuators, after investigating the situation, may begin to see that the picture is less than crystal clear.

At this point, valuators need to call upon their informed judgment and experience to spot the "red flags."[1] Maybe low tax liabilities are too good to be true. Perhaps balance sheet ratios in comparison to industry benchmarks look unusual. Or maybe rosy business projections in a long-range plan are hiding a current problem or are overreaching.

Valuators need to call upon their inquisitiveness and their desire to ferret out the truth, and they need to remember that their long-term reputations depend upon consistently producing good valuations, instead of valuations that merely please a client in the short term. Valuators with integrity, a strong self-identity, an independent mind, and a commitment to the valuation profession will find it easiest to resist the temptations of quick-fix answers in the short term.

HOW VALUATION INDUSTRY TRENDS ARE LIKELY TO AFFECT VALUATION JOBS

We believe that there is a set of trends in the valuation industry that will have an impact on the types of valuation careers and jobs that are likely to exist in the near future.

First, we expect that the valuation specialty will continue to grow as more clients and users of valuations come to appreciate expert valuation skills. As we have discussed throughout the book, valuation combines a science and an art, and it is increasingly clear that valuations differentiate the relevant strategic information that drives the value of a business from the required information that tax and financial authorities demand. Of course, the two types of information are related, but valuators, when doing their best work, focus on the relevant strategic information.

Second, we expect that valuators will display greater specialization. As the level of expertise continue to rise in valuing specific industries, it will be increasingly important to hire a valuation firm that has experience in and understanding of the specific industry in question. In the real estate appraisal industry, this type of specialization already exists between commercial and residential real estate as well as within each sector.

Third, we expect that more courses and certificate programs on valuation will be offered by educational institutions. Professional organizations already provide a broad array of valuation and appraisal courses. As the field of valuation continues to develop and as more theory surrounding valuation develops, colleges, universities, and business schools will create courses, continuing education, and maybe even a major or minor that addresses the needs of the valuation industry.

Fourth, continuing professional education is becoming increasingly important for business valuators. The field is growing and developing in sophistication. The valuator who does not make an investment of time to stay on top of new developments in the field will be at a distinct disadvantage to his or her competitors who do. This is an advantage for those companies that focus on business valuations full time, as these companies can usually better afford to make the investment in human capital that is necessary to become a first-class business valuation company.

Fifth, we expect that a set of widely accepted appraisal principles (WAAP) will begin to evolve to the point that there will be a greater number of broadly accepted standards for valuations. GAAP stands as one model toward which widely accepted appraisal principles may evolve. As these professional standards are discussed and tested, it is likely that there will be some significant disputes among various members and organizations of the valuation profession, but over time, with good faith among the combatants, we expect that broad valuation concepts will be accepted and recognized not only within the profession but also outside the profession.

These trends in the valuation industry and the valuation profession have implications for careers and jobs in valuation. First, as the breadth of course offerings expands in professional organizations and institutions of higher learning, valuation expertise will become an identifiable hiring criterion. Currently, when a valuation firm wants to bring on a new valuator, it takes a long time and substantial investment to figure out the extent of the person's qualifications. As the education and training for valuators become more institutionalized, the process of determining a prospective valuator's qualifications will become easier.

Second, those individuals with training in industries that require a lot of education and training will be highly compensated.

For instance, a valuator who has a computer science or management information systems degree and who has earned an MBA and/or a CPA is likely to be highly sought after and highly compensated for valuations in the high-technology industry. By contrast, a valuator with experience and training relevant to valuations of small, independently owned dry-cleaning businesses will not be able to attract such a high salary; the amount of industry-specific knowledge and expertise is much higher in the high-technology industry.

One last industry trend deserves to be mentioned. Competition in the valuation industry is increasing as the overall number of business valuators grows. If economic theory is correct, the price of valuation services will decrease as the supply of individuals and firms performing business valuations increases. It is our expectation that as this occurs, the industry will adapt through the use of technology and education to maintain its margins and profitability.

ETHICS

This section reflects our opinion of how valuators should integrate ethical concerns into their practices and how valuation businesses may run into ethical problems.

A valuator should follow the standards and code of ethics of an accredited association[2] that he or she is a member of, and express estimates of value in accordance with the canons of ethics related to the process. The Appraisal Standards Board of the Appraisal Foundation develops and publishes the Uniform Standards of Professional Appraisal Practice.[3] Also, some states are regulating this area through statute, so valuators should check with the appropriate state governing society for the applicable regulations and ethics.

From our experience, there is a common profile of private companies that run into ethical problems. Valuations for these types of companies can quickly become expensive, because valuators have to take a lot of time to get to the bottom of the problems. The profile generally gets started by the "tax tail" wagging the "business dog": owners making short-term decisions to save taxes that handicap the business in the long run. The impact of these decisions expands to taint management policy. In turn, these policies finally undermine the basic spirit of the organization and its value.

Employees are usually much smarter than owners realize, so that if the owner/manager sets an example of bad business ethics, employees may view this behavior as a license to be unethical too.

After all, if the owner is lifting money from the till or shorting the tax collector, there is little to stop the employee when the owner is absent.

Consider the owner of a tavern who maintains two cash registers—one for reporting to the government and one for personal use. How does the owner then represent to the buyer, without compromise, what the real sales of the tavern are? If the tavern owner underreported sales to the IRS, is he or she overreporting sales to the prospective buyer?

Similarly, abusive tax practices are advantageous to no one and can lead to serious consequences for the unsuspecting. Remember, anyone who will risk going to prison will probably not hesitate to lie to a valuator. If a valuator discovers such practices and the client is unwilling to take corrective action, the valuator should seriously consider disengaging from the project.

There is debate over the ethical responsibility regarding the knowledge of tax fraud. Valuators who become aware of tax abuse under a protective court order in which it has been agreed to keep all information confidential should call their attorney and/or the risk management department of their malpractice insurer to receive guidance.

In too many cases, abusive tax practices run directly counter to increasing business value. For instance, a buyer may generally assume that if a business owner would cheat the government and risk a substantial fine or imprisonment for evading taxes, then the owner might also cheat the buyer. This situation creates unnecessary doubt and is a short-term decision contrary to maximizing the long-term value of the company.

When we spot a business with abusive tax practices, we may respectfully decline the engagement; it is not worth the time and effort or the risk to our livelihood for a short-term economic benefit. The federal government is issuing directives to state boards of accountancy to seek aggressive disciplinary actions against CPAs who are caught assisting with even the simplest of fraud scams.

Besides tax fraud, there is civil fraud. White collar crime is rampant and doing serious economic damage to our economy. The damage associated with financial statement fraud—such as revenue recognition schemes, inventory and cost-of-goods sold fraud, intentionally overstating assets and understating liabilities, and skimming, is costing consumers billions of dollars every year. In fact, the investigative niche of the accounting industry is flourishing because of the need to crack down on these outright illegal and unethical acts.

A well-run company with sound business ethics is worth more than a company that requires expensive housecleaning. Besides reaping the obvious benefits of being a good citizen, a company may take advantage of a few percentage points on a loan interest rate (bankers are usually astute businesspeople, and it is their job to assess risk and price it accordingly). Lower borrowing costs or a higher estimate of value can be worth a substantial amount of money. And if money is kept in the business, certain profits may end up being taxed at favorable capital gains rates rather than at ordinary income tax rates.

One of the classic examples of a situation gone wrong is portrayed in an article describing an investor who made a multimillion dollar corporate acquisition. After taking over the company, he claimed that the audited financial statements misrepresented the company's financial status. He sued two prominent New York–based CPA firms for $115,000,000, claiming that their audit of the company contained "errors, omissions, and irregularities."[4] Attorney's for the CPA firms denied any wrongdoing by the accountants.

ADVOCACY

Advocacy can be dangerous territory for a valuator. If a valuator does decide to take an advocacy engagement, he or she should make appropriate disclosure to the client—and perhaps the opposing side and the court, if relevant—that he or she is not a disinterested party. Overall, though, only the careless embrace extreme positions, and they are bound to be discovered in the long run.[5] Though this point may appear obvious, we must emphasize it, given what we see in many of our colleagues' reports.

If a valuator is involved in a sensitive valuation of a business that has stepped on the edge (or over the edge) of indiscretions, it makes sense to lay all the cards on the table immediately instead of letting them surface through dispute later. Be proactive and begin with the end in mind. A valuator will maintain the respect of other parties if he or she continually shares relevant information and findings early rather than later.

Clients do not need a "hired gun" who has been trained by and gained experience through advocacy work. In the past, it was common for the legal community to engage a valuator merely to support a particular position, not to search for the best estimate of value. Although this practice still exists, we believe it is occurring less frequently. In the long run, the advocacy bias creates disharmony between parties trying to reach a good-faith agreement on the value of a business.

Although legal counsel is ethically obligated to be its client's advocate, a valuator does not have the same role. While it may be easy to fall into the trap of trying to look like a hero, it is the valuator's responsibility to defend his or her estimate of value, not to defend the client. A valuator should not put his or her reputation at stake and risk potential legal liability by issuing a biased estimate of value.

Choosing an advocacy position adds nothing to the negotiation process; it can only slow it down, increase the cost, or even end it. The assumption is that the other side's valuator is equally intelligent, and with time and the right amount of hard work, he or she will uncover the truth and the best estimate of value. A valuator can impress a client, as well as the opposing expert, if the estimate of value is reasonable and can be defended.

SUMMARY

A career in valuation requires a wide range of skills, positive personality characteristics, and interests. It also demands ethical business practices and a willingness to stand behind a valuation, not necessarily to please the client. If a potential valuator possess these traits and embraces the paradigm, a career in valuation will be rewarding in many ways.

NOTES

1. National Association of Certified Fraud Examiners, *Fraud Examiners' Manual*, Austin, TX: NACFE, 1989.
2. Internal Revenue Service Regulation 1.170A-13, (c)(6)(ii).
3. Appraisal Standards Board, *Uniform Standards of Professional Appraisal Practice*, Washington, DC: Appraisal Foundation, 1995.
4. "Certain-teed Faces its Valley Forge." *Business Week*, June 1, 1974, p. 29.
5. Tax Court Memo 1996–372, *Estate of Ross H. Freeman v. Commissioner*, August 13, 1996.

CHAPTER 11

The Anatomy of a Business Valuation

When we began our business, we lacked a tool that we believe would have assisted us in our development. The purpose of this chapter and the three sample reports in the Appendix is to give our readers a taste of what valuation reports look like—that sample is the tool we were missing. For the most part, it is difficult to obtain reports of any kind, let alone reports where the estimate of value was followed. (*Note:* It is quite possible for the end user of a valuation report not to accept the estimate of value it contains. This could occur if the IRS rejects the value and begins audit procedures or if a proposed merger did not occur reasonably close to the estimate of value in the report. It might also occur, in a litigation setting with more than one valuation report on the same company, if one valuator's report was followed as correct and the other report was not followed.) As authors and professionals, we struggled over whether we should provide sample reports, but our sense of responsibility to our peers and those entering the profession won out over our concerns. This chapter is designed to inform and stimulate thought and discussion in the valuation community. Not everyone agrees with our approach to report writing. Remember, though, that in most dispute situations, our reports ultimately prove persuasive and our estimate of value is followed.

THEME

The underlying theme of our reports is to inform the reader in a simple and straightforward manner. They are purposely packaged to resemble something familiar and easy to read without the feeling of a cold, dry, "here we go again" report. The readers of our reports are assumed to be people who are not familiar with such matters as valuation, and wish to be informed in a clear and understandable way about the industry, the business being valued, and the methodology and assumptions that we followed in reaching our conclusion.

The consumer of our services is paying a substantial amount of money for the valuation and deserves something of substance and readability. The report is copyrighted with all rights reserved, as each report is authored by ValueNomics® employees for ValueNomics®. Each report is therefore authored by the collective efforts of all those who worked on the engagement, and the authors are given credit. The writing of the report is approached as though it were going to become a published document for general readership by the public. All too often we see reports written by others which are at one of two extremes. At the one end are the highly technical jargon-laden reports that are barely decipherable. At the other extreme are reports that appear to be written by a junior high school student who sleeps through English class.

TYPICAL INDEX

Our reports generally follow an index outlined as follows:

> Title Page
> Letter Report
> Executive Summary
> Table of Contents
> Introduction
>> Purpose of Valuation
>> Approach to Valuation
>> Limiting Conditions
> Background
>> Ownership and Structure
> National Economic Review
> Industry Overview
> Financial Review
> Estimate of Value
> Appendix

The reports also include footnotes so that the reader can readily go to the source document.

Rather than write on each of these topics in isolation, we decided to dissect and annotate a hypothetical business valuation for our readers.

ANNOTATION

THE REPORT

Whether you are a member of the National Association of Certified Valuation Analysts (NACVA), the American Institute of Certified Public Accountants (AICPA), the American Society of Appraisers (ASA), the Institute of Business Appraisers (IBA), or some other organization dedicated to the business of valuation, you may be required by its rules (and possibly by USPAP, the Uniform Standards of Professional Appraisal Practice) to include certain information in reports. Please consider those rules carefully when writing your reports if you are a certified or accredited member. The following hypothetical report generally uses the guidelines set out by NACVA. In using them, we are not stating an opinion as to the appropriateness of NACVA guidelines over any other guidelines.

In this regard, it is important to put into perspective that the final report you issue is yours and that these organizations are not Congress, your state legislature, the courts, or an authoritative government agency with ruling and regulatory authority. They are private associations of individuals, each having its own agenda, opinions, requirements, and enrollment criteria. There is disagreement among these organizations on such issues as the proper content of a written report. Of importance to you is this: Can you defend your estimate of value? None of these organizations is going to be sitting next to you in court when you testify; their level of assurance on your work and liability if you lose is zero. There are no Generally Accepted Appraisal Standards as there are Generally Accepted Accounting Standards (GAAS) or Principles (GAAP). For the most part, when you sign your name, you are on your own. *Remember that!*

ANNOTATION

Title Page. The title page is a place for the reader to begin. This page defines what is being valued, for whom it is being valued, what the valuation date is, the date of the report, who authored the report, the purpose, and the copyright.

EXAMPLE

VALUATION[1]

Valuation of
A xx.x% Common Stock interest in Brew and Chew, Inc. (a California corporation, "the Company"), General Partner in Brew and Chew, Ltd. (a California limited partnership).

For
The Law Offices of Legal Eagles in the matter of: Myron Dygert v. Brew and Chew, Inc. (a California corporation), Brew and Chew, Ltd. (a California limited partnership), & Herman Brewmeister, in the Superior Court of the State of California, in and for the County of Franklin, Case # 9.

Valuation Dates
As of July 4, 199x; January 18, 199x; July 24, 199x; and the date as near as practicable to the time of trial, March 31, 199x.

---

1. Copyright 1997, ValueNomics Research, Inc. All rights reserved.

Purpose

The purpose of the valuation is to estimate the "fair value" of a xx.x% interest in the Company at the four valuation dates requested.

Prepared by
ValueNomics Research, Inc.

May 5, 199x

Gary E. Jones
Certified Valuation Analyst

Dirk E. Van Dyke
Senior Quantitative Analyst

Alisa Marienthal
Senior Analyst

Benjamin Chiu
Analyst

ANNOTATION

Letter Report. The letter contains a narrative of what we were engaged to do, the purpose, the relevant dates, the standard of value followed, and the estimate of value. This hypothetical report has a series of dates and events to demonstrate the complicated nature a valuation might take. Note the footnote reference to the standard of value as fair value. It is important not to articulate any opinion or interpretation regarding the standard of value. Simply define it; don't try to explain it and do use the exact quote. Explaining it may appear to be a legal opinion, and this could get you in trouble. (It is important for a valuation analyst not to provide a legal opinion; if any issues arise when you are conducting a business valuation requiring legal interpretation, please consult your legal counsel.) The information in the letter report should be short and to the point, giving the reader a brief and up-front understanding of the results of your engagement and the estimate of value. The report that follows the letter is meant to explain how you got there.

EXAMPLE

David R. Schneider, Esq.
The Law Offices of Legal Eagles
2000 Bohemian Blvd., 49th Floor
Washington, DC 22002

Dear Mr. Schneider:

We have prepared, and enclosed herewith, our valuation report of a xx.x% shareholder Common Stock interest in Brew and Chew, Inc. ("the Corporation" or "the Company"), a California corporation, and General Partner in Brew and Chew, Ltd. (hereinafter "the Partnership"), dated May 5, 199x. The purpose of the valuation is to estimate the "fair value" of a xx.x% shareholder Common Stock interest in the Company at the four valuation dates requested: (1) July 4, 199x; (2) January 18, 199x; (3) July 24, 199x; and (4) the date as near as practicable to the time of trial, March 31, 199x.

Section 2000 of the California Corporations Code calls for a valuation that:

> Shall be determined on the basis of the liquidation value as of the valuation date but taking into account the possibility, if any, of sale of the entire business as a going concern in a liquidation.[2]

Estimate of value July 4, 199x
Based on our study and analytical review procedures, we have concluded that a reasonable estimate of the "fair value" of a xx.x% shareholder Common Stock interest in Brew and Chew, Inc. as of July 4, 199x is zero (see page ___).

Estimate of value January 18, 199x
Based on our study and analytical review procedures, we have concluded that a reasonable estimate of the "fair value" of a xx.x% shareholder Common Stock interest in Brew and Chew, Inc. as of January 18, 199x is zero (see page ___).

Estimate of value July 24, 199x
Based on our study and analytical review procedures, we have concluded that a reasonable estimate of the "fair value" of a xx.x% shareholder Common Stock interest in Brew and Chew, Inc. as of July 24, 199x is more than zero (see page ___).

See the Valuation Report with Limiting Conditions

---

2. Cal. Corp. Code §2000, Subd. (a).

David R. Schneider, Esq.
The Law Offices of Legal Egals
Page 2

Estimate of value for the date as near as practicable to the time of trial
Based on our study and analytical review procedures, we have concluded that a reasonable estimate of the "fair value" of a xx.x% shareholder Common Stock interest in Brew and Chew, Inc. as of March 31, 199x ranges from $xxx (Exhibit J) to $xxx (Exhibit K).

ValueNomics Research, Inc.

Gary E. Jones
President

Cupertino, CA
May 5, 199x

See the Valuation Report with Limiting Conditions

A N N O T A T I O N

Executive Summary. Following the letter report, we recommend that you have an executive summary of how the estimate of value was derived. The reader should have some basic foundation before proceeding with the detailed report. We believe this foundation should be set at the beginning. The report is not a mystery novel in which the surprise ending is critical to sales. The reader simply wants to know what the value of the business is and why you believe that is a good estimate of value. The letter report and the executive summary are meant to inform the reader in a few minutes of your result and to provide the foundation for understanding the detailed report that follows.

We also believe that many of the readers of our reports are not business-oriented or financially inclined and may not understand the detailed schedules in the report appendix. They may not have the time, the inclination, or the business acumen to read and understand the entire report. Consider that the reader of the report may be an out-spouse in a divorce action, a minority shareholder who is not active in the business, a trier-of-fact such as a juror (remember the jury in the O.J. Simpson trial), or an heir with no financial background. The executive summary is designed to provide this individual with an overview of the estimate of value without having to wade through the report.

EXAMPLE

ESTIMATE OF VALUE OF BREW AND CHEW—LOWER RANGE OF VALUE

Total Liabilities and Equity at March 31, 199x	($xxx)
Adjustments:	
Entry to record payoff of current liabilities	(xxx)
Entry to adjust legal expenses	xxx
Entry to adjust legal fees	xxx
Adjusted net book value at March 31, 199x	$xxx
Estimate of value for a xx.x% interest in the Company	xxx

ESTIMATE OF VALUE OF BREW AND CHEW—LOWER LIMIT OF RANGE OF VALUE

$xxx

ESTIMATE OF VALUE OF BREW AND CHEW—UPPER RANGE OF VALUE

Total Liabilities and Equity at March 31, 199x	($xxx)
Adjustments:	
Entry to record payoff of current liabilities	(xxx)
Entry to adjust legal expenses	xxx
Entry to record present value of discounted cashflow	xxx
Adjusted net book value at March 31, 199x	$xxx
Estimate of value for a xx.x% interest in the Company	xxx

ESTIMATE OF VALUE OF BREW AND CHEW—UPPER LIMIT OF RANGE OF VALUE

$xxx

ANNOTATION

Table of Contents. Along with the need to understand is the need to seek information quickly and backtrack when necessary. This is particularly true with complicated reports that contain over 100 pages, including text and exhibits on different topics. Most word processing programs have a table of contents function with floating page numbering features. We find this a helpful tool when a report has been dormant for several years after completion and someone calls us to get a quick answer over the phone. We simply grab the report, look in the table of contents, and move right to the relevant section page. This can also be a helpful quality review feature for the reviewer who was not intimately involved in the process.

EXAMPLE

ANNOTATION

Body of Report. There is a school of thought which holds that the less helpful you are and the less information you provide, the better your chances of having your estimate of value followed. We do not subscribe to this doctrine. We believe just the opposite— that the better you explain your work and articulate it through easily understood terms and concepts, the more likely you are to have your estimate of value followed. In addition, your written report may become a second chance to testify. Consider that the trier-of-fact takes your report and may read it again after you have testified. If your report is well written, you are in effect testifying a second time as the individual rereads your work. If your report is skimpy, vague, and in an outline format with little cross-referencing and footnoting, then someone may choose not to reread it. Even if he or she does look at it again, if that person cannot follow what you have done he or she may place little weight on your results. Our experience and feedback from end users of our reports is very positive.

In fact, there is a second reason to write a good report (in legal matters). It is typically the goal of both sides to settle prior to undertaking an expensive and time-consuming trial. We have found our reports to be helpful in this regard. When the opposition presents a skimpy, lackluster report with vague information, the deposition of this individual is almost certain. This is an added expense for the consumer of our services and for the most part is unnecessary. If both reports met the high standards of Federal Rule 26, we believe there would be more settlements because of the level of understanding of the valuations prior to a deposition being taken. Most matters appear to settle and follow our estimate of value after taking the deposition of the opposing expert. Our deposition is rarely taken in this regard. Why? We believe and have been told that our reports are helpful, that our analysis is substantive and thorough, and that we clearly explain how we arrived at our estimate of value. Therefore, counsel is able to proceed without taking our deposition. It is clear from our reports where we stand on a particular issue, and how we derived or calculated the key numbers and factors that drive the estimate of value. Perhaps some valuators are purposely vague about certain issues because it was not clear in their own minds how or why they came up with a certain factor (e.g., a discount rate). We share this experience not to puff ourselves in your eyes, but hopefully to encourage you to adopt a higher standard in your report writing. It appears to be worth it.

Introduction. While it may appear redundant to go over the sub-headings of this section, thus far in our report we have introduced only the topics. This is where we briefly explain our valuation approach—the internal and external factors affecting value, including marketability and control. We also provide the reader with the limiting conditions underlying our work.

The following mock report is an example of what might be presented in a shareholder dispute litigation. Note that the standard of value here is fair value, not fair market value. Since the definition of fair value varies by state, it is important that you know what the definition of fair value is in the state in which the subject company is incorporated. In this hypothetical instance, we assume the corporation is a California corporation, so we use the definition of fair value for the state of California.

EXAMPLE

INTRODUCTION

PURPOSE OF VALUATION

This report has been prepared for the specific purpose of determining the "fair value" of a xx.x% shareholder Common Stock interest in Brew and Chew, Inc. (hereinafter "the Corporation" or "the Company," a California corporation, and General Partner in Brew and Chew, Ltd., hereinafter "the Partnership"), at the four valuation dates requested: (1) July 4, 199x; (2) January 18, 199x; (3) July 24, 199x; and (4) the date as near as practicable to the time of trial, March 31, 199x.

Section 2000 of the California Corporations Code calls for a valuation that:

> Shall be determined on the basis of the liquidation value as of the valuation date but taking into account the possibility, if any, of sale of the entire business as a going concern in a liquidation.[3]

APPROACH TO VALUATION

Our approach has been to determine an estimate of value which would provide a fair and reasonable return on investment under

---

3. Cal. Corp. Code §2000, Subd. (a).

hypothetical sales conditions, in view of the facts available to us at the time. Our estimate of value is based on, among other things, our estimate of the risks facing the General Partner, the business of the Partnership, the terms of the Partnership Agreement, and the return on investment which would be required on alternative investments with similar levels of risk at the valuation dates.

Both internal and external factors which influence the value of the Company were reviewed, analyzed, and interpreted. Internal factors include the Company's and Partnership's financial position, results of operations, and size. External factors include, among other things, the status of the restaurant and brew-pub industries and the position of Brew and Chew (the restaurant), relative to those industries.

For purposes of this valuation we have not included a review, analysis, and interpretation of control, or lack thereof, associated with the xx.x% Common Stock interest being valued.

[**ANNOTATION:** We did this because this is a Section 2000 valuation, and in the state of California, there is no discount for lack of control for fair value.]

For purposes of this valuation we have not included a review, analysis, and interpretation of marketability associated with the xx.x% shareholder Common Stock interest being valued.

[**ANNOTATION:** This is because this is a Section 2000 valuation, and in the state of California, there is no discount for lack of marketability for fair value. Actually, this is a very contentious issue within the business valuation community. The definition of fair value in the state of California, and in many states—be sure to check the appropriate state law and to consult with an attorney before moving ahead on this issue—is not particularly clear. As of the date we are writing this, there are no written guidelines stating the exact factors that business valuators are to consider when estimating the fair value of a minority interest in a corporation. Most valuators and attorneys would agree that a lack of control adjustment is not appropriate in a fair value valuation, because it would not be fair to the minority shareholder to apply one to his or her interest. However, the marketability adjustment is not so straightforward.

There is one camp of valuators which believes that no lack of marketability is appropriate. The other camp believes that, to estimate fair value accurately, one has to apply a quick-sale adjustment, which some would consider to fall under the broad heading of a marketability adjustment. The statute and case law in the state of California does not directly state if a quick-sale adjustment is appropriate. This area is one of many in the field of valuations that is still open to debate.

For those of you considering a career in valuations, if you do not like ambiguity, and if you want everything to be cut and dried, this may not be an appropriate career move for you. Analysts who are used to applying rote formulas or deferring their analytical skills to rules and regulations promulgated by others, and who want to find the precise and exact right answer, will find that this is not how things are done in the artful field of valuations. On the other hand, if you want to enter an intellectually stimulating industry where there is still plenty of opportunity to assist in the development and interpretation of ever-changing standards, valuations can be a very exciting area of work.

We find valuations to be challenging and interesting. However, it takes a substantial investment of time for one to stay abreast of all the developments, including court cases, new research, databases, studies, and surveys. We do not generally believe that valuations are a good part-time service area to enter into on your own. You need to form an alliance to work with others, your peers, or a mentor. It takes a committed professional devoting all of his or her resources to be a well-rounded valuation analyst. Those who do one or two valuations a year, without proper support and peer review, are not necessarily going to perform at the same level as those who do 10 or more valuations per year with the complement of an organization focused on valuations to assist them.]

ANNOTATION

Limiting Conditions. The limiting conditions section of the report is where you can state how your conclusions were limited. For example, if you used financial statements prepared by a CPA firm, here is the appropriate place for you to state that your firm did not perform an audit or review of the financial information underlying the financial statements. We believe that it is better to err by including more limiting conditions than by leaving some out. It is also a good place to state that your report is not intended to be legal, financial, investment, or any other type of professional advice or counsel unless specifically stated otherwise in the body of the report. In other words, this section of the report is where you want to Cover Your Assets. If your firm was limited in the amount of time or information it had to prepare the report, state that here. We also state some assumptions that we made in the course of our valuation, when appropriate.

There are times when it is necessary for us to qualify reports. It does not happen often, but when it does we qualify the report in the letter and in the limiting conditions. One reason for qualification is a lack of access to specific information. We also single-space this section of the report to set it out on its own. The reader needs to see it as separate from the analysis. We believe this style accomplishes that.

EXAMPLE

Limiting Conditions

This report is based on historical and prospective financial information provided to us by management and other third parties. Had we audited or reviewed the underlying data, matters may have come to our attention which would have resulted in our using amounts which differ from those provided. Accordingly, we take no responsibility for the underlying data presented in this report. Users of this business valuation should be aware that business valuations are based on future earnings potential that may or may not materialize. Therefore, the actual results achieved during the projection period could vary from the projection used in this valuation, and the variations may be material.

We have no present or contemplated financial interest in the Corporation or the Limited Partnership, or with any known petitioner or respondent. Our fees for this valuation are based upon our normal hourly billing rates, and are in no way contingent upon the results of our findings. We have no responsibility to update this report for events and circumstances occurring subsequent to the date of this report.

This report has been prepared for the specific purpose of valuing a xx.x% Common Stock interest in Brew and Chew, Inc. It is to be used solely in the depositions, proceedings, hearings, administration and trial of the Superior Court of Franklin County Case # 9, and is intended for no other purpose. Furthermore, no aspect or conclusion of this report is meant to be construed as legal advice, or any other type of professional advice or counsel, unless specifically stated to the contrary in this report. It is not to be copied or made available to any person(s) without the written consent of ValueNomics Research, Inc., other than for the use of: Plaintiff's legal counsel, Defendant's legal counsel, other valuation expert(s), a special master(s) appointed by the Court, and the Superior Court of California, County of Franklin, Case # 9.

We have relied upon the representations of the Company and Partnership management and other third parties concerning the value and useful condition of all equipment, real estate leases, investments, and any other assets or liabilities except as specifically stated to the contrary in this report. We have not attempted to confirm whether or not all assets of the business are free and clear of liens and encumbrances, or that the business has good title to all assets. The estimate of value included in this report assumes that the existing business of the Partnership will achieve operational and financial goals as projected by management.

ValueNomics Research, Inc., does not purport to be a guarantor of value. Valuation of private, closely held companies is an imprecise science, with value being a matter of the interpretation of specific facts related to the company and partnership business being valued, and reasonable people may differ in their estimates of value.

ValueNomics®, however, performed conceptually sound and commonly accepted methods and procedures of valuation in determining the estimate of value included in this report. ValueNomics Research, Inc., and its employees are liable only to the client, and this liability is expressly limited to the amount of the fee for this engagement. ValueNomics® does not assume any liability, obligation, or accountability to any third party under any circumstances. The client agrees to hold ValueNomics® and its employees harmless in the event of a lawsuit initiated by any party other than the client.

ANNOTATION

Background. This section of the report is intended to provide the reader with a brief history of the company. For a valuation that is performed as part of a legal proceeding, this section can be particularly important. Be sure that your facts and history are correct before releasing your report. This part of the report can help the reader understand the history and the background of the company.

EXAMPLE

BACKGROUND

GENERAL

The concept of Brew and Chew was originally conceived by Trevor Lauren. Frank Lee joined Mr. Lauren in the venture, and they later became associated with Myron Dygert. On June 9, 199x, the group signed an "Agreement to Form Brew and Chew, Inc." ("the June 9, 199x, Agreement"), which specified that each party would receive xxx shares of Common Stock in exchange for investments of $xxx apiece. The agreement further stated that each party would receive xx.x% of both the voting shares and the profits. The Articles of Incorporation of Brew and Chew, Inc., were officially filed and stamped on June 29, 199x. Messrs. Lauren, Lee, and Dygert were involved in ongoing negotiations for a restaurant location with a prospective landlord, Jacob Hunter, 6740 Pub Avenue, New Carrollton ("the premises"), the potential future site for the restaurant. On June 21, 199x, Mr. Dygert allegedly made various declarations to the effect that he would not do any further business with Mr. Lauren. On July 4, 199x, the parties signed a "Release and Settlement Agreement" whereby the three purported to resign as Officers and Directors of Brew and Chew, Inc., although the three were never actually elected Officers or Directors of the Corporation. In addition, the three released each other from any claims they might have against each other with respect to the June 9, 199x, Agreement and otherwise. Sections 3.9 and 3.10 of the Release recited that each group (Mr. Dygert, or Messrs. Lauren and Lee) had an equal right to pursue the procurement of a lease and the development of a restaurant at the Pub Avenue location. It was further specified that whichever part(ies) entered into a lease at the premises would be entitled to the corporate shell and name, after reimbursing the other part(ies).

On or about July 4, 199x, a Blain Downer paid Mr. Hunter $xxx for a one-month rental agreement, hoping to lease the premises. Messrs. Lauren, Lee, and Downer signed a second "Agreement to Form Brew and Chew, Inc.," on August 9, 199x. On August 29, 199x, Messrs. Downer (as company President) and Lauren (as company Secretary) signed a lease agreement on behalf of the Corporation with Hunter, Inc., Mr. Hunter's corporation (Exhibit N).

During November 199x, the Corporation formed Brew and Chew, Ltd. (hereinafter "the Partnership", Exhibit M), and sold xxx Limited Partnership units at $xxx apiece to private investors as a means of providing equity financing for development. In January of 199x, Mr. Brewmeister was introduced to the project by Mr. Lauren. On February 9, 199x, he purchased two of the xxx Limited Partnership units for $xxx.

The General Partner was Brew and Chew, Inc., with stockholders Blain Downer, Trevor Lauren, and Frank Lee owning xx.x% of the outstanding Common Stock, respectively. In early 199x, Mr. Lee passed away and the remaining stockholders purchased an equal share of Mr. Lee's xx.x% Common Stock interest in the Corporation. On July 9, 199x, Mr. Brewmeister agreed to arrange a loan for $xxx to the then substantially undercapitalized Limited Partnership. As part of this agreement, Mr. Brewmeister acquired shares of stock in Brew and Chew, Inc., to bring his ownership interest to xx.x%.

Messrs. Lauren and Downer were then reduced to a xx.x% interest each in the outstanding Common Stock of the Corporation.

Mr. Dygert filed the subject lawsuit in July 199x, just prior to the opening of the Restaurant on August 31, 199x. The Restaurant has been in business continuously since that time. Mr. Brewmeister, in February 199x, purchased Mr. Lauren's then xx.x% interest in the outstanding Common Stock of the Corporation and any/all claims of Mr. Lauren's against the Corporation and Partnership. Mr. Brewmeister paid consideration for this Common Stock and rights of a $xxx payment to Mr. Lauren on January 9, 199x.

ANNOTATION

Ownership and Structure. This part of the report explains to the reader who owns what percentage interest in the Company. Typically, the ownership as of the valuation date is the only information provided in this section of the report, so it is relatively short. For this mock report, there are four potential valuation dates, so the ownership structure must be described as of each valuation date. Unfortunately, we have seen reports in which an appraiser valued an incorrect percentage of ownership in the company and at the wrong valuation date. Needless to say, the client was not impressed.

EXAMPLE

OWNERSHIP AND STRUCTURE

Ownership at Valuation Date #1, July 4, 199x

An Agreement to Form Brew and Chew, Inc., dated June 9, 199x, was signed by Trevor Lauren, Frank Lee, and Myron Dygert. On June 21, 199x, Mr. Dygert allegedly made various declarations to the effect that he would not do any further business with Mr. Lauren. On July 4, 199x, the three parties entered into a Settlement Agreement and Mutual Release, releasing each other from any liabilities arising out of the breach of the June 9, 199x, Agreement and otherwise leaving the Corporation unorganized. July 4, 199x, was selected as a valuation date because the Settlement Agreement and Mutual Release, dated July 4, 199x, contained a list and agreed value of the assets associated with the project.

Alleged Ownership of Brew and Chew, Inc., at July 4, 199x	
	Percent
Trevor Lauren	xx.x%
Frank Lee	xx.x%
Myron Dygert	xx.x%

Ownership at Valuation Date #2, January 18, 199x

On January 18, 199x, Trevor Lauren, Frank Lee, and Blain Downer signed a second "Agreement to Form Brew and Chew, Inc.," with the three men owning the above percentages of the then outstanding Common Stock (Exhibit L).

Ownership of Outstanding Common Stock at January 18, 199x	
	Percent
Trevor Lauren	xx.x%
Frank Lee	xx.x%
Blain Downer	xx.x%

Ownership at Valuation Date #3, July 24, 199x

On February 9, 199x, Herman Brewmeister purchased Frank Lee's Common Stock interest in the Corporation for $xxx. Subsequently on March 3, 199x, Messrs. Lauren, Downer, and Brewmeister jointly purchased Mr. Lee's Common Stock for $xxx. The Common Stock ownership of the Corporation after this transaction is listed above.

We were instructed by counsel to value the restaurant–brew pub as of July 24, 199x.

Ownership of Outstanding Common Stock at July 24, 199x	
	Percent
Trevor Lauren	xx.x%
Blain Downer	xx.x%
Herman Brewmeister	xx.x%

Ownership at Valuation Date #4, March 31, 199x

On July 9, 199x, Mr. Brewmeister agreed to arrange a loan for $xxx to Brew and Chew, Ltd. To induce Mr. Brewmeister to arrange the loan, Messrs. Lauren and Downer each transferred xx.x% of the total issued and outstanding Common Stock shares of the Corporation to Mr. Brewmeister. On January 9, 199x, Mr. Brewmeister purchased Mr. Lauren's then remaining xx.x% Common Stock interest in the Corporation for the consideration discussed earlier in this valuation report (Exhibit L).

Ownership of the Corporation as of the Date of This Report, May 5, 199x		
	# Shares	Percent
Herman Brewmeister	xxx	xx.x%
Blain Downer	xxx	xx.x%
Total shares of common stock issued and outstanding (Exhibit L)	xxx	100.0%

Structure

California Corporation

Tax Structure

C Corporation

ANNOTATION

National Economic Review. Revenue Ruling 59-60 states that a valuator should consider the prevalent economic conditions at the valuation date. The national economy should be considered. The important thing to remember here is: What is the impact of the national economy on the subject company? If the overall economy is booming and people are increasing their spending on luxury items, and if the subject company is a high-priced cigar humidor store, the impact could be substantial. You have to dig into the economic statistics to determine what factors influence the subject company. If you are valuing a bank, then a careful consideration of interest rates is in order. You would probably also want to discuss interest rate risk somewhere in your report, so that your economic overview ties in with the estimate of value. In the 1980s, a report that failed to analyze interest rate risk for a savings and loan would probably not have been a good report.

However, there are businesses that are more influenced by the region and/or industry than they are by the national economy. We believe that this is the case for the hypothetical Brew and Chew. At the valuation date, Brew and Chew was in an industry that was in a fairly rapid growth phase for the number of brew pubs. However, same-store sales is one of the most important industry/economic factors affecting long-term value. The overall strength of the U.S. economy was not as significant as the industry trends, although the fact that the economy was fairly strong overall has most likely helped increase sales.

EXAMPLE

NATIONAL ECONOMIC REVIEW [4]

GENERAL ECONOMIC OVERVIEW

Real Gross Domestic Product ("real GDP"), the output of goods and services produced by labor and property located in the United States, increased at an annualized rate of xx.x%, or about $xxx billion, in the fourth quarter of 199x, according to preliminary estimates released by the Department of Commerce's Bureau of Economic Analysis ("BEA"). In the third quarter of 199x, revised

---

4. Timothy L. Lee, *National Economic Review,* Mercer Capital.

growth in real GDP was xx.x%, or about $xxx billion, and slightly lower than the originally reported annualized rate of xx.x%. Growth in real GDP for all of 199x was xx.x%, up from 199x's xx.x% rate but lower than the xx.x% rate in 199x. According to the BEA, the fourth-quarter GDP results reflected rapid acceleration in personal consumption expenditures and increased export activity.

The Composite Index of Leading Economic Indicators, the government's primary forecasting gauge, ended the fourth quarter with a x.x increase in December to xxx (199x=100), near all-time highs for the measure, according to The Conference Board. The index attempts to gauge economic activity six to nine months in advance. Multiple consecutive moves in the same direction are said to be indicative of the general direction of the economy. The index has either increased or remained stable 11 of the last 12 months and hasn't declined since January of 199x. Measures over the last six months have been modestly lower than those of the first and second quarters, suggesting a moderation of economic growth during the first half of 199x.

Stock markets declined in early December after surging in November. Comments in early December from Federal Reserve ("Fed") Chairman Alan Greenspan regarding his assessment of the market's "irrational exuberance" had investors hinging on possible action by the Fed to tighten interest rates. However, by the end of the year most investors, believing the market to have a strong foundation and supported by the Fed's lack of action to tighten interest rates, were resuming their bullish buying. The bond markets were generally favorable during October and November as yields dropped, but hints of strong economic growth reversed the trend with bond prices dropping throughout much of December.

The outlook for the economy through the first half of 199x is for modest growth with the possibility of increasing inflationary pressures. Growth in GDP is estimated to be near or just above xx.x%, with inflation falling between xx.x% and xx.x% and unemployment levels remaining below xx.x%.

CONSUMER SPENDING AND INFLATION

According to the Bureau of Labor Statistics ("BLS"), the Consumer Price Index ("CPI") increased to xxx.x in December (CPI—all urban consumers, 198x–198x=xxx, before seasonal adjustment). The seasonally adjusted annualized rate of inflation for the fourth quarter was xx.x%, compared to xx.x% (1st), xx.x% (2nd), and xx.x% (3rd), respectively, for the prior three quarters. For all of 199x, the rate of inflation was xx.x%, reflecting an increase from the xx.x% level measured in 199x. Seasonally adjusted increases of xx.x% for each month of the fourth quarter were consistent with expectations of somewhat higher inflation. The core rate of inflation (that rate net of the volatile fuel and energy sectors) was consistently lower than overall quarterly inflation rates measuring xx.x% for 199x after increases of xx.x% and xx.x% in 199x and 199x, respectively. The xx.x% core rates of inflation for 199x and 199x are the lowest measured since 196x.

The Producer Price Index ("PPI"), generally considered a good indicator for near-term consumer price trends, increased by x.x in December after climbing x.x in both October and November (PPI for finished goods, seasonally adjusted). Energy prices were the primary reason behind the PPI's recent increases. Unlike the CPI, advancing energy prices are considered significant, because higher producer costs for energy represent future pressure on core consumer pricing. The outlook among most economists is for inflation to remain relatively steady through the first half of 199x at approximately xx.x% to xx.x%.

According to the Commerce Department, retail sales for the November to December period were revised downward from an originally reported increase of xx.x% to an increase of xx.x%. Retail sales during the 199x holiday season were generally weaker than expected but still favorable for many retailers. Personal consumption expenditures, which represent approximately two thirds of total economic activity, rebounded from a lackluster increase of xx.x% in the third quarter to xx.x% in the fourth quarter and contributed to the overall strong growth in GDP for the period. Durable-goods purchases were primarily responsible for the strong gains. Analysts cite higher personal income for the fourth-quarter consumption increase. Savings rates also climbed in the fourth quarter and are expected to provide a degree of protection for the economy from a near-term decline in personal consumption. Current indications suggest that 199x consumer spending will continue at a modest rate despite increasing personal income as consumers continue to save and to show restraint in taking on additional credit obligations.

SUMMARY AND OUTLOOK

Economic growth, as measured by growth in GDP, increased to xx.x% in the fourth quarter of 199x, after registering a moderate xx.x% annualized rate in the third quarter. Consensus estimates of growth in GDP for 199x are xx.x% to xx.x%. Equity markets experienced their second consecutive strong year, while bond markets exhibited mixed directions throughout the second half of the year after a generally poor first half. Inflation results for the fourth quarter reflected a seasonally adjusted annualized rate of xx.x%, representing an increase from the third quarter level of xx.x%. Inflation signals remain somewhat mixed but generally favorable enough that no eminent Federal Reserve action is expected in the near term. Many analysts and economists anticipate overall inflation levels will fall in the xx.x%-to-xx.x% range for the first half of 199x.

ANNOTATION

Industry Overview. Of all the opposing experts' reports that we come across in the course of doing our work, this is the section that is usually the least well done. For example, one appraiser's report on a company he valued at over $3 million had a one-paragraph section on the industry, with the apparent conclusion (the paragraph was rather vague, actually) that the industry was riskier than most industries. In our analysis, we took the time to perform extensive industry research, after interviewing company management about where the company was heading. During the management interview, we determined that the company exported products to Asia, and had been successful in selling to mainland China, a country which had, in the last few years, opened up to exports from foreign countries for the products the company sold. Further research demonstrated that demand from China had been a substantial portion of U.S. exports (of the subject company's best-selling product), and that demand was most likely going to continue increasing from China. We used this information in our estimate-of-value section to develop a healthy growth rate in revenues for the Company. The other valuator's report did not mention the prospects for exports of the company's products to China, although it did state that relevant aspects of the U.S. and state economy did not affect the value of the company one way or the other! We believe that, for the valuation of this specific company, it would be impossible to accurately assess the company's growth prospects without an analysis of sales to China, which the other evaluator totally ignored. Our advice: Do not skimp on this section of the report.

There are three things we try to accomplish with our industry section. First, give the reader an understanding of the industry, including risks and rewards. Second, interview key individuals in the industry rather than just rely on our research. This has proved to be very helpful over the years and hundreds of reports we've done. Some of the best sources of information have been calls to CFOs, controllers, or vice presidents of marketing. Believe us when we tell you that they love to talk and are very knowledgeable. They are usually very proud of their accomplishments and want to, on a confidential basis, share them with someone they can trust. In all the years we've done valuations, we know of only a couple of instances that became difficult. Third, once the research, analysis, and written sections are finished, the report is completed with a link to our estimate of value. After all, it makes no sense to inform the reader of the industry and its current status unless we connect it to our thinking and result. In other words, how was the estimate of value affected by the current status and outlook of the industry? Unless we're missing something, that is what Revenue Ruling 59-60 recommends we do.

Failure to research, analyze, and report the industry outlook can be harmful to your result. Let us give you a war story. We were valuing a software developer and distributor of prepackaged or shrink-wrapped software in Silicon Valley. The opposing expert had not done his research and had valued the company using an SIC code for custom software developers, not understanding the difference. The industry section of his report and discussion of what the company did were completely incorrect. His valuation of the company was off by millions of dollars as a result. Prepackaged software companies have profit margins in the xx.x%-plus range once they have covered fixed costs, while custom software companies have much lower margins, say xx.x%, for the contract work they typically perform. Needless to say, it is the dream of every software developer to come up with a commercially viable software package.

In the hypothetical report we are dissecting in this section, a similar problem arises. At the time of our research a substantial proportion, if not all, of the articles on the brew-pub industry were very positive on the growth and future of the industry. The problem arises when the analyst who doesn't understand the industry fails to ask the question "How are same-seat sales performing?" Answer: They're declining. It turns out that the industry reports of fantastic growth were from new restaurant units being opened at a very rapid pace, while existing store units were experiencing downtrending sales from the competition and consumers moving on to newer, more exciting restaurants. In our hypothetical report, let's assume for a minute that an opposing expert fails to recognize this in valuing a single unit with no plans or room to expand. Let's also assume that the unit stabilizes and is expected to begin downtrending in the near future because of over 2000 new seats opening in the market area within a year of the valuation date closest to trial. You can begin to understand the need to do your research. If you don't and assume the growth rate of the industry without examining the trend in same-seat sales, you could overvalue the brew pub.

In further analysis of guideline public brew pubs, it was determined that the bloom had indeed fallen off the rose for the investment community. Almost all public companies mentioned in our report have experienced declines in the price of their stock since our initial research. Much of this is attributed to declining same-seat sales and increased competition. The industry section below is included to frame a hypothetical situation, and its data are derived from a time period other than the dates used in the hypothetical. This is done to allow us the latitude to apply real-world data in this example rather than fictitious data. Some of the citations were changed to protect the sources of information.

EXAMPLE

INDUSTRY OVERVIEW: RESTAURANTS OFFERING SPECIALTY BEER

THE RESTAURANT INDUSTRY

Sales at full-service restaurants are projected to reach $xxx billion in 199x—up xx.x% over 199x or a xx.x% advance in real terms.[5] There are, however, some caveats regarding this growth including (1) low chance of long-term success for restaurants in general, and (2) changes in the employee labor pool.

Many restaurants are subject to lack of customer loyalty. Consumers tend to frequent the new concept or theme restaurant for a short period of time before moving on to the next, albeit that some concepts have survived the test of time. Some prime examples are hamburger restaurants, healthful concept restaurants , ethnic restaurants (Mexican, Asian, and European), and many more. But many other restaurant styles will emerge, and be in heavy demand when they do, only to be preempted by a new restaurant craze within a few years, months, or even less time. For instance, the "sports restaurant and bar," whose 199x's popularity has been waning, has been

---

5. "The Nation's Restaurants," National Restaurant and Brew-Pub Association, October 199x, p. 151.

eclipsed by renewed interest in family-style pizza restaurants with sports entertainment.

The restaurant patron is a fickle consumer whose loyalty lasts according to the courtesy and service exhibited by restaurant employees, the quality and consistency of the food, condition of the facility, and the demographics of the area the restaurant serves. Two examples of long-term success are Bakers Heaven, which has consistently maintained all these factors while others have failed (such as Apple-Pear Pies and Earthly Delights), and Tacos Mexicana Restaurant. While the cofounder's brother, Carlos, tried and failed to expand the Tacos concept beyond the original restaurant located in New York, the family has continued to operate the tremendously successful regional Mexican food and bar concept in its original location. The original location has proven demographics, embellished by consistently high standards for food, service, and physical appearance (four updating remodels) during its 20-plus years of operations.

Another potential blight on the horizon is that the restaurant industry's prime employee labor pool—xx-to-xx-year-olds—has been steadily shrinking. This age group, which comprises nearly half of food service employees, has shrunk by more than xx.x%, from about xxx million in 198x to xxx million today, according to Census Bureau data. Compounding the effect of this declining labor pool, the restaurant industry's labor needs have grown in recent years. Between 199x and 199x, the number of eating and drinking establishments increased xx.x%.[6]

Before Cowboy Bank was acquired, then President Jonathan Jones was asked, "Why doesn't your bank pursue the restaurant industry more with respect to lending?" His reply: "There are three major reasons bankers do not like to lend to restaurants: (1) the labor pool is generally uneducated and dishonest; (2) the entrepreneur typically lacks business operating experience and has generally underestimated the capital required to develop the restaurant and the working capital needed to reach profitability; and (3) the volatility of the industry."

RESTAURANTS WITH SPECIALTY BEER

In-house specialty brewery operations brew beer on premises as a value-added feature to food service, and typically have beer sales of less than xx.x% of the restaurant unit's total sales. Consumer

---

6. Ibid.

interest in high-quality, flavorful beer has resulted in growth in the number and profitability of restaurant-breweries ("brew pubs"). According to the Institute for Brewing Studies, the number of restaurant-breweries has increased to approximately xxx in the United States in 199x,[7] an increase from only eight in 199x.[8]

Restaurant-breweries feature handcrafted beer, along with a wide selection of quality wines, both of which are draws for high-volume food sales. A Restaurant Industry Operations Report published by the National Restaurant Association in 199x indicated that revenues per check are greater in restaurant-breweries (average $xxx) than in full- and limited-menu restaurants as a whole (average $xxx and $xxx respectively). This can be extended to conclude that revenues per seat, and revenues per square foot, are generally higher for brew pubs than for restaurants. While this does not speak directly to profitability, it does show that brew pubs are generally better revenue generators than full- and limited-service restaurants.

Brewery USA, a publicly traded company, has xx Brewery USA brewery-restaurants and xx Swamp City restaurants, including planned units, whose restaurants feature over xx handcrafted brews. Janet Sieger, whose securities firm handled two public offerings for Brewery USA, reiterated the preeminence of the *restaurant* concept: "First and foremost [Brewery USA] is a restaurant. The restaurant concept is what drives the business. A lot of brew pubs are primarily brewing operations; however, just brewing good beer is not good enough, especially if you want to survive. You have to be able to lure your customers on the restaurant side to have a viable and successful concept."[9] Brewery USA's strategic use of specialty beer as a hook for food customers has garnered the company total annual revenues in excess of $xxx million.

Other successful restaurant-brewery concepts include Spring City, South Dakota-based BBQ Grill & Beer Bar, with xx units open and several more planned, averaging $xxx million per unit; Grille & Brewing, Inc., with two operating units grossing $xxx million apiece, and a contract for a third unit in the Carver's Funny World; and Boston-based John Jacobs Brewing Company, with four units and a recently opened Manila unit which is projected to gross over $xxx million in 199x.[10]

---

7. Charles Lonnie, "Brew Pub: Fad or Fashion," *Restaurant News,* January 27, 199x, p. 15.
8. Brew Studies of America, "Finding the Right Brew of Beer and People," December 14, 199x, p. 14.
9. Janet Sieger, "Brewery USA," *Restaurant News,* February 27, 199x, p. 24.
10. Lonnie, p. 20.

RESTAURANT–BREW PUBS AS HIGH-RISK START-UPS

Restaurants generally are known to have among the highest failure rates of any industry. Restaurant breweries, as a subset of the restaurant industry, are not immune to these trends in the long run: "Some industry analysts believe that the brew-pub phenomenon has long-range potential limits."[11] While restaurant–brew pubs are opening at a fast and furious rate, so too are they closing. In 199x, California had xx such restaurants opened and xx closed. Ralph David, co-owner of Una Brew, Inc., which brings in $xxx million at an New Orleans unit, was unable to turn a profit at a similar operation in Idaho and closed shop last year. High failure rates in the restaurant business are often closely associated with the lack of a link between the success of a start-up and the intangible qualities of an entrepreneur: willingness to accept risk, drive, propensity for organization, discipline, and access to capital reserves to finance contingencies and growth. A new "expertise for equity" trend has emerged, whereby successful entrepreneurs like Eva Bonkoski, founder of Bonkoski's Pub & Brewing, are hired to assist would-be entrepreneurs get started in exchange for a piece of the profits when the start-up becomes successful. According to Bonkoski, "A brew-pub owner who wants to make her business sustainable needs business experience, brewing experience, restaurant experience, and access to capital. Very few people have all four."[12]

With respect to capital needs, restaurant–brew pubs require a substantial capital investment. The up-front investment averages $xxx.[13] Larger and more elaborate units can cost up to $xxx million, with brewing facilities as high as $xxx. According to J. J. Whitlock, chief executive of Christian's Brewhouse in Pittsburgh, "I anticipate a shakeout in the industry, because a lot of people are getting into the business without sufficient capital and resources. People who think that a brew pub is pure gravy will find that just isn't true."[14] Indeed, a study by the Institute for Brewing Studies, a leading beer industry association, indicates that it takes a restaurant–brew pub an average of xx months to attain operating profitability.[15] Adding to the startup costs are state and federal regulations, which, in some cases, preclude

---

11. Ibid.
12. Jackilyn Chen, "Brew Pubs: Hops on the Wave of the Future," *The New Brew-Pub Alliance*, September 1995, p. 56.
13. Institute for Brewing Research, *Industry Examined*, Benville, ID: Brewers Research Publications, Inc., 199x ed., p. 33.
14. Chen, p. 61.
15. Ibid.

entrepreneurs from finding sites for their ventures. Walter Visher, a New York consultant, returned $xxx million that he had raised from investors when two proposed restaurant–brew pub locations were shot down by Hoboken officials.[16]

Another risk factor in the brew pub industry is a trend toward declining or stabilized same-unit sales. Heidi Boid, an analyst with Boid-Chen and Co., believes that same-unit sales for brew pub–restaurants will most likely decline or stabilize. She believes that sales are destined to decline on same-unit sales as the young/single population, currently enamored with the concept of boutique beers, moves on to the next latest and greatest concept to come along. Her statements are corroborated with data and statistics from the National Restaurant Statistical Center. Over the most recent six-month period in 199x, same-unit sales have decreased by xx.x%. Furthermore, interviews with the typical brew-pub patron reveal that on average he or she visits a brew pub less often than what he or she did just a year ago. One interviewee, in a national newspaper, stated, "The whole concept [of brew pubs] was a fad; the initial thrill of brew pubs is gone. All my friends are now socializing at the café scene."[17]

OUTLOOK

Continued restaurant–brew pub growth is on the horizon from new units opening while established units ("same-unit sales") may begin to show signs of slowed growth. Since xx states have either partially or entirely legalized brew pubs as of the end of 199x, we anticipate continued growth in the industry and the opening of many new units in the short-term future. The industry segment does not have a long track record, as the first restaurant–brew pub opened in the early 1980s, and the average large restaurant–brew pub has been in business for only x.x years.[18] This trend will be combined with other risk factors, including business failure rates for restaurants generally and competition that will intensify with new unit growth. Approximately xxx brew pubs are scheduled to be opened by June 199x, a xx.x% increase in the number of units over the previous year.[19] In addition, there is the need for success-driven entrepreneurs

---

16. Michael Johnson, "Brew Pubs: Some Pubs Simply Can't `Hop' to It," *Financial Journal*, February 14, 199x, p. B1.
17. Janet Jerome, "Generation X and the Concept of Brew Pubs," *National Evening Times*, April 14, 199x, p. 5, col. 1.
18. Ibid.
19. *Brew Pubs National!*, BeerCount, 199x, accessed via Internet.

and high levels of investment, all of which raise uncertainty as to whether restaurant–brew pubs are the wave of the future, a new niche, or merely another restaurant fad. The brew-pub industry is currently favorable, but risky as a result of slowed growth, competition, and probability of business failure. We have taken these industry trends into consideration in calculating the estimate of value.

ANNOTATION

Financial Review. The purpose of the financial review is to analyze a company's financial performance at the valuation date. Ideally, one would like to have financial statements as of the valuation date. However, things don't always work out that way. Often you will be working with financial statements as of an earlier date, and an interim financial statement as of a date closer to the valuation date. It is important to compare the interim-period financial statements with the most recent full year's to determine if any material changes have taken place. This is what we did in our valuation of Brew and Chew.

We typically begin our financial analysis with a look at the balance sheet. We examine the current and quick ratios for the subject company relative to its industry to determine the liquidity of the company. The stronger the company's ability to meet its short-term obligations, the less risk there is, all other factors being equal. A company with relatively low current and quick ratios could have trouble meeting its short-term obligations. The next factor that we examine is a company's debt-paying ability. The ratios that we examine here include the debt-to-equity ratio and the interest coverage ratio. The more debt that a company has (as a percentage of total assets) and the lower the company's interest coverage ratio, the higher the level of financial risk associated with the company. A company with very high levels of debt may find itself in a position where it cannot make its debt payments. (Remember the companies that were taken over via leveraged buyouts back in the 1980s, some of which filed for bankruptcy?) The turnover ratios can be used to examine how efficiently a company is using its assets, or if inventory is piling up in the back rooms.

We next turn to the income statement. The compound growth rate in revenues is a good starting point to obtain an idea of the company's growth, although it is important to consider any extraordinary items which may have influenced growth. (Actually, the effect of extraordinary items should be considered throughout the financial analysis, not only in the growth rate.) The historical growth rate may provide information about the company's future prospects for growth. However, the industry and economic factors must also be considered when examining a company's prospects for future growth. We often compare the company's gross profit margin to the industry, and in the Brew and Chew valuation this was particularly important, since the subject restaurant–brew pub's gross profits were lower than the industry average for brew pubs. This led us into analyzing why gross profits were lower than the industry average, and we determined that beer sales—which are very profitable—were much lower than the average beer sales for brew pubs. When there is a large difference between the industry averages and the results of the company, it is typically a good idea to explain why the difference arose.

We also like to examine income before taxes of the subject company relative to the industry average. Obviously, there is a positive correlation between the profitability of a company and its value. We examine pretax income to eliminate the effects of special tax situations. Two other useful measures to examine are return on assets and return on equity. Return on assets becomes more meaningful for companies that have more assets; it is not a particularly useful measure for, say, a professional service firm, such as an accounting or law firm. This brings up another point for the financial review section of the report. If a particular ratio is not meaningful for a company in a certain industry, it is probably better left off the financial review. For example, there is probably no need to examine accounts receivable for a fast-food restaurant.

The industry data that we use are actually an average of industry medians. We use comparative financial ratios from the usual industry sources as well as data from publicly traded corporations, if we believe they are applicable to the subject company. That is the case for Brew and Chew.

We typically end our financial review section with a summary of our conclusions and a link to the estimate of value.

EXAMPLE

FINANCIAL REVIEW

This analysis of the business is based on the Partnership's reviewed financial statements and tax returns (both of which were prepared by the Partnership's Certified Public Accountant, Allen, Euclid,

Jurgenson & Mozart, Washington, DC) and unaudited Partnership interim financial statements. We used the financial statements and tax return for the year ending December 31, 199x, as the last full accounting year to conduct our analysis. The interim 199x financial statements from January 1, 199x, to March 31, 199x, were also considered. After analyzing the 199x financial statements and the 199x interim statement, we determined that it was appropriate to use the full-year 199x financial statements and 199x tax return in conducting our analysis, since this was the last full-year financial statement available to us dated prior to the valuation date of March 31, 199x. We found no significant reason or changes that occurred between these two periods that would substantially change our findings.

In conducting our financial and comparative analyses, we compared the financial statements and tax returns of the Partnership with the average of the industry medians. Industry medians for the brew-pub industry are based on publicly available financial information on Brewery USA, Inc. Industry medians for the restaurant industry are based on data from restaurant industry ratios (RIR) and the general restaurant index (GIR) (Exhibit D).

BALANCE SHEET

The Partnership displays a positive balance sheet when examining the asset composition, level of debt and equity. Although current assets are slightly below the average of the industry medians, the Partnership more than makes up for it in its positive cash balances. Current assets as a percentage of total assets are xx.x%, compared with the average of the industry medians of xx.x%, while cash as a percentage of total assets is xx.x% compared with the industry average medians of xx.x%. Current liabilities are xx.x%, comparable to the average of the industry medians at xx.x%. Total debt as a percentage of total assets is xx.x%, compared with the average of the industry medians at xx.x%. As a result of lower debt than the average of the industry medians, the Partnership's equity is higher at xx.x% of total assets, compared with xx.x% for the industry.

Liquidity

The current ratio and the quick ratio are measures of liquidity. These calculations provide evidence of the Partnership's ability to meet its short-term obligations. The Partnership's current ratio as of December 31, 199x was x.x:x, compared with the average of the industry medians of x.x:x. The Partnership's current ratio reveals an unfavorable liquidity position relative to the average of the industry medians. Profitable operations depend upon sufficient current assets to cover current debts and maintain adequate working capital to support ongoing operating activities. The Partnership's quick ratio of x.x:x is favorable compared with the average of the industry medians of x.x:x, indicating the adequacy of short-term obligations covered by "cash" assets. The Partnership's overall liquidity position appears to be adequate, with a favorable amount of "cash" balances.

Debt-Paying Ability

Long-term debt is xx.x% of total assets, compared with the average of the industry medians of xx.x%. This lower debt is reflected in the Partnership's interest coverage ratio. The Partnership has a x.x:x interest coverage ratio compared with the industry's x.x:x. This ratio indicates the degree of safety or protection against the possible ramifications of default on the Partnership loans and debts. Because the interest coverage ratio is adequate, it appears that the Partnership will be able to continue meeting its debt service obligations in the near future.

Turnover

Relevant turnover ratios for the Partnership include turnover of inventory, fixed assets, and total assets. The Partnership's inventory turnover of x.x times is unfavorable compared with the average of the industry medians of x.x times. In today's fast-moving marketplaces, a company with slow turnover of inventory represents a higher risk, because the company could be at a competitive price and cost disadvantage. In addition, a company expending liquid assets to produce or purchase its inventory can be a costly venture, in terms of higher interest rates. Excessive inventory may occur from product obsolescence, incorrect product mix on shelf, long shelf life, lack of inventory controls, or overproduction (capacity).

Turnover on fixed and total assets are x.x and x.x times, respectively, compared with the average of the industry medians of x.x and x.x times. The turnover ratios of these assets are a physical measure of the efficiency of management in utilizing assets at its disposal. Turnover on fixed assets is positive, while turnover on total assets is negative. However, the differences in the comparison to the average of the industry medians is nominal.

INCOME STATEMENT

Brew and Chew's net sales were $xxx million during 199x, a figure commensurate with sales at other similarly sized restaurant–brew pubs and average sales per square foot. Brew and Chew's gross profit margin is xx.x%, while the same margin for the brew-pub industry (as measured by Brewery USA's xx units) is xx.x%. The industry brew pubs' superior margin is due to the large proportion of sales of beer—a very high-margin product (a glass selling for $xx to $xx costs about xx¢ in raw materials to produce). While Brewery USA and other brew pubs' beer sales are nearly xx.x%, Brew and Chew's beer sales are averaging xx.x% of gross sales and declining. The result of Brew and Chew's disappointing beer sales is that the Company's xx.x% gross profit margin is high for the restaurant industry, but low for the brew-pub industry.

Brewery USA, like other publicly held multiunit concepts, faces high operating expenses. Overhead costs, including administration, area management, legal fees, marketing, and the multitude of costs associated with central offices, result in a xx.x% operating expense ratio. Brew and Chew, a privately held partnership with only one unit, avoids much of the overhead that is borne by its public competitors, and thus has operating expenses of only xx.x% of its sales. If Brew and Chew went public, or expanded the scope of its restaurant–brew pub concepts to other units, or attempted to market its specialty beers through retail outlets, it too would incur high operating expenses. Brew and Chew's operating profit (the profit after operating expenses) is xx.x%, more than four full percentage points higher than the industry average for a brew pub (xx.x%), but slightly below the average of the medians of the restaurant industry (xx.x%).

Brew and Chew's income before tax (sales minus operating expenses and interest expense) is xx.x%, higher than both brew pubs (xx.x%) and restaurants (xx.x%). This is to be expected, since a single-unit restaurant incurs a lower level of overhead than larger, public entities. In 199x, before-tax return on assets was xx.x%, representing a return more than three times greater than the average of the industry medians. This ratio is an indicator of the Partnership's ability to utilize its assets to generate profits and is often used as a measurement of financial performance. Similarly, before-tax return on equity was xx.x% in 199x, about twice the industry average. Return on equity indicates whether the equity owners are being provided with an adequate reward for their assumption of risk. Given the two measurements of profitability, it appears that the Partnership is more profitable than the average of the industry medians.

OVERVIEW

In summary, the Partnership's operating performance is well balanced and similar to the average of the industry medians. The Partnership has both positive and negative aspects in regard to the balance sheet, income statement, turnover ratios, and risk. Profitability of the Partnership is generally superior when compared with industry data. Our analysis of the restaurant–brew pub business provides evidence that the Partnership will continue to perform at a profitable level subsequent to the valuation date.

A N N O T A T I O N

Estimate of Value. The estimate-of-value section is the meat of the report. We believe that it is important to clearly explain how the estimate of value was developed. State the assumptions used, explain how they were developed, show how the discount rate was calculated, and state how the industry and other factors affect the value of the company. We have seen a number of reports that simply adjust officers' compensation to arrive at an earnings number, increase this earnings amount by an unexplained growth rate ("we increased earnings by xx.x% for the next xx years..."), and then discount these projected future earnings back to a present value using a discount rate which may as well have been plucked out of the air, with no explanation of how the rate was calculated, let alone the analysis specific to the valuation at hand.

You want to be sure that you use an appropriate valuation method to value the company. Typically, you would not value a reasonably profitable operating company with an asset-based approach. Note that in the mock valuation we used earnings from operations before taxes. We used this type of earnings instead of operating cashflows, because our industry research and interviews with industry experts indicated that the assets of restaurant–brew pubs deteriorate relatively quickly. We therefore used a measure of income that included depreciation as an expense.

We adjusted the historical financial statements to arrive at an earnings number representative of the company's future earnings capacity. One adjustment that we made that is typical for litigation situations is to remove the expenses associated with the lawsuit, since this is (hopefully) a nonrecurring expense. We believe that it is important to explain how and why the specific line items were adjusted, so that the reader can readily understand where the final earnings number comes from.

Note how we use the information from our industry research to assist us in developing the future projections for operating earnings. The discount rate was developed by consideration of the pertinent risk factors discussed in the report. If you can determine the value multiples for which companies are actually being bought and sold for the subject company's industry than you have accomplished quite a bit. For this valuation, new restaurant–brew pubs were formed by those interested in owning and operating one. There was little evidence of already existing restaurant–brew pubs being acquired. Therefore, we used the buildup summation method to determine the discount rate.

EXAMPLE

ESTIMATE OF VALUE

DEVELOPMENT STAGE ENTERPRISE

Prior to July 4, 199x, when the restaurant–brew pub opened, the Company was a development stage enterprise. "An enterprise shall be considered to be in the development stage if it is devoting substantially all of its efforts to establishing a new business and either of the following conditions exists:

a. Planned principal operations have not commenced

b. Planned principal operations have commenced, but there has been no significant revenue therefrom"[20]

The Company was devoting substantially all its efforts to establishing its start-up restaurant business, and the planned principal operations had not commenced prior to July 4, 199x. There was no revenue generated by the Company prior to this date.

At each of the first three valuation dates (7/4/xx, 1/18/xx, and 7/24/xx) the Company was in the "start-up," or development stage. For a company to emerge from this embryonic stage to a successful

---

20. *Accounting Standards, Volume II: Industry Standards*, Norwalk, CT: Financial Accounting Standards Board, June 1, 1994, p. 54511.

business takes considerable effort, expertise, capital, and time. It requires an entrepreneur.

ENTREPRENEURSHIP AND WHAT IT TAKES TO BE A SUCCESSFUL ENTREPRENEUR

It isn't easy taking an idea for a business and bringing it to fruition. According to Jon P. Goodman, director of the University of Southern California's Entrepreneur Program, "Good ideas are common; the people who can implement them are rare. . . . I have listened to literally thousands of business ideas and continue to hear more every day. The great majority of the people who tell you about them can't turn their ideas into businesses."[21] Given that most would-be entrepreneurs do not end up developing their ideas into successful businesses, there must be something special about those individuals who are successful in developing a start-up company. In fact, researchers have discovered several traits that are prevalent among effective entrepreneurs.

Successful entrepreneurs are described in a 199x *Business Week* report as having a number of common personality traits. They are willing to accept risk, and they are driven, organized, and disciplined. They are passionate about what they are doing, which helps alleviate the fears of being on their own. According to Paul Shipman, the founder of the successful Red Hook Ale Brewery in Seattle, entrepreneurs are driven by both positive and negative forces. On the positive side, they have the ability to formulate strategy and implement effectively. Entrepreneurs typically find failure intolerable. "[Succeeding in my own business is] a very powerful competitive issue," said Shipman. "It's primal stuff."[22]

Entrepreneurs are willing and able to do what it takes to get the job done. The word entrepreneur is derived from the French verb *entreprendre*, which means "to undertake."[23] Entrepreneurs are doers, not just owners. An absentee owner is not an entrepreneur.

This paragraph is a brief synopsis of the definition of an entrepreneur provided in an article published in the January 199x issue of the *Journal of Small Business Management*. The successful entrepreneur has "strong drives for independence and success, with high levels of

---

21. Jon P. Goodman, "What Makes an Entrepreneur," *Inc.*, October 199x, p. 29.
22. Michael O'Neal, "Just What Is an Entrepreneur?" *Business Week/Enterprise*, 199x, pp. 105, 112.
23. J. Barton Cunningham and Joe Lischeron, "Defining Entrepreneurship," *Journal of Small Business Management*, January 199x, p. 50.

vigor, persistence, and self-esteem." The following traits help define (or perhaps make) a successful entrepreneur: energy, perseverance, the ability to inspire and motivate, vision, and single-mindedness. Research on entrepreneurs has consistently come up with three personality characteristics: "(1) . . . honesty, duty, responsibility, and ethical behavior; (2) risk-taking propensity; and (3) the need for achievement." The act of entrepreneurship is defined by the process of doing as opposed to the owning of a business. An important attribute of a successful entrepreneur is the ability to develop and mentor people. "Because of the importance of the mentoring process, the entrepreneur is more than a manager, but also a leader of people."[24]

Howard W. Stevenson is an endowed professor and senior associate dean at the Harvard Business School, where he is also considered the "point man on entrepreneurship." He believes that an important ability for entrepreneurs is presentation. Professor Stevenson "would argue that most of life is selling. Selling myself to my banker, selling my product to a customer, selling myself to my suppliers."[25] Being a skilled promoter/salesperson is a very important part of the entrepreneur's skill set.

There are individuals who are repeat entrepreneurs, who "identify a business opportunity, form a company, succeed, then sell out, often completing this cycle repeatedly....[This is an] ultrapreneur, a restless, driven, energetic, hard-working, brave, easily bored, lateral thinking, enthusiastic, and opportunistic hard-charger."[26] These individuals obviously have the skill set of successful entrepreneurs.

The authors of a study published in *Fortune* magazine traveled around the United States for several months interviewing nearly 100 CEOs of small businesses to ascertain what being an entrepreneur is all about. The world of the entrepreneur was described by the entrepreneurs as "life without a safety net—thrilling and dangerous. When competition gets tough, small businesses feel it first. Financing is hard to find, sometimes impossible. . . . Owners lie awake at night worrying about what irrational government and a tort system run amok will do to them next: A bureaucratic trampling or a lawsuit can break a small company. . . . 'In small business there are no small mistakes'—it's a phrase that comes up time and again when [talking to entrepreneurs]."[27]

---

24. Ibid.
25. Michael Warshaw, "The Mind Style of the Entrepreneur," *Success,* April 199x, p. 30.
26. Carroll Chateau, "Here Come the Ultrepreneurs," *Management-Auckland,* from an abstract located in ABI/Inform under the subject of entrepreneur.
27. Charles Burck, "The Real World of the Entrepreneur," *Fortune,* April 5, 199x, p. 62.

A primary reason that would-be entrepreneurs have to be risk-tolerant is that it is very difficult to start a business from scratch. "The challenge [of starting a new business] is a difficult one, and as a result, about half of the ventures launched won't last more than a few years. Indeed, most entrepreneurs eventually decide their businesses aren't going anywhere and close up shop."[28]

Mr. Brewmeister is the driving force behind the success of Brew and Chew, Inc., the partnership and the business operations of the restaurant–brew pub. After our interview of Mr. Brewmeister and his son, numerous trips to the restaurant, and an extensive tour of the facility, including interviews with key restaurant personnel, it is apparent that Mr. Brewmeister's skill set matches the profile of not just the entrepreneur but the ultrapreneur as well.

Mr. Brewmeister was on the scene during the development process and managed the design, construction, preopening, and opening phases. Included in this process is the difficult management of the relationships with the various licensing and government agencies necessary to open a restaurant–brew pub. These agencies are the Department of Alcohol, Tobacco, and Fire Arms; the State Department of Alcohol Beverage Control; the Town of New Carrollton (known to be one of the most difficult cities in the area to deal with and obtain an opening permit); the Fire Department; the Health Department; and the State Board of Equalization.

The preopening of a restaurant is also a phase that requires the discipline of time and experience of managing people. This phase must occur simultaneously with the construction phase. As one phase is reaching closure, the other phase is beginning, and the entrepreneur/project manager must be at his or her best.

The next phase, opening to the public, is a Herculean task requiring inordinate strength of character. Mr. Brewmeister had to manage the licensing and permit closure, the construction closure, which extends for several months past opening to the public, the employee workforce (management), the execution of the concept of two businesses in one (restaurant–brew pub) and the relationship as host to the public. To add to this scenario of complexity and confusion for the customer, the law requires that the operation be open and the in-house specialty beer be tested for two months after opening, before it can be served to the public. During those months, the employee(s) and owner must defend and sell the *promise* of a product which is not available when the customer arrives to sample and judge.

---

28. Marcel Cote, "Enter the Entrepreneur," *CA Magazine,* August 199x, p. 68.

Mr. Brewmeister and his team have not only accomplished this difficult process, they have accomplished it well. To make the assumption that someone else could have accomplished it, or could purchase the New Carrollton restaurant–brew pub and continue to execute the concept without Mr. Brewmeister and his people, is speculation. The ability to purchase a restaurant–brew pub and operate it profitability is an unproven event. We were not able to locate any market evidence to support this scenario. Consultant Bill Owens, publisher of *Beer, the Magazine,* agrees with this and believes that the pub takes on the character of the owner/driving force and it may be all but impossible to transplant to a new owner or management team. Further, there is the risk that the old management team would disband upon a merger/acquisition in the event the old owner's bond was as strong as Mr. Brewmeister's.

Mr. Brewmeister lives in the New Carrollton community, has for many years established relationships with hundreds if not thousands of individuals and businesses here and outside the region, and is one of the best-known personalities in the area. His relationships with sports figures and national sports team management have assisted him in promoting the growth and stabilization of sales.

To have removed, or to remove, Mr. Brewmeister from the formula of success of the Brew and Chew restaurant–brew pub at any stage would be almost certain disaster for all involved. This would create financial harm to close to 100 employees. The investors in the original concept (Messrs. Lauren, Lee, and Downer), who failed in their effort to adequately capitalize and develop a complex business, were saved only when Mr. Brewmeister stepped forward with his personal capital and expertise to bail out the restaurant and see it through to profitable operations. These are the actions of an entrepreneur.

METHOD OF VALUATION EXPLAINED

The *Guide to Business Valuations* states that asset-based valuation methods should be employed when "the company has . . . a questionable ability to continue as a going concern (such as a start-up company or troubled business)."[29] Start-up companies are valued by a method that does not focus on the earnings potential of the company. According to the *Litigation Services Handbook: The Role of the*

---

29. Jay E. Fishman et al., *Guide to Business Valuations,* Fort Worth, TX: Practitioners Publishing Company, 1995, ¶705.02.

Accountant as Expert, the expected profits of a company about to "enter a perfectly competitive business . . . are, at first approximation, zero. This analysis violates the expectations of some people . . . but it makes common sense. *Most start-ups fail.* [Emphasis added]"[30] "A start-up offers only financial speculation. . . . It takes considerable effort to put a start-up together and get it off the ground. . . . A start-up may lose considerable money until it reaches breakeven sales."[31]

For the first three valuation dates, the value of the Corporation's General Partner interest is affected by the provisions in section x.xx of the Partnership Agreement that provide for the Limited Partners to receive xx.x% of the cash available for distribution until such time as the Limited Partners have received total distributions equal to xx.x% of their capital contributions. This provision increases the length of time it would take for a hypothetical buyer of the Corporation General Partner to receive back his or her original investment.

VALUATION DATE # 1: JULY 4, 199X

The Corporation did not exist at this date. Although Articles of Incorporation had been filed, it had no directors, no officers, no shareholders, no assets, no lease, and no money. A use permit for the future location of the restaurant–brew pub (with a required closing time of xx:xx p.m.) had been approved by the New Carrollton Town Council on May 29, 199x. There is no value indicated by the existence of a use permit.

VALUATION DATE # 2: JANUARY 18, 199X

Some of the Partnership units had been sold prior to this date. If the Partnership were dissolved, the assets of the Partnership would be distributed according to section x.x of the Partnership Agreement. "Upon the dissolution of the Partnership, winding up its affairs, and payment of all debts of the Partnership (including without limitation any debts owed to any General Partner or its affiliates), the assets of the Partnership shall be distributed to the Partners in accordance with the positive balances in their capital

---

30. Peter B. Frank, Michael J. Wagner, and Roman L. Weil, *Litigation Services Handbook: The Role of the Accountant as Expert*, New York: John Wiley & Sons, 1990, pp. 31–32.
31. Arnold S. Goldstein, *Buying and Selling a Business...Successfully*, Homewood, IL: Dow Jones–Irwin, pp. 14–15.

accounts." As there was no business generating any revenue or profits, the upper limit on the value of the Company is the past contributions made by the owners of the Corporation. There is no value in excess of this amount.

VALUATION DATE # 3: JULY 24, 199X

At this date there is no balance sheet. Therefore, we used the financial statements dated June 30, 199x, which were prepared externally and on an unaudited basis by the Partnership's CPA. The net worth of the Company/General Partner is negative, after the current liabilities and the Limited Partner's capital contributions are paid and returned. As there was no business generating any revenue or profits, the upper limit on the value of the Company is the past contributions made by the owners of the General Partner Corporation. There is no value in excess of this amount.

VALUATION DATE # 4: MARCH 31, 199X (AS NEAR AS PRACTICABLE TO THE TIME OF TRIAL)

The restaurant–brew pub had been in business for approximately 3½ years as of March 31, 199x. Our approach for this valuation date differs from that used prior to the restaurant's opening. Specifically, we conducted the valuation in three progressive steps. First, we valued the restaurant–brew pub via the discounted earnings method. Second, we analyzed the capital accounts of the Partnership. Finally, we computed the value of a xx.x% Common Stock interest in the corporate General Partner.

[ANNOTATION: In this sample report, we do not include an analysis of the Partnership capital accounts or estimate the value of the corporate General Partner.]

VALUATION OF THE RESTAURANT–BREW PUB BUSINESS

Discounted Earnings Method

We utilized the widely accepted discounted earnings method to estimate the value of the restaurant. The discounted earnings method is an income-oriented approach, and is based on the theory that the total value of a business is the present value of its projected future earnings from operations before tax, plus the present value of the terminal value.

The projected future earnings and the terminal value are discounted back to the present using an appropriate discount rate. The discounted earnings method is the valuation method we see used most frequently in the merger and acquisition arena (the real world) for pricing/valuation issues.

The first step in calculating discounted earnings is to choose the type of earnings. We used earnings from operations before tax. We chose earnings from operations rather than operating cashflows to account for rapid physical deterioration of the Company's assets owing to high customer traffic and to probably match revenues and expenses. Our research and interviews with industry experts indicate that restaurant–brew pubs have to substantially remodel and renovate/update their restaurant and brewery every five to eight years. Depreciation is a measure of the decrease in the remaining productive life of an asset, so we used an income measure that includes depreciation expense.

The next step is to adjust the earnings to a normalized level. We made the following adjustments to the financial statements:

1. *Management Fees/Officers Compensation*

We made an adjustment to Management Fees and Officers Compensation. The hypothetical buyer of the restaurant–brew pub will deduct a reasonable living wage from earnings when valuing the business. We reclassified Management Fees paid to the General Partner (which are then paid to the principal Officer) to Officers Compensation. We then made an adjustment to the Officers Compensation figure using data from the Economic Research Institute.[32] The data reflects the average industry compensation paid to officers given the specific level of sales for the restaurant–brew pub in each year. The industry chosen as a basis for comparison was the restaurant industry (SIC Code 5812). We examined Chief Executive Officer salaries for 199x, 199x, and 199x. While a wide range of salaries is reflected in the data, we based our adjustment on the mean (average) salary in each year. We believe this is a conservative approach considering Mr. Brewmeister's level of expertise and experience.

2. *Insurance/Workers Compensation Dividend*

Workers Compensation Dividend was reclassified as Insurance in 199x and 199x so that the Insurance line item would accurately reflect Insurance expense during those years of comparison.

---

32. Economic Research Institute, *The Assessor Series Software*, Redmond, WA: ERI, 1995.

3. Selling Expense/Advertising and Donations

In 199x, Advertising and Donations were reclassified as Selling Expense so that these line items would be consistent with 199x and 199x classifications for comparison.

4. Professional Expense

For all three years we adjusted Professional Expenses to provide for actual accounting fees for accounting and tax services and to provide for a reasonable provision for legal fees of x.xx% of total sales. This adjustment has the effect of removing the cost of legal and other professional fees associated with this litigation.

5. Reserve for Replacement

We introduced a Reserve for Replacement to provide for the remodeling of the restaurant and the update/renovation of brewing technology which needs to occur every five to eight years. A Reserve for Replacement allowance provides for the periodic replacement of business components that wear out more rapidly than the building itself and that must be replaced periodically during the businesses economic life cycle. It is particularly important for the subject business, because the cash distributions to Limited Partners decrease reserves.

6. Interest

We assumed that the hypothetical sale was for all cash and that the new owner would have no debt service. We therefore reclassified Interest expense from an operating expense to a nonoperating expense. Since we valued the restaurant–brew pub using income from operations, this adjustment removes Interest expense, which decreases operating expenses and increases the resulting value of the business.

Given the adjusted historical performance of the restaurant–brew pub and our analysis of the restaurant industry, we believe that the operating results will remain constant (flat) in the future. That is, the restaurant–brew pub's sales and operating earnings will not proportionally change from 199x levels. This is due to both the peak amount of sales being reached on certain nights of the week (capacity), and to two industry factors: the decreasing trend for same-store sales, and the potentially changing consumer tastes for restaurants (nonloyalty of consumers). We projected constant operating earnings from 199x though 199x. The terminal value is the present value of the eighth-year earnings projected into perpetuity. These calculations are located in Exhibit F.

The estimated earnings and the terminal value were then discounted back to a present value by a pretax discount rate of xx.x%.

The discount rate for a stream of future earnings is directly related to the risk of the earnings. We used the buildup method to develop the discount rate. This method adds risk premiums to a safe rate of return to calculate the discount rate. A risk premium is an excess rate of return for a certain class of investment relative to a different specific type of investment. Without this "risk premium" to compensate for the higher risk level for stocks relative to bonds, rational, risk-averse investors would not invest in stocks. In other words, the risk premium is an increase in the expected rate of return to induce investors to make riskier investments.

Specifically, the risk-free rate of return that we used is xx.x%, the rate for 10-year Treasury bonds as of March 31, 199x. To this percentage, we added three risk premiums: (1) an equity risk premium of xx.x% (the historical rate-of-return premium for large-capitalization company stocks in excess of the rate of return for long-term government bonds), (2) a small stock risk premium of xx.x% (the historical rate-of-return premium for small-capitalization company stocks in excess of the rate of return for large-capitalization company stocks), (3) a company-specific risk premium of xx.x% (our estimate of the extra risk for the subject company in excess of a small-capitalization stock). The result is an after-tax discount rate of xx.x%.

[ANNOTATION: We based the company-specific risk premium on specific risk factors pertaining to the subject company, competition, the regional economy, and the industry. The risk factors are not discussed in this sample report.]

We then converted the after-tax discount rate to a pretax discount rate of xx.x%.[33] This calculation begins with the after-tax rate of xx.x%. The estimated sustainable long-term growth rate of x.xx%—a rate slightly higher than that of inflation—is subtracted out. The result of xx.x% is divided by xx.x% (1 minus the effective tax rate of xx.x%), which equals xx.x%. We added back in the long-term growth rate of xx.x%, and the sum is the pretax discount rate of xx.x%. We believe that this discount rate captures the risk commensurate with the projected future earnings.

The present value of projected earnings is $xxx. The present value of the terminal value is $xxx. The sum of projected earnings and the terminal value is $xxx, which is the estimated value of the restaurant–brew pub.

33. Mary Ann Lerch, "Pretax/After-Tax Conversion Formula for Capitalization Rate and Cash Flow Discount Rates," *Business Valuation Review*, March 1990, p. 18.

VALUATION OF BREW AND CHEW, INC.

[ANNOTATION: We are not including these two sections in our sample report, since we do not believe that this would improve the reader's understanding of how to perform a business valuation. However, the reader should be aware that this type of analysis is common for partnerships.]

APPENDIX

FULL-SCOPE VALUATION ENGAGEMENT LETTER

Date

John E. Sample, President
First Corporation
7060 Corporate Lane
Cupertino, CA 95014

Dear Mr. Sample:

This letter outlines our understanding of the terms and objectives of the valuation engagement.

We will perform an estimate of value of First Corporation (a California corporation, the "Company"). The valuation date will be determined. The objective of the valuation will be to estimate the current fair market value of the Company. The term "fair market value" is defined as:

> ...the price at which the property would change hands between a willing buyer and a willing seller, when the former is not under any compulsion to buy and the latter is not under any compulsion to sell, both parties having reasonable knowledge of relevant facts. Court decisions frequently state in addition that the hypothetical buyer and seller are assumed to be able, as well as willing, to trade

CONFIDENTIAL

John E. Sample, President
First Corporation
Date
Page 2

and to be well informed about the property and concerning the market for such property.[1]

Although the valuation is intended to estimate fair market value, we assume no responsibility for a seller's or buyer's inability to obtain a purchase contract at that price. In performing our valuation, we will be relying on the accuracy and reliability of the Company's historical financial statements, projections, and/or budgets of future operations or other financial data of the Company. We will not audit, compile, or review those financial statements, projections, or other data. We will not express an opinion or any form of assurance on them. At the conclusion of the engagement, we will ask you to sign a representation letter on the accuracy and reliability of the financial information used in the engagement. Our engagement cannot be relied on to disclose errors, irregularities, or illegal acts, including fraud or defalcations, that may exist. However, in the event something comes to our attention that we believe to be of interest, we will bring it to your attention.

We will document the results of our findings in a written report. The purpose of this report is to develop a valuation conclusion for estate and tax planning, and the distribution of the report is restricted to this use. This report will not be distributed to outside parties to obtain a loan or credit or for any other purpose unless approved in writing by ValueNomics Research, Inc. Furthermore, no aspect or conclusion of the report is meant to be construed as legal advice, or any other type of professional advice or counsel (such as tax, accounting, or investment advice).

If you fail to comply with any of the provisions of this agreement, we may, at our option, withdraw from the engagement. If for any reason we are unable to complete the valuation engagement, we will not issue a report as a result of the engagement. We have no responsibility to update our valuation report for events and circumstances that occur after the date of its issuance.

Our fees will be based on the activity performed at our standard hourly rates (schedule attached), which range from $xxx for clerical to $xxx for court testimony. For this full-scope engagement,

---

1. Internal Revenue Service Revenue Ruling 59–60, Section 2, background and definitions, ¶.02.

John E. Sample, President
First Corporation
Date
Page 3

the fees will not exceed an estimated $xxx, plus out-of-pocket expenses for the valuation. We require an advance of $xxx with the execution of this agreement. The remainder of the fees and expenses will be rendered on a monthly basis and are payable upon request. All work will be suspended if the account becomes xx days past due, and no work will be resumed until the account is brought current. In any event, the balance of all fees and expenses owing are payable at the time the report is delivered. Unforeseen or changed circumstances might affect our original fee estimate. If that is the case, we will notify you as soon as we become aware of it. Any proposed change in our fees will be in the form of a written change order agreed to and signed by both you and ValueNomics®.

Additional fees for any services that may be required defending our valuation report in audit or litigation, including conferences, deposition, court appearances, and testimony, if required, will be billed in excess to this not-to-exceed engagement at Mr. Gary Jones' expert testimony rate of $xxx per hour.

If any dispute arises among the parties hereto, the parties agree first to try in good faith to settle the dispute by mediation administered by the American Arbitration Association under its commercial mediation rules, before resorting to litigation. Costs of any mediation proceeding shall be shared equally by all parties.

ValueNomics® and its employees are liable only to the client, and this liability is expressly limited to the amount of the fee for this engagement. We do not assume any liability, obligation or accountability to any third party under any circumstances. The client agrees to hold ValueNomics® and its employees harmless in the event of a lawsuit initiated by any party other than the client.

Company policy states that we will not retain notes, draft reports, or work papers that are not relevant to our final opinion. This paragraph is your notification of that policy.

We appreciate the opportunity to serve your Company. If you agree with the foregoing terms, please sign the copy of this letter in the space provided and return the letter, along with the $xxx advance, in the enclosed self-addressed envelope. We will begin the engagement upon receiving the signed engagement letter and

CONFIDENTIAL

John E. Sample, President
First Corporation
Date
Page 4

the advance. We reasonably expect to complete our assignment and present our findings within four to six weeks after receipt of (1) this signed engagement letter; (2) documents sent to us pursuant to our forthcoming document request; and (3) our management interview and tour of your facilities. Delay in this regard will stall the process and our delivery of the final report.

If this engagement letter is not signed and returned within xxx days of the date hereof, this proposal will be null and void, and neither party shall have any further obligations to the other. Further discussion of the matter, our fees, and our ability to complete the assignment in a timely manner would be necessary in order to move forward at a later date.

Sincerely,

Gary E. Jones, President
ValueNomics Research, Inc.

Agreement and Acknowledgment:
This letter correctly sets forth our understanding of the terms of the engagement.

John E. Sample, President   Date

CONFIDENTIAL

LIMITED-SCOPE VALUATION ENGAGEMENT LETTER

Date

John E. Sample, President
First Corporation
7060 Corporate Lane
Cupertino, CA 95014

Dear Mr. Sample:

This letter outlines our understanding of the terms and objectives of this Ltd-Scope Valuation^{SM} engagement.

CONFIDENTIAL

John E. Sample, President
First Corporation
Date
Page 2

We will perform an estimate of value of First Corporation, (a California corporation, the "Company"). The valuation date will be determined. The objective of the valuation will be to estimate the current fair market value of the Company. The term "fair market value" is defined as:

> ...the price at which the property would change hands between a willing buyer and a willing seller, when the former is not under any compulsion to buy and the latter is not under any compulsion to sell, both parties having reasonable knowledge of relevant facts. Court decisions frequently state in addition that the hypothetical buyer and seller are assumed to be able, as well as willing, to trade and to be well informed about the property and concerning the market for such property.[1]

Although the valuation is intended to estimate fair market value, we assume no responsibility for a seller's or buyer's inability to obtain a purchase contract at that price. In performing our valuation, we will be relying on the accuracy and reliability of the Company's historical financial statements, projections and/or budgets of future operations or other financial data of the Company. We will not audit, compile, or review those financial statements, projections or other data. We will not express an opinion or any form of assurance on them. At the conclusion of the engagement, we will ask you to sign a representation letter on the accuracy and reliability of the financial information used in the engagement. Our engagement cannot be relied on to disclose errors, irregularities, or illegal acts, including fraud or defalcations, that may exist. However, in the event something comes to our attention that we believe to be of interest, we will bring it to your attention.

We have been asked to limit the scope of this engagement to save your Company time and money. In general, these limitations result in a reduced analysis of the financial statements of the Company, the industry (local, regional, and national), market comparables, and the competition. If we were engaged to perform a more detailed analysis and given more time, matters might come to

---

1. Internal Revenue Service Revenue Ruling 59–60, Section 2, background and definitions ¶.02.

CONFIDENTIAL

John E. Sample, President
First Corporation
Date
Page 3

our attention that could have a substantial impact on the estimate of value contained in our findings. Accordingly, our level of assurance on the estimate of value is reduced. Our report is not intended to serve as a basis for expert testimony in a court of law or with any other government agency without further research, analysis, and resulting documentation.

We will document the results of our findings in a Ltd-Scope[SM] (informal) report with limited exhibits. The purpose of this report is to develop a valuation conclusion for estate and gift tax planning, and the distribution of the report is restricted to this purpose. This report will not be distributed to outside parties to obtain a loan or credit or for any other purpose unless approved in writing by ValueNomics Research, Inc. Furthermore, no aspect or conclusion of the report is meant to be construed as legal advice, or any other type of professional advice or counsel (such as tax, accounting, or investment advice).

If you fail to comply with any of the provisions of this agreement, we may, at our option, withdraw from the engagement. If for any reason we are unable to complete the valuation engagement, we will not issue a report as a result of the engagement. We have no responsibility to update our valuation report for events and circumstances that occur after the date of its issuance.

Our fees will be based on the activity performed at our standard hourly rates (schedule attached), which range from $xxx for clerical to $xxx for court testimony. For this Ltd-Scope[SM] engagement, our fees are estimated not to exceed $xxx, plus out-of-pocket expenses. We require an advance of $xxx with the execution of this agreement. The remainder of the fees and expenses will be rendered on a monthly basis and are payable upon request. All work will be suspended if the account becomes xxx days past due, and no work will be resumed until the account is brought current. In any event, the balance of all fees and expenses owing are payable at the time the report is delivered. Unforeseen or changed circumstances might affect our original fee estimate. If that is the case, we will notify you as soon as we become aware of it. Any proposed

CONFIDENTIAL

John E. Sample, President
First Corporation
Date
Page 4

change in our fees will be in the form of a written change order agreed to and signed by both you and ValueNomics®.

Additional fees for any services that may be required defending our valuation report in audit or litigation, including conferences, deposition, court appearances, and testimony, if required, will be billed in excess to this not-to-exceed engagement at Mr. Gary Jones' expert testimony rate of $xxx per hour.

If any dispute arises among the parties hereto, the parties agree first to try in good faith to settle the dispute by mediation administered by the American Arbitration Association under its commercial mediation rules, before resorting to litigation. Costs of any mediation proceeding shall be shared equally by all parties.

Company policy states that we will not retain notes, draft reports, or work papers that are irrelevant to our final opinion. This paragraph is your notification of that policy.

ValueNomics® and its employees are liable only to the client, and this liability is expressly limited to the amount of the fee for this engagement. We do not assume any liability, obligation, or accountability to any third party under any circumstances. The client agrees to hold ValueNomics® and its employees harmless in the event of a lawsuit initiated by any party other than the client.

We appreciate the opportunity to serve your Company. If you agree with the foregoing terms, please sign the copy of this letter in the space provided and return the letter, along with the $xxx advance, in the enclosed self-addressed envelope. We will begin the engagement upon receiving the signed engagement letter and the advance. We reasonably expect to complete our assignment and present our findings within four to six weeks after receipt of (1) this signed engagement letter, and (2) documents sent to us pursuant to our forthcoming document request. Delay in this regard will stall the process and our delivery of the final report.

If this engagement letter is not signed and returned within xxx days of the date hereof, this proposal will be null and void, and neither party shall have any further obligations to the other. Further discussion of the matter, our fees, and our ability to complete the

CONFIDENTIAL

John E. Sample, President
First Corporation
Date
Page 5

assignment in a timely manner would be necessary in order to move forward at a later date.

> Sincerely,
>
> Gary E. Jones, President
> ValueNomics Research, Inc.

Enclosure

Agreement and Acknowledgment:
This letter correctly sets forth our understanding of the terms of the engagement.

_____   _____
John E. Sample, President   Date

CONFIDENTIAL

MANAGEMENT REPRESENTATION LETTER

Date

John E. Sample, President
First Corporation
7060 Corporate Lane
Cupertino, CA 95014

Re: Management Representation Letter

Dear Mr. Sample:

Please find enclosed the management representation letter for your review.

Also you will find enclosed a final draft of our report for your review and comments regarding factual matters contained in the report. It is our normal practice to prepare three (3) copies of the final bound report. If you would like additional copies, please do not hesitate to give us a call.

When we receive the signed management representation letter, the initialed draft report and a check for the balance owing on the project ($_____ , invoice attached), it will take only a few days to conclude our assignment and furnish the final written reports as agreed.

John E. Sample, President
First Corporation
Date
Page 2

With best wishes for your continued success, I remain

Respectfully,

Gary E. Jones, President
ValueNomics Research, Inc.

enclosures

[Your Letterhead]

Date

Gary E. Jones
ValueNomics Research, Inc.
10090 Pasadena Avenue, Suite A
Cupertino, CA 95014

Dear Mr. Jones:

In connection with your valuation engagement of First Corporation (a California corporation, the "Company), as of February 14, 199x, the valuation date:

1. We have made available to you all information requested (that is available) and all information that we believe is relevant to your valuation. All significant matters of judgment have been determined or approved by us.
2. The Company has no material commitments or contingent liabilities, including those arising from litigation, claims, and assessments, that have not been disclosed to you.
3. The Company does not have any employment contracts with salaried employees except to the extent indicated in written agreements furnished to you.
4. The Company is not currently negotiating the acquisition of new business interests or the disposition of existing business or fractional interest therein that have not been disclosed to you.
5. We have reviewed the preliminary rough draft of your valuation report, a copy of which is attached (each page initialed as approved), and represent that the information

Gary E. Jones
ValueNomics Research, Inc.
Date
Page 2

about the Company's matters and assets presented therein are accurate and complete.

Sincerely,

_____   _____

John E. Sample, President   Date

S A M P L E   V A L U A T I O N   R E P O R T S

V A L U A T I O N

Valuation of
The Estate of Daryl Lee Departed

Valuation date, January X, 199Y

Prepared by
ValueNomics Research, Inc.

June X, 199Y

Gary E. Jones
Certified Valuation Analyst

Dirk E. Van Dyke
Senior Quantitative Analyst

Disclaimer: The following model valuation report (the "Report") is provided for illustrative purposes only. The Report is a purely hypothetical creation of the authors and any resemblance, including without limitation, resemblance of financial information, to any entity or real person (whether living or dead), is purely coincidental and unintentional.

Although the authors have endeavored to include in the Report information and techniques which they believe to be relevant for the purposes of illustrating valuation analysis, neither the authors nor their publisher makes any representation or warranty as to the efficacy, reliability, or completeness of the Report. The reader agrees that neither the authors nor their publisher shall have any liability to the reader or any other third party resulting from the use of the Report.

The Report is being published solely for illustrative purposes, and the reader should not use or rely on the Report for any other purpose. No part of the Report may be reproduced or transmitted in any form or by any means, electronic or mechanical, including without limitation, photocopying, recording, or information storage and retrieval, without the prior written consent of the authors and the publisher.

Mr. Easy Q. Tor, Executor
Estate of Daryl Lee Departed (January X, 199Y)
706 Estate Way
Cupertino, CA 95014

Dear Mr. Tor:

We have prepared and enclosed, herewith, our valuation report of the estimated fair market value of specific equity interests of the Estate of Daryl Lee Departed. The purpose of the valuation is to render an estimate of the fair market value of these ownership interests transferred as a result of the demise of Daryl Lee Departed on January X, 199Y, the valuation date. The term "fair market value" is defined as

> ... the price at which the property would change hands between a willing buyer and a willing seller, when the former is not under any compulsion to buy and the latter is not under any compulsion to sell, both parties having reasonable knowledge of relevant facts. Court decisions frequently state in addition that the hypothetical buyer and seller are assumed to be able, as well as willing, to trade and to be well informed about the property and concerning the market for such property.[1]

In this report, the term "equity interest" is defined as the Estate's holdings in various entities and investments representing the value of an enterprise over and above the indebtedness against it. The equity interests being valued are in general those holdings in limited partnerships and corporations.

This report is based on historical and prospective financial information provided to us by management and other third parties. Had we audited or reviewed the underlying data, matters may have come to our attention which would have resulted in our using amounts which differ from those provided. Accordingly, we take no responsibility for the underlying data presented in this report. Users of this valuation report should be aware that valuations and their underlying assumptions are generally based on future earnings potential that may or may not materialize. Therefore, the actual results achieved during the projection period will vary from the projections used in this valuation, and the variations may be substantial.

Treasury regulation states that "the term 'qualified appraiser' means an individual . . . who includes on the appraisal summary . . . a declaration that—(A) The individual either holds himself or herself

---

1. Internal Revenue Service Revenue Ruling 59–60, Section 2, Background and Definitions ¶..02.

Mr. Easy Q. Tor, Executor
Estate of Daryl Lee Departed (January X, 199Y)
Page 2

out to the public as an appraiser or performs appraisals on a regular basis. (B) Because of the appraiser's qualifications as described in the appraisal . . . , the appraiser is qualified to make appraisals of the type of property being valued.[2]

We have no present or contemplated financial interest in the Estate of Daryl Lee Departed, the Trust, or any heir of Mr. Departed's.[3] Our fees for this valuation are based upon our normal hourly billing rates and are in no way contingent upon the results of our findings, and we have been paid in full as of the date of this report. We have no responsibility to update this report for events and circumstances occurring subsequent to the date of this report.

This independent valuation report is the property of ValueNomics® and has been prepared for the specific purpose of estimating the fair market value of certain holdings of the Estate. The report is for Federal estate tax purposes and is not intended for any other use. It is not to be copied or made available to any person(s) without the express written consent of Gary E. Jones and ValueNomics Research, Inc., other than for the use in the Estate of Daryl Lee Departed, their legal counsel, the Internal Revenue Service, and Federal Tax Court in the process of administration, meetings, hearings, and trial resulting from the audit of the Estate by the Internal Revenue Service. This report is intended to comply with the local tax court Rule 143 for expert reports.[4]

On the basis of our study, analytical review procedures, and use of the widely accepted adjusted net assets method, we have concluded that a reasonable estimate of the fair market value of these equity interests as of January X, 199Y, is $xxx (Exhibit A).

ValueNomics Research, Inc.

Gary E. Jones, President
Certified Valuation Analyst

Cupertino, CA
June X, 199Y

---

2. Internal Revenue Service Regulation 1.170A–13.
3. Ibid.
4. Federal Tax Court Rule 143 (7/1/90), 1f.

APPENDIX

INTRODUCTION

PURPOSE OF VALUATION

Mr. Daryl Lee Departed, as of his demise and the valuation date, owned equity interests in limited partnerships and corporations. These interests are detailed on page xx of this report. This report has been prepared for the specific purpose of estimating the fair market value of Mr. Departed's ownership interests in these assets on January 1, 199x. The term "fair market value" is defined as:

> . . . the price at which the property would change hands between a willing buyer and a willing seller, when the former is not under any compulsion to buy and the latter is not under any compulsion to sell, both parties having reasonable knowledge of relevant facts. Court decisions frequently state in addition that the hypothetical buyer and seller are assumed to be able, as well as willing, to trade and to be well informed about the property and concerning the market for such property.

APPROACH TO VALUATION

Our approach has been to determine an estimate of value which would provide a fair and reasonable return on investment to an investor or owner in view of the facts available to us at the time.

Our opinion is based on, among other things, an estimate of the risks facing Mr. Daryl Lee Departed at the time of his demise and the return on investment which would be required on alternative investments with similar levels of risk.

Both internal and external factors which influence the value of the Departed investment interests were reviewed, analyzed, and interpreted. Internal factors include the financial position, results of operations and size of investment. External factors include, among other things, the current status and outlook of the industry, the local and national economic factors and the position of the investments relative to these influences.

For the Estate's assets that were located in the earthquake federal disaster areas, we have made an economic condition adjustment to reflect the deleterious effect of the earthquake. This section included an analysis of the earthquake's effect on different types of assets in various locations.

For purposes of the valuation of the private, closely held companies and less than xx.x% control in investments, we have included a review, analysis, and interpretation of control associated with the Departed ownership interests on the valuation date. This review was performed taking into consideration the size of the block and character of ownership.

We have included a review, analysis, and interpretation of marketability associated with the Departed entities as of the valuation date. This review took into consideration both the general factors affecting marketability and specifically the contingent tax liability which further reduces the marketability of C corporations with appreciated assets.

On the basis of the facts of this particular situation, we selected the widely accepted adjusted net assets method, an asset-oriented approach. This method is used to value the equity interest of an entity using the difference between the fair market value of the entity's assets, less all specific and estimated liabilities and other adjustments that are appropriate and relevant under the circumstances. Under this method, we adjusted the appraised value, and then reduced the total adjusted value of assets by any recorded or unrecorded liabilities and other adjustments. This method is used to derive a total value for the equity interest. Adjusted net assets is a sound method for estimating the value of a nonoperating entity (holding or investment company).

LIMITING CONDITIONS

Treasury regulation states that "the term 'qualified appraiser' means an individual . . . who includes on the appraisal summary . . . a declaration that—(A) The individual either holds himself or herself out to the public as an appraiser or performs appraisals on a regular basis. (B) Because of the appraiser's qualifications as described in the appraisal . . . , the appraiser is qualified to make appraisals of the type of property being valued."

We have no present or contemplated financial interest with Easy Q. Tor, Executor, the Estate of Daryl Lee Departed, the Daryl Lee Departed Trust, or any heir. Our fees for this valuation are based upon normal hourly billing rates, and in no way are contingent upon the results of our findings. We have no responsibility to update this report for events and circumstances occurring subsequent to the date of this report.

This independent valuation report has been prepared for the specific purpose of valuing the fair market value of certain assets of the Estate. The report is a valuation for estate tax reporting purposes and is intended for no other purpose. This report is not to be copied or made available to any persons without the consent of Gary E. Jones and ValueNomics Research, Inc., and is restricted to the use of the Estate of Daryl Lee Departed, their legal counsel, the Internal Revenue Service, and Federal Tax Court in the process of administration, meetings, hearings, and trial resulting from the audit of the Estate by the Internal Revenue Service.

Our report is based on historical and prospective financial information provided by management of the Estate's entities and other third parties. Had we audited or reviewed the underlying data, matters may have come to our attention which would have resulted in our using amounts that differ from those provided. Accordingly, we take no responsibility for the underlying data presented or relied upon in this report.

Users of this valuation report should be aware that valuations are based on future earnings potential that may or may not materialize. Therefore, the actual results achieved during the projection period will vary from the projections utilized in this valuation, and the variations may be material.

We have relied upon the representations of the executor/ trustee and other third parties concerning the value and useful condition of all real estate, leases, equipment, investments, and other assets used in the businesses, and any other assets or liabilities except as specifically stated to the contrary in this report. We have not attempted to confirm whether or not all assets of the businesses are free and clear of liens and encumbrances, or that the businesses have good title to all assets. The estimate of value included in this report assumes that Mr. Departed's existing businesses and real estate will achieve operational and financial goals as projected by management.

Gary E. Jones, ValueNomics®, and its professional staff do not purport to be a guarantor of value. Valuation of private, closely held entities and adjustments is an imprecise science, with value being a matter of the interpretation of specific facts related to the entity and adjustment being considered, and reasonable people can differ in their estimates of value.

Gary E. Jones, ValueNomics®, and its professional staff have, however, performed conceptually sound and commonly accepted methods and procedures of valuation in determining the estimate of value included in this report.

The valuation analyst, by reason of performing this valuation and preparing this report, is not to be required to give expert testimony nor to be in attendance in court or at any government hearing with reference to the matters contained herein, unless prior arrangements have been made regarding such additional engagement.

BACKGROUND

NATURE AND HISTORY OF BUSINESS

Mr. Departed, the deceased, was born at the exact moment the century turned, December 31, 1899, and resided in California for most of his life. Mr. Departed was an entrepreneur in real estate. He generally purchased and held real estate through syndication for investment, development, and management. The types of real estate he managed included commercial (both improved and unimproved) and residential (single-family residences and apartments).

The deceased had a tendency to invest in real estate with other individuals. He would invest in a fractional interest and manage the asset. These interests were in different forms and percentage of ownership, depending on where cash was available at the time. He also purchased assets for his own account and on occasion would split the ownership between entities. In general, these ownership

splits were situational and driven by liquidity. The particular entity Mr. Departed chose to purchase an interest in with was determined by where the funds existed at the moment. In addition, he
would on occasion borrow funds from one of the entities and then
repay the loan with an interest in assets rather than with cash. Over
the years, these practices contributed to a mélange of equity interests and diluted control, which explains the diverse ownership percentages and types of entities that date back as far as 192x.

These complicated bundles of asset ownership are uncommon
and present challenges with respect to valuing the adjustments
associated with their structure. However, like most complicated situations, given time and analysis, they can be sorted out and the
adjustments properly measured. Of further complication, the
Departed bundle of assets need to be valued at a point in time
when the economies of the United States and California were in
serious difficulty, one of the worst recessions since the Great
Depression. In addition, Mr. Departed's untimely demise came
only months after the largest earthquake in California history since
190x. By pure chance, Mr. Departed had invested much of his
wealth in areas that were strongly affected by the earthquake.
Several of his properties suffered extensive damage. Some were
demolished and remain fallow as of the date of this report.

As luck would have it, the severe crisis in the lending industry also enveloped Mr. Departed and his Estate, rendering most of
his real estate investments all but totally illiquid. The lending policy of most lenders in the market at the time of his demise was not
to lend funds in excess of the already existing debt on properties.
Subsequent to Mr. Departed's demise, the executor has attempted
to refinance properties with little success, and those properties that
have been refinanced required funds from the Estate to pay costs
and/or reduce the debt.

In addition to the issues discussed above, the illiquidity of the
decedent's assets are well evidenced by the Internal Revenue
Service's acceptance of the installment method of paying estate
taxes under Internal Revenue Code §6166.

In summary, we have valued the Estate's holdings in the following manner. We started with the appraised value of the Estate's
assets. Where necessary, we made an economic conditions adjustment to these values to reflect the economic impact of the earthquake. From these adjusted asset values we then deducted debt to

arrive at the net asset value prior to the ownership and marketability adjustments. An adjustment was then made to take into account the lack of control of certain of the Estate's holdings. The final adjustments were the general marketability adjustment and the adjustment to marketability that was necessary owing to the existence of the contingent tax liability in certain C corporations. The final result of these adjustments is ValueNomics'® estimated fair market value of the assets held by the Estate as of the date of death.

In our determination of the estimate of fair market value, we considered how the specific factors of the Departed Estate would affect the price of the various assets from the perspective of a willing buyer and seller.

OWNERSHIP

The following schedule is referenced to the indexing system used on the Federal Form 706.

Schedule/Item	Description of Asset
A/1	xx% limited partnership interest in Notts Landing, LP
A/2	xx% limited partnership interest in Fly by Night, LP
A/3	xx% GP interest in Ed's Limited Partnership
B/1	xxx shares (100%) of Good Deal Realty, Inc.
B/2	xxx shares (100%) of Really Good Investments, Inc.
B/3	xxx shares (100%) of Get Realty Man, Inc.

STRUCTURE

It is the executor's and management's intent to operate the decedent's properties for the benefit of the Estate.

INDUSTRY OVERVIEW: REAL ESTATE INVESTMENT AND DEVELOPMENT

GENERAL INDUSTRY OUTLOOK

At the valuation date, the real estate industry and the general economy in California were weak. Demand for residential and commercial real estate was in decline and financing for real estate investment was extremely difficult to obtain. Real estate investment and development were at very low levels. The syndication industry was all but dead because of the savings and loan crisis and the 198x Tax Reform Act. There were very few interested real estate buyers at the time of the decedent's death.

California real estate experienced a significant expansion during the mid–1980s. Real estate development was fueled by a combination of liberalized depreciation laws, lower interest rates, and easy credit for mortgages.[5] In 198x, home prices in California started rising at a rate of 15 to 20 percent per year as many households used the increased equity in their homes to trade up to more expensive houses, which further increased prices. "Not until the summer of 198x, when most households simply 'topped out' on their ability to afford financing, did California's speculative home price spiral come to an end."[6]

As of September 198x, the Monterey–Santa Cruz and San Francisco Bay Area real estate markets were in even worse condition than the California market as a whole, which was experiencing a significant slowdown in real estate activity.[7] In San Jose, the number of single-family building permits issued dropped xx.x% from 198x to 198x.[8] The median sale price of an existing home in California dropped xx.x% from June to December of 198x.[9]

Housing prices throughout California's coastal markets increased too much too rapidly during the second half of the 1980s. "Because coastal housing prices rose so far and so fast, they outpaced the ability of many households to meet mortgage lenders' equity and/or income requirements. As a result, it may take several years for incomes and accumulated equity to catch up. In the near term, this means that coastal housing markets will remain soft."[10] By the date of the decedent's death, the residential real estate markets where the deceased owned properties were very weak.

5. John D. Landis et al., "California Real Estate Opportunities in the 1990s: Is California Still a Good Place to Invest?" Reprint No. 93, Center for Real Estate and Urban Economics, University of California at Berkeley, p. 2.
6. Ibid., p. 18.
7. Cynthia Kroll et al., "Economic Impact of the Earthquake: A Focus on Small Business," Working Paper No. 91-187, Center for Real Estate and Urban Economics, University of California at Berkeley, p. 19.
8. Cynthia Kroll and Kenneth Rosen, "California's Housing Market: Which Direction in 1990?" *Quarterly Report: Center for Real Estate and Urban Economics,* University of California at Berkeley, 1st Quarter 1990, p. 2.
9. Ibid., p. 3.
10. Landis, p. 18.

The market for apartments was also depressed at the valuation date. "As in other real estate sectors, multifamily [units] did get exceedingly overbuilt in the mid–198xs, resulting in a lack of demand. . . . "[11] From 198x to 198x the number of multifamily building permits issued in San Jose decreased by xx.x%.[12] In the late 1980s the decrease in construction was mainly in multifamily units.[13] This decrease in the number of apartments built was due to a combination of oversupply of multifamily units and changes to the Internal Revenue Code made in 198x. "The Tax Reform Act of 198x reduced the tax benefits of real estate by increasing its depreciable life, instituting the passive loss rules and changing the tax rates on capital gains, thus killing the (real estate) syndication business. . . . "[14] According to Paul Boneham, a principal with Richard Ellis International, "The first three years of this decade [the 1990s] were absolute disasters for property owners. There was no real estate market. . . . "[15] In 199x, Gary Lucas, a senior regional manager for Marcus and Millichap, said that "the apartment market has been less than spectacular. . . . "[16]

The commercial real estate market in California went through an explosive growth period in the middle of the 1980s. At the beginning of the 1980s, California did not have enough office space, and by the end of the decade there was far too much office space in the state. By 199x the office vacancy rate in California varied from xx% in certain downtown areas to xx% in several suburban markets.[17] Referring to the national market for commercial real estate at the beginning of this decade, David Shulman of Solomon Brothers stated that "we are probably in the worst real estate environment since the 1930s."[18] According to an article in the *Real Estate Review*, "Pessimism is rampant in real estate circles these days.[19]" The San Francisco Bay Area

---

11. Steve Bergsman, "Multifamily Offers Unique Opportunities to Investors Looking for Solid Returns," *National Real Estate Investor*, July 1993, p. 48.
12. Kroll and Rosen, "California's Housing," p. 4.
13. Landis, p. 14.
14. Michael Evans, "Beyond the REIT Boom: Newest REITs Are Property-Specific and Operations Oriented," *Ernest & Young Real Estate Journal*, Fall 1993, p. 28.
15. Bergsman, p. 64.
16. Tim Turner, "San Francisco Bay Area Review: Lack of Lending, Development Has Led to What Could Be the Area's Worst Slump Ever," *National Real Estate Investor*, October 1991, p. 126.
17. Landis, p. 11.
18. "Real Estate's Low-Rise Future," *Fortune*, January 28, 1991, p. 41.
19. William Wheaton and Raymond Torto, "The Prospect for Rebound in the Commercial Real Estate Market," *Real Estate Review*, Winter 1992, p. 91.

commercial real estate market was also in bad shape, as the following title from the October 199x *National Real Estate Investor* indicates: "San Francisco Bay Area Review: Lack of Lending, Development Has Led to What Could Be the Area's Worst Slump Ever." There was clearly little real estate development or investment occurring in northern California as of the date of valuation.

Extremely high inflation and interest rates during the late 1970s limited the ability of regulated savings and loans to compete for deposits. To counter depositors leaving thrifts in search of higher interest rates, Congress deregulated the thrift industry in 198x and 198x so that money would continue to be available for the construction and purchase of homes.[20] Savings and loans were also allowed to make commercial and real estate development loans for the first time ever in the United States. This lack of experience was in part responsible for the vast overbuilding of commercial real estate which was prevalent in the late 1980s. Many thrifts became insolvent as a direct result of making risky real estate development loans that subsequently went bad. To ensure the soundness of the nation's financial system, Congress passed the Financial Institutions Re-regulations Enforcement Act (FIRREA) of 198x. FIRREA placed strict limits on the amount of capital that financial institutions could loan to developers and apartment owners. The effect of FIRREA was that "even those thrifts and commercial banks with strong track records and portfolios stopped making mortgage loans to apartment owners and developers. . . . Financing for new construction . . . was simply nonexistent."[21] The period of time following the passage of FIRREA became known as the credit crunch in the real estate industry because of the dearth of available financing for real estate.[22] The amount of real estate investment that was possible via financing was sharply limited during this period.

In summary, Mr. Departed's assets were predisposed to an environment approximate to that of the assets owned by the Resolution Trust Corporation (RTC). The glut of assets on the market, the depressed California real estate market, the earthquake,

---

20. Garn-St. Germain Depository Institutions Act of 1982.
21. Mary Comerio et al., "Postdisaster Residential Rebuilding," Working Paper 608, Institute of Urban and Regional Development, University of California at Berkeley, February 1994, p. 19.
22. William Wheaton and Raymond Torto, "The Prospect for Rebound in the Commercial Real Estate Market," *Real Estate Review,* Winter 1992, p. 94.

type of assets, and location, along with the lending environment, were all current and relevant market conditions affecting sellers and buyers at the time of Mr. Departed's death. Thus the question: How would a willing buyer and seller behave, if the Departed equity interests were in fact priced and sold at his date of death? Of concern is the issue that the federal government compelled the RTC to sell its assets under the same market conditions and point in time, resulting in material discounts from appraised values. These conditions would directly impact a willing buyer's and seller's purchasing strategies at the point of time in question, and that in itself is sufficient to influence the estimated fair market value as defined by Revenue Ruling 59–60.

ECONOMIC CONDITION

EARTHQUAKE DISASTER AREA

In late 199(Y–1) a massive earthquake occurred in California, the largest earthquake in California history. The damage to property was extensive. There were three cities where substantial damage occurred during the earthquake: Quake Town, Fault City, and Land Fill, California. "Approximately 12,000 housing units were lost or rendered uninhabitable, and another 32,000 were damaged. Of the 12,000 lost, 9,000 were in multifamily (apartment) buildings and about xx% of these have not been repaired or replaced four years after the earthquake."[23] The amount of damage caused by the earthquake to physical structures has been estimated at close to $x billion.[24] In addition, the earthquake caused a significant decrease in property values throughout the area impacted by the earthquake.[25]

The Urban Land Institute described Quake Town after the earthquake as follows: "The total impact on downtown businesses, surrounding lower-income housing stock and the fiscal impact on the city (through loss of sales tax and property tax revenue) is severe."[26] The city of Quake Town lost most of its four-block commercial strip,

---

23. Comerio, p. 19.
24. Kroll, "Economic Impact," p. 3.
25. James Murdoch et al., "The Impact of Natural Hazards on Housing Values: The California Earthquake," *AREUEA Journal*, 1993, 21:2, pp. 167 and 177.
26. Urban Land Institute, *An Evaluation of Development Potential and Land Management Strategies for the City of Quake Town*, Washington, DC: The Urban Land Institute, 1990, p. 3.

and xx% of its residential housing was severely damaged or destroyed. Prices for rental units dropped in the year following the earthquake.[27] Because of the unprecedented amount of planning and redevelopment necessary for recovery from the earthquake, the city of Quake Town requested assistance from the Urban Land Institute.[28]

Paradise County experienced the most severe damage from the earthquake. Fifteen percent of the county's housing stock was damaged, and over one-fourth of the commercial and industrial buildings located in the county were either damaged or destroyed.[29] "The city of Quake Town was in something of a state of shock after the earthquake. . . . [In fact] . . . one year later, nothing had been rebuilt."[30] The number of home sales in Paradise County dropped over xx% from the fall of 198x to the fall of 198x.[31] The Paradise County Housing Authority determined that "housing demand actually deteriorated and rental prices fell x–xx% in the two years following the earthquake."[32]

Since the value of apartments is driven by rental income, a conservative adjustment for the effects of the earthquake on the price of income-producing apartments in Paradise County is x%. This adjustment is necessary to reflect a material change in economic conditions that was not taken into consideration by all the appraisals of assets owned by the various Departed entities. Thus the equity interests reported with the filing of the Form 706 were overstated.

Traditional real estate appraisal methodology involves the use of comparable sales data. This technique arrives at a value for a particular property by using the actual sales price of similar properties that have sold in the same general location as the subject property. It is essential for the comparable sales to have taken place close to the appraisal date. Real estate appraisals incorporate changes in the market value of real estate on a relatively gradual basis. That is, "the appraisal process imparts a lag or 'gradualness' in incorporating real estate market changes. . . . "[33] Real estate mar-

---

27. Comerio, p. 47.
28. Urban Land Institute, p. 6.
29. Kroll, "Economic Impact," pp. 3–5.
30. Comerio, p. 46.
31. Kroll," Economic Impact," p. 23.
32. Comerio, p. 46.
33. Michael Giliberto, "Measuring Real Estate Returns: The Hedged REIT Index," *The Journal of Portfolio Management,* Spring 1993, p. 96.

ket values change faster than the appraised value of the real estate does. This occurs because real estate appraisers frequently rely on the use of actual sales price (market value) of properties comparable to the one being valued to derive the appraised value of the subject property. To the extent that the sales of comparable properties are close in time to the date of appraisal, this lag or gradualness is minimized. Conversely, when the sales of comparable properties are further away in time from the date of appraisal, this lag will increase. The more that market conditions have changed from the date of the comparable sales to the date the subject property is being appraised, the more that the appraised value will be showing what market conditions were like in the past, and the less the appraisal will reflect the actual market conditions prevalent at the absolute appraisal date.

All the comparable sales used on the appraisals for apartment buildings located in the earthquake zone were sales that occurred prior to the earthquake. In fact, the same nine sales were used as comparables for each of the apartment buildings appraised for the Departed entities and for which ValueNomics® has made an economic adjustment to equity for the earthquake. All the sales were from 198x. The appraisals of the apartment buildings do not consider any of the detrimental effects of the earthquake on the equity value of the properties. Furthermore, comparable real estate "transactions occurring over one year are usually not indicative of a changing marketplace."[34] Therefore, the Estate's equity interests do not reflect the deleterious economic conditions caused by the earthquake. An adjustment to the values of certain of the Estate's assets is necessary to arrive at the estimated true fair market value for these entities.

The Estate's real estate appraisers used comparable sales data from after the earthquake to arrive at their value for residential property in Paradise County, which does adjust for the effects of the earthquake on the price. We therefore did not make an earthquake adjustment for any residential property located in this area.

For commercial land, no adjustment is necessary to accurately value the Departed's equity interest. This is because the appraisals already consider the effects of the earthquake on the value of the properties. For the undeveloped commercial land contained in the

---

34. Martin Shenkman and Cal Feingold, "Minority, Marketability Discounts Affect Valuation of Partnership Interest," *The Real Estate Finance Journal*, Summer 1993, p. 20.

Get Realty Man limited partnership, the Estate's appraisal report examines the effect of the earthquake on the value and places more weight on the comparable sale that occurred after the earthquake.

While there was substantial publicity surrounding the collapse of the Highway interchange in Idyllic City, there was little other material damage caused in the area from the earthquake. We therefore did not take an earthquake adjustment for the properties located in Idyllic City, since there was no empirical evidence that a diminution in value actually occurred.

To recapitulate, for the property types where the real estate appraisals did not take into account the economic impact of the earthquake, we have taken an adjustment of x% to do so. This adjustment was based upon empirical market evidence.

OWNERSHIP STRUCTURE

CONTROL

The control adjustment is recognized because the holder of a fractional interest may lack operational or dispositional control over the underlying assets and the entity itself. The owner of a xx.x% interest would not receive a control adjustment, because the owner has complete control over the assets and the entity. Mr. Departed, as a limited partner, had very little operational or dispositional control over the partnership's assets. Therefore, an adjustment to the value of the limited partnership interests held by the Departed Estate is necessary to arrive at an estimate of the fair market value of the equity owned by Mr. Departed at the valuation date.

In *Estate of Berg,* the Federal Tax Court specified that the control adjustment for owners of fractional interests of real estate holding companies should preferably be calculated using the "REIT Approach."[35] We are utilizing this approach to quantify the size of this adjustment for the Estate's fractional interests in property owned via limited partnerships and corporations. The Federal Tax Court, in *Moore v. Commissioner,* states that "we see no reason for a different rule for valuing partnership interests (compared to corporate shareholder interests). The critical factor is lack of control, be it as a minority partner or as a minority shareholder."[36]

---

35. T. C. Memo 1991–279.
36. T. C. Memo 1991–546.

The first step in the REIT approach is to locate the publicly traded real estate entities that are comparable to the entities being valued. This group is then narrowed down to those entities that publish data on the appraised value of their real estate holdings. Then for each entity, subtract the net book value of real estate assets from the book value of equity, add back the appraised value of the real estate assets, and then divide this sum by shares outstanding at the closest possible date to the valuation date. The resulting figure is the fair market value of the net assets per share. Then compare this value with the market price per share on the same date to calculate the market's control adjustment from fair market value of the net assets per share.[37]

In a study published in the June 1986 issue of *Business Valuation News*, on December 31, 198x, five publicly traded real estate companies were selling at a xx% discount to the net asset values of their real estate.[38] There is an adjustment because investors are acquiring a noncontrolling fractional interest in the REIT. For their fractional interest, investors were willing to pay only 76 cents for each dollar of real estate owned by these companies. After extensive research, we were able to obtain the appraised value of the real estate holdings of two REITs approximate to the Estate's holdings: Lincoln N. C. Realty Fund (LRF), and the Northern Cal Properties (NCP).

There are three properties in LRF, and all three are in California. One apartment building comprises xx% of LRF's real estate holdings, and one of the other properties is land. Therefore, the properties in the decedent's Estate are similar to the holdings of the Lincoln REIT in that they are located entirely in California. Northern Cal Properties (NCP) has 50 properties, and in terms of dollar amounts, xx% of the properties are apartments. The other properties consist of office buildings and undeveloped land. Geographically, xx% of the properties are located in northern California.

For each of the Departed entities, these market-derived adjustments for lack of control are adjusted by comparing its financial performance with that of the REITs. Specifically, an adjustment is made for the relative profitability, leverage, cash distributions, size of the ownership interest, and location of the assets.

---

37. James Hitchner and Kevin Rudd, "The Use of Discounts in Estate and Gift Tax Valuations," *Trusts & Estates*, August 1992, p. 55.
38. Robert Oliver, "Moving Beyond the Real Estate Appraisal: Valuing Fractional Interests in Closely Held Real Estate Companies," *Business Valuation News*, June 1986, p. 17.

For both REITs we calculated the lack of control adjustment as of December 31, 198x, in the manner described above (Exhibit G–1). The adjustment for LRF is xx.xx% and the adjustment for NCP is xx.xx%.

As of December 31, 199(Y–1), these REITs were selling, on average, at a xx.x% discount to the net asset values of their holdings. This means that in December 199(Y–1) investors were willing to pay an average of only xx.x cents for each dollar of real estate held by these companies. This figure is in line with results of a study conducted by Coopers & Lybrand that found adjustments of up to xx% in the publicly held real estate companies analyzed. The Coopers & Lybrand study goes on to state that the market prices used to calculate the lack of control adjustment are indicative of a liquid interest, and that if a lack of marketability adjustment is warranted it would be taken in addition to the lack-of-control adjustment.[39] To value the equity interests owned by Daryl Lee Departed on January 199Y, it is much more relevant to use the adjustment calculated on December 31, 199(Y–1) for the LRF and NCP REITs than an adjustment calculated in 198x. The market for real estate and REITs was in an "explosive period"[40] from 198x to 198x, which was definitely not the case in January 199x. (This is established in the Industry Overview section of this study.) Furthermore, "transactions occurring over one year are usually not indicative of a changing marketplace."[41] The adjustments determined for LRF and NCP on December 31, 199(Y–1) were calculated less than three months from the date of valuation.

To obtain the size of the lack-of-control adjustments for each Departed Estate equity interest, we used the lack-of-control adjustment calculated for the specific publicly traded REITs as a starting point (Exhibit G–1). It was necessary to make adjustments to these values (xx.xx% and xx.xx%) to account for the differences between these entities and the equity interests in the Departed Estate. Specifically, we made adjustments for the following factors: (1) distribution/dividend yield, (2) leverage, (3) size of interest, and (4) profitability. Each of the four factors is discussed in more detail below. The overall lack-of-control adjustment for each of the Estate's equity interests is the simple average of the four factor adjustments (Exhibit G).

---

39. Ibid.
40. Evans, p. 26.
41. Shenkman and Feingold, p. 20.

There is a minimum adjustment that a willing buyer will accept. This minimum adjustment is directly related to the other investment opportunities that a hypothetical willing buyer has. This minimum adjustment is empirically derived below from capital market data.

There are basically two equity markets that one can invest in: the efficient, public market or the inefficient market for private, closely held entities. There must be a good reason for an investor to put his or her money into a closely held entity when (s)he could be investing in less risky investments in an efficient market. An investor in closely held entities will do so only with the expectation that (s)he will be compensated for the extra risk and lack of liquidity with a higher expected return on investment (ROI) than if (s)he had invested in a publicly traded company or portfolio in an efficient market. There is a minimum threshold level of return for investments in closely held entities in an inefficient market. When the ROI for the subject entity in the inefficient market is approximate to this level of expected rate of return for the efficient market, investing in the target closely held entity is not a particularly good investment in terms of the risk/reward relationship.

The average compound rate of return for small-company stocks for the 20-year period ending December 29, 198x (the last trading day of 198x) was xx.xx%.[42] The 20-year period was chosen because, statistically, it is better to use more rather than less data. The use of a longer data series decreases the effect of short-term fluctuations in the rate of return. Thus, using 20 years of return data provides a more accurate estimate of the underlying series than a shorter return series would.

If the expected rate of return in an investment in a closely held entity is approximate to this threshold of xx.xx%, an investor will most likely invest elsewhere. The investor would then have the same (or higher) expected rate of return than with the small, private entity and the added benefit of being in an efficient market. Therefore, the risk floor for each of the following four adjustment factors is xx.xx%.

1. Distribution/dividend yield (equal to cash distribution divided by investors equity). For investors in REITs (or any type of income-producing real estate), an important factor to consider is the distribution or dividend yield. Investors are concerned with the

---

42. *Stocks, Bonds, Bills, and Inflation 1994 Yearbook*, Chicago: Ibbotson Associates, 1994, p. 44.

yield of the cash distributions they are going to receive from their investment. For the Lincoln REIT, investors received distributions of xx.xx% versus x.xx% for the Northern Cal REIT. Not surprisingly, the discount for Northern Cal (xx.xx%) was more than one and one-half times the discount for Lincoln (xx.xx%). We are calculating the adjustment for the Departed equity interests by a mathematical formula (Exhibit G) that generates a factor adjustment that is proportional to the size of the dividend yield. For the Departed entities where the distribution yield is x% or higher, we are setting this factor equal to the aforementioned risk floor of xx.xx%. This means that the higher the cash distributions as a percentage of investors equity, the lower the lack of control adjustment will be for this factor. This is in accordance with what a willing buyer will pay for a fractional interest in an entity whose primary asset is real estate. Investors will pay more in the expectation of higher cash distributions.

2. Leverage (equal to book debt divided by appraised asset value). Investors prefer investments with lower leverage because higher leverage means more risk. A willing buyer will pay less money for an investment with higher risk, all other factors being equal. This is reflected in the REITs. Northern Cal (xx.xx%) was more leveraged than Lincoln (xx.xx%) and had a larger lack-of-control discount. The equity interests in the Estate which are more (less) leveraged receive higher (lower) adjustments for the leverage adjustment factor.

3. Control. This factor adjusts for the relevant sections in the partnership agreement, if any, and the fact that the control an investor has increases as the size of the investor's fractional interest increases. A willing buyer will pay more for an interest that has more operational control. A typical investor in a publicly traded REIT owns less than x% of the total market value of the REIT, and there are numerous other investors who own shares of the REIT. The Departed interest in the various entities was larger than x%, and there are fewer than 10 limited partners in the partnerships in which Mr. Departed was a limited partner, so we are setting this factor adjustment equal to the risk floor of xx.xx%. For all three of the corporations which are owned xx.x% by Mr. Departed, and for Ed's Limited Partnership, where the partnership agreement provided Mr. Departed with basically all the powers of control, there is no adjustment for lack of control.

4. Profitability (net income divided by revenues). A willing buyer will pay more for a more profitable investment than a less profitable one. The formula that is used to calculate this factor

adjustment gives a higher (lower) adjustment for less (more) profitable entities. For the REITs, both with losses, Northern Cal (–xx.xx%) was losing more than Lincoln (–xx.x%). Because both of the publicly traded REITs were unprofitable in 198x and given the relatively poor condition of the real estate market at the valuation date, the risk floor adjustment of xx.xx% is applied to the Departed Estate entities that generated profits in 198x.

The final result is an adjustment that is derived in two steps. First, the lack-of-control adjustment for the publicly traded REITs was calculated (Exhibit G–1). These figures were then adjusted for differences in the cash distributions, leverage, control, and profitability of each of the equity interests compared with the REITs (Exhibit G). The willing buyer and seller perspective was analyzed in the derivation of the individual factor adjustments. These factor adjustments were then combined to arrive at the final unweighted lack-of-control adjustments for the limited partnership interests in Notts Landing and Fly by Night.

The numerical percentages for the four factor adjustments are not meaningful on an individual basis. It is the combination of these adjustment factors that results in an accurate quantification of the lack-of-control adjustment for each entity.

LIMITED PARTNERSHIPS

1. Notts Landing—apartment building (Form 706 reference A/1). Daryl Lee Departed owned a xx% limited partnership interest. Distribution yield was xx.x%. This is exactly halfway between the distribution yield for Lincoln (xx.xx%) and National (x.xx%), so this adjustment factor is equal to xx.xx, which is halfway between the control adjustment for Lincoln (xx.xx%) and National (xx.xx%). Leverage was xx%, so this limited partnership is less leveraged than either Lincoln (xx.x%) or National (xx.xx%). This means that this limited partnership has less financial risk than either of the comparable REITs, which are more highly leveraged investments. The adjustment for this factor is xx.xx%, as calculated by the formula listed under Leverage in Exhibit G.

Mr. Departed did not have control over the disposition of the partnership's assets as a holder of a xx% limited partnership interest, which is larger than a typical investor in an REIT. Since there were only five limited partners in this partnership, Mr. Departed

had potentially more operational influence over the management
of the partnership than an investor in a REIT would have over
management of the REIT, which typically has many more than five
shareholders. This adjustment factor is set at the risk floor of
xx.xx%. Profitability was negative xx.x%, which was less negative
than either REIT. A willing buyer will pay more for a less unprofitable investment than for a more unprofitable investment. This
factor adjustment is xx.xx% (from the formula under profitability
in Exhibit G, which is lower than the adjustment for either REIT.

The final lack-of-control adjustment is the simple average of
the four factor adjustments equal to xx.xx% (Exhibit G).

2. Fly by Night—apartment building (Form 706 reference
A/2). Daryl Lee Departed owned a xx% limited partnership interest. Distribution yield was xx.xx%. A willing buyer will pay more
for an investment that is generating higher cash distributions, so
this adjustment factor is set at the risk floor of xx.xx%. Leverage
was xx.x%, which is a fairly high amount of leverage, meaning
more risk than an investment with less leverage. Since investors
prefer less risky investments, this factor adjustment is set at
xx.xx%, from the formula under Leverage in Exhibit G.

Mr. Departed did not have control over the disposition of the
partnership's assets as a holder of a xx% limited partnership interest, which is larger than a typical investor in an REIT. Since there
were only nine limited partners in this partnership, the holder of
the Estate's interest could have more potential influence over the
management of the partnership than an investor in an REIT would
have over management of the REIT, which typically has many
more than nine shareholders. This adjustment factor is set at the
risk floor of xx.xx%.

Profitability was xx.xx%, which was considerably higher than
the REITs that were losing money. A willing buyer will pay more for
a profitable investment than for a less profitable (or unprofitable)
investment. This factor adjustment is set at the risk floor of xx.xx%.

The final lack-of-control adjustment is the simple average of
the four factor adjustments equal to xx.xx% (Exhibit G).

3. Ed's Limited Partnership—commercial land (Form 706 reference F/3). Daryl Lee Departed, the general partner, owned xx%.
The partnership agreement for this entity does not place any limits
on the powers of the general partner. In fact, there are restrictions
on what the limited partner can do. The limited partner "may

assign his Limited Partnership interest only with the consent of the general partner. . . . " and "The retirement, expulsion, bankruptcy or insanity of a Limited Partner shall not work a dissolution of the Partnership. . . . " The general partner of this partnership had control of the property—there is no lack-of-control adjustment.

C CORPORATIONS

The three C corporations were Good Deal Realty, Really Good Investments, and Get Realty Man. These corporations were all wholly owned by Departed. No lack-of-control adjustment is applied to the equity interests of these corporations.

MARKETABILITY

FACTORS AFFECTING MARKETABILITY

This section, along with the section on contingent tax liability that follows, quantifies the size of the lack-of-marketability adjustment for the limited partnerships and C corporations that are part of the Departed Estate. The quantification for this section uses data from the liquidity adjustment on properties sold by the Resolution Trust Corporation (RTC) as a proxy for the size of the lack-of-marketability adjustment for the equity interests of the Estate. We believe that this is an appropriate technique to use, since the asset holdings of the Departed entities consist primarily of real estate and extensive data are available from the RTC on the dollar amount that illiquid properties were appraised for compared with their actual sales price. Real estate is commonly recognized to be an illiquid asset. The sales price of the RTC assets was consistently lower than their appraised value because of the illiquidity of these assets. The difference between what the properties were appraised for and what a willing buyer actually paid for these properties is equal to the marketability adjustment for the Departed equity interests.

"By the fourth quarter of 198x, the California economy had begun to experience a significant slowdown in real estate activity. . . . "[43] Considerable price increases in coastal California throughout the 1980s meant that many households simply could not afford a

---

43. Kroll, "Economic Impact," p. 19.

house, so a significant number of people moved inland, where houses were more affordable.[44]

A paper published in the *Journal of Real Estate Research* in 199x measured the liquidity adjustments for over 43,000 sales of properties across the United States and Puerto Rico.[45] This paper utilized data from the Resolution Trust Corporation to compare the actual sales price of the properties with their most recent appraised value. A total of 43,785 sales were recorded from August 198x to June 199x. The dollar value of sales in California was $xxx.x million, which was xx.x% of the total amount of RTC sales. California had the third highest dollar amount of sales compared with the other states, the District of Columbia, and Puerto Rico. The mean sale price for all properties was $xxx, compared with the mean appraised value of $xxx. The average liquidity adjustment was therefore xx.x%. This is less than the xx% adjustment that was derived as being appropriate for the sale of illiquid, distressed real estate in a 199x analysis.[46] Data are provided later in this section on the empirical adjustment for the equity of the entities contained in the Departed Estate.

During 198x Congress required the RTC to sell its assets for at least xx% of the estimated market or appraised value. There were very few buyers willing to pay this much. In 198x only 181 sales occurred, which was less than one-half of one percent of the total number of sales included in this study. This is compelling evidence that the appraisals consistently overvalued the properties relative to their actual market value. The conclusion of the RTC liquidity adjustment paper states: "This paper's importance relies most heavily on the finding that realistic market adjustments over time (i.e., Congress permitting the properties to be sold at increasingly lower percentages of their appraised values with the passage of time) helped to achieve a higher degree of *liquidity* in RTC real estate asset sales."[47] [Emphasis added.] In other words, buyers were willing to purchase these properties only at a substantial downward adjustment to their appraised value.

---

44. Landis, p. 10.
45. Fred A. Forgey et al., "Implicit Liquidity in the Disposition of RTC Assets," *Journal of Real Estate Research*, Summer 1993, pp. 347–363.
46. Schilling et al., "Estimating Net Realizable Value for Distressed Real Estate," *Journal of Real Estate Research*, 5:1, 1990, pp. 129–140.
47. Forgey, p. 362.

One purpose of asset sales is to reflect an unbiased assessment of the information available to market participants.[48] When no data are available for what a property sold for on the open market, the next best thing is the actual price at which comparable properties sold for. This section provides evidence on the appraised value and the actual market price from over 43,000 sales. All the different types of property sold at a value less than the appraised value of the property. The percentage difference is the empirically derived proxy for the lack-of-marketability adjustment for the Estate's equity interests.

When the Congress created the RTC in 198x, one of the implied duties of the RTC was the disposition of its assets during its seven-year existence.[49] Those less informed might therefore argue that the RTC was compelled to sell its assets. While the RTC may have been required to sell its assets during its seven-year life, this does not mean that the prices at which it sold its assets can be ignored. In fact, the prices at which the RTC's assets sold for provide some of the best information available concerning the actual market values of those and other assets like the Estate's. In the conclusion to the paper on the disposition of the RTC's assets, Forgey states: "The findings of this paper confirm . . . that real estate properties acquired by the government are disposed of [by the RTC] at the highest dollar value possible."[50]

The RTC's pricing policy for its real properties allow the sale price to be reduced in stages if a given asset has not been sold after a specified period of time. For example, the lower limit the RTC will accept for an asset starts at xx% of the appraised value and then drops to xx% of appraised value if the asset remains unsold after four to six months. According to the chief of the mortgage and consumer finance section of the Federal Reserve Board, John L. Goodman, Jr., "This is not a plan for selling below market price, or dumping, but rather a method for trying to determine what the market price is in circumstances in which appraisals and other methods for estimating market value are imprecise."[51] When

48. John H. Crockett, "Workouts, Deep Pockets, and Fire Sales: An Analysis of Distressed Real Estate," *AREUEA Journal,* Spring 1991, p. 85.
49. Forgey, p. 347.
50. Ibid., p. 362.
51. John L. Goodman, Jr., "RTC Real Estate Sales: Just Do It," *Real Estate Review,* Winter 1991, p. 28.

appraisals are imprecise, it is preferable to look at the actual price at which transactions took place in assessing market values.

Given the task of the RTC, "it is clear that properties held by the RTC cannot be taken off the market until conditions improve. And it is also clear that what [the] properties were valued at . . . is irrelevant to what they can and should be sold for in the current market."[52]

The most reliable indicator of market conditions for a specific time period are actual market transactions that take place during that period. "Markets can generally be relied on to provide transactions on terms that reflect unbiased adjustments of the information available to market participants. In fact, by conveying price information, the occurrence of transactions can aid market participants in assessing conditions."[53] The Forgey paper used price and appraisal data from over 43,000 sales to determine the actual market value of the RTC's assets as a percentage of the appraised value of those real properties.

The liquidity adjustment varied depending on the type of property, with the size of the adjustment ranging from x.x% to xx.x% of the appraised value. The liquidity adjustment paper breaks down the data into 44 categories. The liquidity adjustments used are reported here for the equity interests in various property types contained in the report. Apartments sold at xx.x% less than appraised value for the 869 sales that occurred during the period studied. The 735 parcels of unimproved commercial land sold at an average value of xx.x% less than their appraised value. Office buildings sold at an average discount of xx.x% in 1038 sales. There were 348 sales of single-family residences in California, with an average discount of x.x%. Fifteen parking garages/lots sold for xx.x% less than their appraised value. These are the lack-of-marketability adjustments to the equity interests in the Departed Estate that contain the various types of assets.

The Federal Tax Court in *Estate of Dougherty* has "recognized that the value of an interest in an investment company is not always equal to its proportionate share of the company's net asset value. We acknowledge that we have in the past applied discounts for minority interests and for the nonmarketability of an investment company's stock, particularly where its assets consist of real

---

52. Forgey, p. 349.
53. Crockett, p. 85.

estate or other nonliquid assets."[54] The purpose of this adjustment to the equity interests is to reflect the fact that ownership interests in small, closely held entities do not have an institutional, efficient marketplace for sales or transfers.

Mr. Departed held equity interests in highly illiquid properties as of his demise. The assets held by the Estate's entities were negatively impacted by the sharp decrease in sales volume in real estate markets, which directly and dramatically affected the marketability of the equity interests held by the Departed Estate.

For the purpose of this valuation, we are not assuming that the Departed Estate was under any compulsion to sell. We have utilized data from the sales of illiquid RTC properties as a proxy for the size of the marketability adjustment to the equity interests in the limited partnerships, corporations, and cotenancies of the Estate. This technique was used because the asset holdings of these entities consist primarily of real estate, and we believe that these percentages accurately reflect the adjustment for market illiquidity that a willing buyer and seller would have accepted in negotiating a fair market price for the Departed equity interests at the valuation date.

In addition, the adjustments to the Estate's equity interests in the limited partnerships and corporations are almost certainly understated by the RTC liquidity proxies. The RTC liquidity adjustments are for sales of entire properties, which are more liquid than properties burdened by ownership via complex entity structure.

ENTITY-SPECIFIC MARKETABILITY

Partnerships—Evidence of a Market

There is evidence of a limited market for the limited partnership interests owned by Mr. Departed. "Private partnerships [that predominately hold real estate] which are neither traded in generally recognized markets nor traded by most of the secondary market firms have the smallest market of all and are rarely traded. . . . An interest worth over $xxx may be difficult to dispose of at all."[55] The secondary market for real estate limited partnerships is

---

54. T. C. Memo 1990–274.
55. Brad Davidson, "Valuation of Fractional Interests in Real Estate Limited Partnerships—Another Approach," *The Appraisal Journal*, April 1992, p. 189.

Estate of Daryl Lee Departed   June X, 199Y   Page 24

described in a book written by Richard Wollack and Brent R. Donaldson, two of the seminal figures in this relatively small market. Major purchasers of real estate limited partnerships in the secondary market are pooled investment funds, which are limited to those individuals who possess a high degree of investment sophistication. "These funds purchase units at an average discount of xx% to xx% from "break-up" value, [which is defined as] what the units of the partnership would actually be worth if the partnership were immediately liquidated."[56] Break-up value is comparable to the net asset value of the equity interests of the Departed entities before any adjustments. The value of the limited partnerships trading in the secondary market after the xx% to xx% discount from break-up value is applied is comparable to the fair market value of the Departed equity interests after the appropriate adjustments have been taken. Investors in these pooled funds are buying fractional, noncontrolling interests of a limited partnership in a market where there is virtually no liquidity without material discounting. The xx% to xx% adjustment reported above is the combination of the lack-of-marketability and the lack-of-control adjustment for the limited partnerships actually being traded in the secondary market. The average combined adjustments for the two limited partnerships held by the Estate where both a lack-of-marketability and a lack-of-control adjustment were taken is xx%. This is reasonably approximate to the range of adjustments reported for equity interests in limited partnerships trading in the secondary market.

C CORPORATIONS

"By definition, ownership interests in closely held companies are typically not readily marketable compared to similar interests in public companies."[57] The extent to which this statement is true can vary materially depending on many factors: the extent to which there is a market for the subject corporation, probability of a public offering, dividend history, and size of the block.

---

56. Richard Wollack and Brent R. Donaldson, *Limited Partnerships: How to Profit in the Secondary Market*, Chicago: Dearborn Financial Publishing, 1992, p. 52.
57. Jay E. Fishman et al., *Guide to Business Valuations*, 3rd ed., Fort Worth, TX: Practitioners Publishing Company, ¶.815.22.

Probability of Public Offering

Evidence suggests that as the probability of a public offering of a company's shares of stock increases, the adjustment related to liquidity of the investment decreases. However, this adjustment will most likely still be material if the shares being offered for registration must be sold prior to the initial public offering (IPO). There is also the probability that shares which remain unregistered at the time of the IPO will subsequently suffer material adjustment from the public market price if they are sold prior to registration or if there is the maturing of some restriction on transfer.

Examining the profile of the corporations in the Departed Estate as of the valuation date, we find that none of the corporations had any prospect of going public in the short or long term. There is no market for shares of stock in a private, closely held corporation. Thus, the liquidity of the ownership interest in the shares being valued is materially impaired.

Evidence of a Market

There is no efficient market for the shares of stock owned by an investor in the C corporations that are part of the Estate.

Dividend History

None of the six corporations issued any dividends in the five years prior to the valuation date.

Size of the Block Transferred

The decedent owned a xx% interest in the corporations. This would tend to make the corporations more marketable, because the new owner could have control of the corporation. However, this factor is accounted for by not applying a lack-of-control adjustment to the equity interests in the corporations.

QUANTIFICATION OF ADJUSTMENT

The size of this adjustment will be set equal to the lack-of-marketability adjustment—as measured by the RTC proxy—plus an

additional adjustment for the decrease in marketability of the corporations due to the contingent tax liability. This adjustment,
which is calculated after deducting the lack-of-marketability
adjustment from the equity interests, is discussed in another section of this report. Data on the lack-of-marketability adjustment
from private transaction studies compare the price of a corporation's stock during private stock transactions with the stock price
at the time of the subsequent IPO. These data were used as a consistency check of the total marketability adjustment for the C corporations in the Estate.

The market data that are most relevant for comparison with the
C corporations come from private transaction studies, which compare the stock price of a private, closely held corporation with the
price of the stock at the time of the same corporation's initial public
offering (IPO). The difference between the public and private price
per share measures the adjustment for lack of marketability, since no
public market exists for the shares of the company's stock prior to
the IPO. The result of this technique is a lack-of-marketability adjustment that is derived from actual market transactions.

The size of the adjustment derived in this manner may under-
state the lack-of-marketability adjustment for private, closely held
corporations. This will occur when the private transactions used in
the studies took place within a few months of the IPO. If this is the
case, there is a reasonable chance that the buyer knew about the
high probability of a public market for the shares in the near future.

The best private transaction studies that quantified the lack-
of-marketability adjustment were conducted by Williamette
Management Associates. These studies used only transactions that
were conducted on an arm's-length basis, which is appropriate for
this fair market valuation. These studies were done competently
and professionally. A total of nine studies were conducted over the
time period from 197x to 198x, excluding calendar year 198x. The
range of median lack-of-marketability adjustments in these studies
was xx.x% to xx.x%.[58]

The overall marketability adjustment for the corporations in
the Departed Estate is xx.x%, which is approximate to the midpoint
of the above range. We expected these estates to be less marketable

---

58. Fishman, 4th ed., Exhibit 8–18.

than the average private, closely held corporation, given the decreased marketability resulting from the contingent tax liability for the corporations held by the Estate.

CONTINGENT TAX LIABILITY

For the closely held corporations owned by Mr. Departed, there is an additional adjustment for marketability. This adjustment is necessary to adequately quantify the overall lack of marketability for the corporations. As discussed in the previous section, there are certain characteristics of stock in private, closely held corporations that make it a particularly illiquid investment. Certain of the C corporations owned by Mr. Departed are further burdened by the existence of a contingent tax liability that would have to be assumed by a willing buyer upon the purchase of the corporation. This "prospect of phantom gains induces buyers to significantly cut their bid prices to offset the expected tax liability."[59]

The closely held corporations of the Estate are being valued at fair market value, which is defined as the price at which a sale would take place, assuming a willing buyer and seller. Without a hypothetical sale, the concept of fair market value, as defined by Rev. Ruling 59–60, has no meaning. To arrive at the estimated fair market value for a particular asset, it is imperative to consider the value of that asset to a hypothetical willing buyer and a willing seller. If a value is calculated without taking into account the economic value of the asset to a hypothetical willing buyer and a willing seller, this value will not be the fair market value. For example, to place a value on a company by assuming that it changes its corporate status from C to S and holds on to all its assets for 10 years is not the correct approach to reach the fair market value of that corporation's stock unless this value is adjusted to reflect present value. This scenario, while it does make two potentially erroneous assumptions, does not involve a sale, nor does it consider what a willing buyer would currently be willing to pay for the company as a C corporation.

At this time, because of general economic and specific market conditions, the heirs do not have any plans to sell the corporations. The pertinent fact is that nobody can reasonably predict if the heirs will sell the properties during the next 10 years, and there is no valid

---

59. Wollack, pp. 59–60.

technique to statistically estimate the probability of this occurring. Furthermore, if only one shareholder dissented to elect S corporation status, the corporations could not make the election, because all shareholders must consent to such election.[60] The companies that are part of the Departed holdings are being valued according to their "fair market value." If the corporations were to be valued as if we knew the future, a future where the heirs of the Departed Estate elected S corporation status and held onto the assets for not less than 10 years, then a substantially higher lack-of-marketability adjustment would have to be taken to reflect the fact that none of the real estate assets could be sold for 10 years without the "built-in" tax being incurred, hence the present value calculation.

However, since this is a valuation of the Departed Estate's assets as of January X, 199Y, there must be an adjustment for the decreased marketability of the corporations resulting from the contingent tax liability that would have to be assumed upon the purchase of the corporations, in addition to the other factors discussed in the previous section. This adjustment is necessary to reflect the fact that willing buyers will decrease the price that they are willing to pay for a corporation owing to the existence of a contingent tax liability on appreciated property that the corporation holds. There are a number of reasons that ownership of a C corporation with real estate as its primary assets is not the same as direct ownership of the underlying real estate.[61] The first is that the assets are owned by the corporation and not directly by the shareholder. This means that the ordinary income and the capital gains derived from these assets would be taxed at the corporate level. The net effect is that the rate of return is lower for an investor in the shares in the corporation than it would be for direct ownership of the assets outside of a corporation. This decreases what a willing buyer will pay for shares of the corporation. Another difference is that the tax basis in the assets remains the same with a change in ownership. This results in less cashflow to an investor in the corporate stock than to an investor who directly holds the assets. This factor will also reduce the amount a willing buyer will pay for the corporate stock.

To accurately determine the fair market value of the C corporations, one cannot ignore the fact that "investors will pay less to acquire

---

60. Internal Revenue Code Section 1362 (a), (b); Treasury Regulation Section 1.1362–6.
61. John R. Gasiorowski, "Is a Discount for Built-In Capital Gains Tax Justified?" *Business Valuation Review,* June 1993, p. 77.

an interest in a real estate holding company organized as a C corporation than for an equivalent interest in an identical entity organized differently. Because corporate-level taxes affect strategic outcomes, the impact of corporate taxes must be considered in the valuation."[62]

To further quantify the effect of a contingent tax liability on marketability, we undertook the task of conducting a survey of professionals specifically dealing with the issue on a day-to-day basis. The survey asked questions of over 2000 certified public accountants, attorneys specializing in business transactions, and business brokers.

The results from the survey of the treatment of a contingent tax liability continue to support the essence of simplicity and penetrating truth of this 35-year-old statement: Fair market value is "the price at which the property would change hands between a willing buyer and a willing seller, when the former is not under any compulsion to buy and the latter is not under any compulsion to sell, both parties having reasonable knowledge of relevant facts."

This report contains an analysis and conclusions derived from the results of the ValueNomics'® survey in which we asked three sample audiences (CPA valuation experts, business attorneys, and business brokers) their opinions regarding the valuation treatment of a contingent tax liability on highly appreciated property owned by private, closely held corporations. The primary conclusion that can be drawn from the survey is that a large majority of buyers will, *ceteris paribus,* discount the stock price of a corporation because of the existence of a contingent tax liability on the appreciated property that the corporation holds.

For the entire sample, there is an xx% probability that a willing buyer will discount the price paid for stock by the contingent tax liabilities described. This conclusion is based on the response from an equally weighted average of questions 2 through 5. There is a xx% probability that the response for the entire population would fall between xx% and xx%. In other words, it is highly likely that over xx% of the entire population would discount the stock price because of the contingent tax liability. To be exact, there is only 1 chance in 40 that this is not the case.

It isn't very often that a survey will yield a unanimous result. For all three populations and for the entire sample, the results to the second half of question 4 were unanimous. For those who

---

62. Ibid., p. 79.

answered that a buyer of corporate stock would be influenced by the fact that the buyer does not receive the tax benefit associated with an increase in basis on the appreciated assets within the corporation, every single respondent indicated that the buyer will attempt to negotiate the price downward. Clearly, the lack of the tax benefit described decreases the price a buyer is willing to pay for the corporation.

The average discount for stock based on the responses from the entire population, including those who believe that a discount is inappropriate, would be xx% of the contingent tax liability. By group, attorneys responded with a discount of xx%, CPA expert valuators xx%, and business brokers xx%.

In our opinion, the survey results and our experience provide sufficient empirical substantiation to support a xx% deduction of the contingent taxes from the fair market value of the corporation's equity interests. This adjustment is necessary to incorporate the effect of the decreased marketability of the corporations as a result of the existence of the tax liability. See Exhibits D, E, and F for detailed computation.

ESTIMATE OF VALUE

ADJUSTED NET ASSETS METHOD

For purposes of this valuation we selected the widely accepted adjusted net assets method, an asset-oriented approach. This method is used to value the equity interest of an entity on the basis of the difference between the fair market value of the entity's assets less its liabilities and other adjustments. Under this method, we adjusted the appraised value, and then reduced the total adjusted value of assets by any recorded or unrecorded liabilities and other adjustments. This method is used to derive a total value for the equity interest. Adjusted net assets is a sound method for estimating the value of a nonoperating entity (holding or investment company).

The fair market value of certain specified Departed equity interest valued using the adjusted net assets method at the date of death is $xxx. To arrive at this value, we began with the appraised value of the assets of the entity, which is $xxx. We then made adjustments to the appraised value of the assets to reflect economic conditions, debt, lack of control, and marketability to arrive at the fair market value of the equity interests.

The first adjustment that we made is an economic condition adjustment, the earthquake disaster adjustment. This adjustment, which results in asset values that appropriately incorporate the economic conditions prevalent at the date of death, reduced the total value by $xxx (x.xx%) to $xxx. We then deducted from this figure $xxx of debt to arrive at an adjusted appraised value of $xxx after the economic condition adjustment and debt. This number is the value to which we applied the adjustments for ownership structure (the control adjustment of $xxx (xx.x%)) and for lack of marketability (the combined marketability adjustments of $xxx (xx.xx%) for general marketability factors and the contingent tax liability). The final result of these adjustments is the fair market value at the date of death of $xxx.

Appraised Value	**$ xxx**
Economic Condition	
Earthquake disaster adjustment	\<xxx\>
Debt	
Debt	\<xxx\>
Ownership Structure	
Lack-of-control adjustment	\<xxx\>
Marketability	
Factors affecting marketability, including the contingent tax liability	\<xxx\>
Value at Date of Death	**$ xxx**

Estate of Daryl Lee Departed	June X, 199Y	Page 32

VALUATION

Valuation of
Occupational Health Care Company

Valuation date, October 31, 199x

Prepared by
ValueNomics Research, Inc.

March 9, 199x

Gary E. Jones
Certified Valuation Analyst

Dirk E. Van Dyke
Senior Quantitative Analyst

Paul B. Jones
Senior Analyst

Benjamin Y. Chiu
Analyst

Mary O'Leary, M.D.
Occupational Health Care Company
1234 Health Drive
Berkeley, CA 94765

Dear Ms. O'Leary:

We have prepared and enclosed, herewith, our estimate of value of a xx.x% minority interest in Occupational Health Care Company (a California corporation, the "Company"). The objective of the valuation is to estimate the fair market value of a xx.x% interest in the Company as of the valuation date, October 31, 199x. The term "fair market value" is defined as:

> . . . the price at which the property would change hands between a willing buyer and a willing seller when the former is not under any compulsion to buy and the latter is not under any compulsion to sell, both parties having reasonable knowledge of relevant facts. Court decisions frequently state in addition that the hypothetical buyer and seller are assumed to be able, as well as willing, to trade

and to be well informed about the property and concerning the market for such property[1]

This report has been prepared for the purpose of estimating the fair market value of a xx.x% minority interest in the Company for the hypothetical purchase/sale of Dr. Charles Chiu's minority interest, and is intended for no other use.

On the basis of our study and analytical review procedures, we have concluded that the estimated "fair market value" of a xx.x% minority interest in the Company, as of October 31, 199x, is $xxx (Exhibit A).

ValueNomics Research, Inc.

Gary E. Jones, President
Cupertino, CA
March 9, 199x

EXECUTIVE SUMMARY

		199x	199x	199x
Adjusted earnings before interest, depreciation, and taxes (EBDIT)	$xxx $xxx	$xxx	$xxx	$xxx
Present value of adjusted EBDIT	$xxx			
Present value of terminal value	$xxx			
Estimated investment value of a 100% interest	$xxx			
Value of a xx.x% minority interest in the Company before adjustments for ownership structure and marketability	$xxx			
Adjustment for ownership structure as a percentage	x.x%			
Adjustment for ownership structure in dollars	$xxx			

---

1. Internal Revenue Service Revenue Ruling 59–60, Section 2, Background and Definitions ¶.02.

Subtotal	$xxx
Adjustment for marketability as a percentage	x.x%
Adjustment for marketability in dollars	$xxx
Estimated fair market value of a xx.x% interest	$xxx

APPENDIX

INTRODUCTION

APPROACH TO VALUATION

Our approach has been to determine an estimate of value which would provide a fair and reasonable return on investment under hypothetical sales conditions, in view of the facts available to us at the time. Our estimate of value is based on, among other things, our estimate of the risks facing the owners, the Company, and the return on investment which would be required on alternative investments with similar levels of risk at the valuation dates.

Both internal and external factors which influence the value of the Company were considered, analyzed, and interpreted. Internal factors include the Company's financial position, results of operations, and size. External factors include, among other things, the industry and the position of the Company relative to the industry. We considered a variety of valuation methods to value the Company. We believe that the discounted earnings method is the appropriate valuation method (see the Estimate of Value section for a more detailed explanation).

For purposes of the valuation of the Company, we have included a review, analysis, and interpretation of control associated with a xx.x% minority interest in the Company as of the valuation date.

For purposes of the valuation of the Company, we have included a review, analysis, and interpretation of marketability associated with a xx.x% minority interest in the Company as of the valuation date.

LIMITING CONDITIONS

This report is based on historical and prospective financial information provided to us by management and other third parties. In this valuation, we have relied on reviewed financial statements provided by the Company's CPA and financial projections developed by Company management. Had we audited or reviewed the underlying data, matters may have come to our attention that would have resulted in our using amounts which differ from those provided. Accordingly, we take no responsibility for the underlying data presented in this report. Users of this business valuation should be aware that business valuations are based on future earnings potential that may or may not materialize.

We have no present or contemplated financial interest in Occupational Health Care Company. Our fee for this valuation is based upon hourly billing rates and is in no way contingent upon the results of our findings. We have no responsibility to update this report for events and circumstances occurring subsequent to the date of this report.

This report has been prepared for the specific purpose of estimating the fair market value of a xx.x% interest in the Company, for the possible purchase/sale of Dr. Charles Chiu's xx.x% interest, and is intended for no other use. This report may not be used to obtain a loan, credit, or financing in any form. Furthermore, no aspect or conclusion of this report is meant to be construed as legal advice, or any other type of professional advice or counsel (such as tax, accounting, or investment advice), unless specifically stated to the contrary in this report. It is not to be copied or made available to any person(s) without the written consent of ValueNomics Research, Inc.

We have relied upon the representations of the Company's management and other third parties concerning the value and useful condition of all equipment, real estate leases, investments, and any other assets or liabilities except as specifically stated to the contrary in this report. We have not attempted to confirm whether or not all assets of the Company are free and clear of liens and encumbrances, or that the Company has good title to all assets. The estimate of value included in this report assumes that the existing business of the Company will achieve operational and financial goals as projected by management.

ValueNomics Research, Inc. does not purport to be a guarantor of value. Valuation of private, closely held companies is an imprecise science, with value being a matter of the interpretation of specific facts related to the company being valued, and reasonable people may differ in their estimates of value. ValueNomics® has, however, performed conceptually sound and commonly accepted methods and procedures of valuation in determining the estimate of value included in this report.

ValueNomics® and its employees are liable only to the client, and this liability is expressly limited to the amount of the fee for this engagement. ValueNomics® does not assume any liability, obligation, or accountability to any third party under any circumstances. The client agrees to hold ValueNomics® and its employees harmless in the event of a lawsuit initiated by any party other than the client.

BACKGROUND

GENERAL

Occupational Health Care Company is a medical service company that has provided high-quality, cost-effective outpatient occupational medical care to various companies since 198x. The Company provides occupational medical services to patients from its two medical centers in California: Occupational Health Care Clinic I in Berkeley, California and Occupational Health Care Clinic II in Richmond, California. Both of these clinics were founded in 198x. The Company is currently in the process of opening a new clinic in the San Francisco Bay Area. Furthermore, management is planning on opening two more clinics by the year 200x.

The medical services provided to employees of the Company's customers include treatment of occupational injuries, occupational therapy, drug screening, and physicals. Approximately xx.x% of patient fees are billed to insurers under workers compensation, while the remaining xx.x% is billed directly to employers requesting the services. Patient fees billed under workers compensation insurance are regulated by California state law. Patient fees billed to employers are based on negotiated rate and fee schedules.

Management is pursuing an aggressive growth strategy to increase market share of the occupational medicine in its region. This strategy will involve purchasing and buying other occupational medical clinics as well as opening new ones in the region.

In March of 199x, the Occupational Health Care Medical Group relinquished its certification as a professional medical corporation to form a management service organization (MSO) under the name Occupational Health Care Company. A different group called the Occupational Health Care Medical Group is the organization that employs the doctors of the Company.

OWNERSHIP AND STRUCTURE

Ownership

Owner	Percentage of Shares
Dr. Charles Chiu	xx.x%
Dr. Mary O'Leary	xx.x%

Legal Structure

Medical service organization (MSO), a California corporation

Tax Structure

Corporation (C corp)

NATIONAL ECONOMIC REVIEW[2]

GENERAL ECONOMIC OVERVIEW

Real gross domestic product ("real GDP"), the output of goods and services produced by labor and property located in the United States, increased at an annualized rate of xx.x%, or about $xxx billion, in the third quarter of 199x, according to preliminary estimates released by the Department of Commerce's Bureau of Economic Analysis ("BEA"). In the second quarter of 199x, revised growth in real GDP was xx.x%, or about $xxx billion, and higher than the originally reported annualized rate of xx.x%. Growth in real GDP for all of 199x was xx.x%, down from xx.x% and xx.x% for 199x and 199x, respectively, and the lowest since a xx.x% recessionary decline in 199x. According to the BEA, the third-quarter GDP results reflected a moderation in personal consumption expenditures and a downturn in government spending.

The Composite Index of Leading Economic Indicators, the government's primary forecasting gauge, ended the third quarter with a x.x increase in September to x.x (198x = 100), an all-time high for the measure, according to The Conference Board. The index attempts to gauge economic activity six to nine months in advance. Multiple consecutive moves in the same direction are said to be indicative of the general direction of the economy. The index has increased eight months consecutively and nine of the last ten months beginning with December of 199x. The increases of the last several months have been modestly lower than those measured in the first and second

---

2. Timothy L. Lee, National Economic Review, 3rd quarter 199x, Mercer Capital, 199x.

quarter, suggesting further moderation in growth during the rest of the year and throughout the first half of 199x.

Stock markets surged in September after recovering in August from a July plunge. Early volatility was attributed to speculation regarding the Federal Reserve's direction on monetary policy. Concerns about inflationary pressure from continuing strong growth and low unemployment prompted the markets' early-quarter declines. Late-quarter reports revealed less vigorous activity in several business and consumer segments and markets appeared to reach consensus that a prenational election shift in rate policy was a low probability. Given currently favorable near-term expectations, many analysts believe equity markets will remain at near-record levels but will likely exhibit higher volatility. Bond markets generally followed suit as yields dropped in July and August, sending prices higher. Midquarter revisions to several economic measures (showing higher than previously reported growth, etc.) sent yields back up where they leveled off on late-quarter reports of significant moderation in economic growth.

The consensus outlook for the economy through the end of 199x suggests modest growth with somewhat increasing inflationary pressures. Growth in GDP is estimated to be near or just above xx.x%, with inflation falling between xx.x% and xx.x% and unemployment levels remaining below xx.x%.

EMPLOYMENT

According to the Labor Department's Bureau of Labor Statistics, unemployment levels during the third quarter remained below the xx.x% levels measured during most of the first half of the year. The September unemployment rate was xx.x%, following xx.x% and xx.x% in July and August, respectively. Strong employment data, generally believed an indicator of higher future inflation, were the primary negative component in the financial markets, starting the quarter with generally higher than 199x job creation thus far in 199x. Most analysts estimate that unemployment levels below xx.x% are likely to persist through the end of 199x.

SUMMARY AND OUTLOOK

Economic growth, as measured by growth in GDP, slowed to xx.x% in the third quarter of 199x, after registering a vigorous xx.x% annualized rate in the second quarter. Consensus estimates of growth in GDP for 199x are xx.x%–xx.x%. After a dismal start in the third quarter, equity markets finished strongly, while bond pricing exhibited mixed directions throughout the period. Inflation results for the third quarter reflected a seasonally adjusted annualized rate of xx.x%, representing a respectable decrease from the second-quarter level of xx.x%. Inflation signals remain somewhat mixed but generally favorable enough that no eminent Federal Reserve action is expected in the near term. Many analysts and economists anticipate that overall inflation levels will fall in the xx.x%–xx.x% range for 199x.

The impact of the economy on occupational health care providers is explained in the Industry Overview section of this report.

INDUSTRY OVERVIEW: OCCUPATIONAL HEALTH

BACKGROUND

The American health care system is in a state of rapid change, brought about in equal measure by economic trends and by public policy imperatives. Increasingly, primary medical care in the United States is provided by groups of physicians and other health care providers organized into corporate entities. These entities market their services to groups of patients with common characteristics such as employer, residence, or demographic group. Today, these services are also increasingly likely to be paid for by a fixed fee (capitation allowance), with financial risk accepted by the provider rather than the third-party payer.

Occupational medicine is a field of preventive medicine concerned with the medical problems and practices related to the health of workers. The growth of managed care in traditional health settings has put pressure on the occupational health system to move toward a managed care model. The occupational health care industry is largely driven by workers compensation, in which physicians are usually compensated on a fee-for-service basis according to a state-determined schedule. Under the current workers compensation system, employers select physicians and approve treatments for injured workers, but only for 30 days. After 30 days, the employee can seek medical care elsewhere.

In 1993, California State Senate Bill 30 for Workers Compensation passed. This bill resulted in a series of radical reforms in the state's workers compensation model and opened the door to managed care by deregulating premium rates and stiffening penalties for fraud. In addition, the new legislation set up a certification procedure for so-called HCOs (health care organizations). HCOs are networks of physicians and other professionals who specialize in treating injured workers. Nearly every HMO (health maintenance organization) in California has attempted to set one up or find another way into the growing, billion-dollar workers comp business. Well-Point Health Networks Inc., Health Systems International Inc., and Kaiser Foundation Health Plan Inc. have all acquired a workers comp insurance company, become allied with one, or set up a network of occupational physicians.[3] Currently, however, the concept of HCOs has not had its desired effect, particularly in northern California. Critics say that the legislation is flawed because the legislation was designed to treat employees by the same medical group for 360 days; however, employees have the option to switch medical groups at specific times, even after zero days of treatment by the designated HCO.

OUTLOOK

"The clinical discipline of occupational medicine . . . underwent unprecedented rejuvenation in the 1980s," and is predicted to continue to improve through the 1990s.[4] The rise in occupational injuries shows no signs of slowing, especially with an increase in white collar injuries, such as carpal tunnel syndrome and chronic low back pain. Companies are spending millions in benefits, and are contracting with primary care doctors more than ever to help them stem these costs. Physicians are doing preplacement physicals, drug screening, and medical surveillance services, as well as the traditional evaluation and treatment of injuries or illness occurring in the workplace.

Occupational health specialists are evolving into a group of highly trained experts with widespread interdisciplinary knowledge. Despite increased demand, evidence indicates that there has been, and continues to be, a shortage of physicians with this expertise. At present, there is approximately one board-certified specialist for every 140,000 workers. This also raises the threat that in addition to a real deficit in trained occupational health specialists,

---

3. Rhonda L. Rundle, "Benefits: Mending Workers Comp in California," *Wall Street Journal,* August 17, 1995, p. 1B.
4. Philip L. Polakoff, "Agenda for Occupational Medicine Will Remain Full Throughout the 90's," *Occupational Health & Safety,* January 1992, p. 54.

some deficiency probably exists in the qualifications of many practicing physicians who spend a significant portion of their time in the field. The Institute of Medicine Subcommittee on the Physician Shortage in Occupational and Environmental Medicine places the deficit of trained professionals at 3100–5500 physicians, 1600–3500 fully trained specialists, and 1500–2000 primary care physicians with special competence in occupational medicine.[5]

Occupational health, perhaps more than any clinical specialty, is tied to the state of the economy. Correspondingly, regional occupational health practices are tied to the economic forecasts for the regions they serve and remain volatile to severe swings in employment. For example, California's East Bay economy is currently at high levels with low unemployment, and "there is an understanding that there is a void for this type of medicine [in the East Bay]."[6] The current trend in health care is consolidation, and occupational health care clinics are no exception. "Consolidation is the name of the game right now, and that's the direction we're headed."[7]

CONCLUSION

There is currently a high demand for quality occupational health care clinics, staffed by board-certified physicians. Clinics that provide quality care and have a strong reputation in their local communities will be able to gain a competitive edge over competitors. However, occupational health care remains a volatile industry, subject to workers compensation policies and rules dictated by the state government. "As community care networks emerge, the success of hospitals and other medical settings will depend on how well they establish partnerships for health promotion with local businesses, government agencies, and schools."[8] Important factors to the success of an occupational health clinic include client retention, a strong information system to manage programs for multiple

5. Jeffrey K. Pearson et al., "We're All Practicing Occupational Medicine," *Patient Care*, 30:3, February 15, 1996, p. 42(12).
6. Pete Barlas, "Health Care Firms Vying to Lead in Occupational Medicine," *Business Journal–San Jose*, April 24, 1995, Sec. 1, p. 5.
7. Interview of Bob Cimasi, "A New `Paradigm' in Health Care: Current Trends in Medical Practice Consolidation," *Shannon Pratt's Business Valuation Update*, 10:10, October 1996.
8. Daniel Stokols, Kenneth R. Pelletier, and Jonathan E. Fielding, "Integration of Medical Care and Worksite Health Promotion," *Journal of the American Medical Association*, April 12, 1995, p. 1143.

employers, effective internal protocols and quality control, and strong leadership that stays in the forefront and educates the business community on emerging issues in occupational health.

FINANCIAL ANALYSIS

The source documents for our financial analysis of the business are the Company's reviewed financial statements (which were prepared by the Company's certified public accountant) for the four years from January 199x to December 199x. We also used an interim 199x financial statement (prepared by the Company bookkeeper) for the 10-month period ended October 31, 199x. After analyzing the 199x financial statements and the 199x interim statement, we determined that it was appropriate to use the interim 199x financial statement in conducting our analysis, as October 31, 199x is the valuation date. We annualized the 199x interim profit and loss statement. We adjusted the financial statements as described in the Estimate of Value section of this report. The following financial analysis is based on the Company's adjusted financial statements.

BALANCE SHEET

As of October 31, 199x, the Company's total assets were approximately $xxx million. Current assets totaled $xxx, or xx.x% of total assets. The Company's primary current asset is accounts receivable, which has historically been in the range of xx.x% to xx.x% of total assets. This high level of accounts receivable could signal risk in the event of a question about the quality of the receivables.

The current ratio and the quick ratio are measures of liquidity. These calculations provide evidence of the Company's ability to meet its short-term obligations. The Company's current and quick ratios were both equal to x.x:x as of October 31, 199x.

Total current liabilities of the Company are approximately $xxx, or xx.x% of total assets, while long-term debt is $xxx, or xx.x% of total assets. Stockholders equity constitutes xx.x% of total assets, or $xxx.

INCOME STATEMENT

The Company's adjusted net revenues have increased over the five-year period from approximately $xx.x million in 199x to an annualized figure of $xxx million in 199x, a compounded growth rate of xx.x%.

The Company's most significant cost as a percentage of revenue is salaries and wages. Salaries have been variable, accounting for anywhere between xx.x% and xx.x% of revenues, averaging xx.x% over the five-year period considered.

The Company reported favorable profitability over the past five years, on an adjusted basis. Earnings before depreciation, interest, and taxes (EBDIT) has an average compounded rate of xx.x%. EBDIT was $xxx in 199x and grew to an annualized $xxx in 199x. As a percentage of revenue, earnings before depreciation, interest, and taxes has averaged xx.x% over this period.

ESTIMATE OF VALUE

DISCOUNTED EARNINGS METHOD

We utilized the widely accepted discounted earnings method to estimate the value of Occupational Health Care Company. This method is an income-oriented approach and is based on the theory that the value of a business or an interest in a business is contingent upon the future benefits that will accrue to it. In other words, the total value of a business is the present value of its projected future earnings, plus the present value of the terminal value. The projected future earnings and the terminal value are discounted back to the valuation date, using a discount rate commensurate with the risk associated with the prospective economic income stream. The discounted earnings method is the valuation method used most frequently in the merger and acquisition arena for pricing/valuation issues.[9]

Adjustments

Company management developed a projection for a five-year period beginning at the valuation date. ValueNomics® made normalizing adjustments to revenues and expenses. ValueNomics® analyzed the major underlying assumptions in the projected revenues and expenses and reconciled these assumptions with external data.

---

9. Shannon P. Pratt, *Valuing a Business: The Analysis and Appraisal of Closely Held Companies*, Homewood, IL: Business One Irwin, 1989, p. 152.

In general, the assumptions were consistent with and corroborated by the external data employed in the analysis.

Some assumptions in management's model to project future revenues, expenses, and profits are:

1. The Company will continue to invest in the overhead of a CEO and certain marketing and administration expenses.

2. The opening of a new clinic next year will temporarily increase certain expenses (e.g., start-up salaries) as a percentage of revenues, causing a one-time drop in earnings for the fiscal year. As future capacity needs arise, new clinics will be opened or current clinic capacity will be expanded with more optimal timing to minimize short-term earnings variances.

3. The Company will achieve some economies of scale and efficiencies which will lower labor costs as a percentage of revenues over the next five years. The decline in labor as a percentage of revenues will also occur because of the fixed nature of some general and administrative expenses (i.e., officers compensation or corporate management office facilities).

4. The Company's revenues will grow faster than expenses as a result of increased fees for workers compensation services. The Industrial Medical Council of the Department of Workers Compensation, a government agency, is responsible for setting the fees for workers compensation. These fees have not increased for the past 14 years, and the council will recommend an increase in fees for workers compensation in the near future.

5. The Company is adequately capitalized to fund the growth.

ValueNomics® made the following adjustments to the Company's projected earnings to arrive at the adjusted projected earnings discounted in this valuation:

1. We removed depreciation, interest, and taxes from the Company's projected earnings to arrive at earnings before depreciation, interest, and taxes (EBDIT). EBDIT is widely accepted and used by analysts and acquisitions managers in this industry niche.

2. We adjusted the compensation of officers and key members of management to an industry living wage.

3. We amortized forward the extra start-up phase salaries related to the opening of a new clinic in 199x by xxx years.

Adjustments 2 and 3 above convert the Company's projection from a projection of accounting earnings to a projection of economic earnings.

Discount Rate

These projected earnings and the terminal value were then discounted back to a present value by a before-tax discount rate of xx.x%. This discount rate was developed using market evidence and interviews of industry experts, and corroborated via the Black/Green Buildup Summation Method.[10]

We conducted interviews of key individuals in this industry, including acquisitions directors of national occupation health care providers, including TheraTx, Meridian Occupational Healthcare Associates, Occusystems, and the Company Doctor. Our interviews of these individuals provided strong evidence for the type of earnings we used and the discount rate we developed. The type of earnings that these industry experts use to value occupational health care clinics is earnings before depreciation, interest, and taxes, which is the type of earnings we used to value Occupational Health Care Company. The valuation method mentioned most frequently during our interviews was the capitalization of earnings method. These industry experts stated that occupational health care providers are currently being valued at a multiple between xxx to xxx times EBDIT. The interviewees stated that a clinic with a strong reputation and the profile of the subject Company would sell at a multiple in the upper end of the range. A multiple of xxx to xxx translates into a capitalization rate in the range of xx.x% to xx.x%.

We did not, however, use the capitalization of earnings method to value the Company. The capitalization of earnings method, which is basically the same as applying a multiple to a single earnings amount, was considered and rejected for the following reason.

---

10. Black & Isom Associates, *Business Valuation: Fundamental, Techniques & Theory,* Salt Lake City, Utah: National Association of Certified Valuation Analysts, 1995, Ch. 5, pp. 19–23.

Occupational Health Care Company   March 9, 199x   Page 12

This method works well provided that "the economic income variable is expected to have a constant average annually compounded rate of growth in perpetuity."[11] This is not the case for Occupational Health Care Company, where economic income is expected to grow at a fairly strong rate in the short run, and then level off to a more stable long-term growth rate after five years. We do capitalize earnings at the end of the five-year period, because earnings are then expected to grow at a constant rate of x%. This is a more typical application of capitalizing earnings. Since companies rarely grow at a constant rate in the short run, the capitalization of earnings model is "often used only as one stage of a multistage discounted economic income model. For example, it is common to make specific income forecasts for some period (often, five years or until the company is expected to reach a reasonable stable state), and then use the constant growth model to reflect income expectations from that point onward."[12]

Capitalizing "is a process applied to an amount representing some measure of economic income for some single period to convert that economic income amount to an estimate of present value."[13] Because this method capitalizes a single measure of economic income, we believe it is not an appropriate method to use, since it does not capture the Company's relatively high growth projected for the short run. Instead, we used the discounted earnings method. This method is a more appropriate technique to use when relatively high growth is expected for a number of years prior to more stabilized growth in the long run. With this method, earnings "forecasts should be continued until a point at which the anticipated rate of growth has stabilized. Widely accepted practice is to cause the interim period to be five years."[14] The discount rate is a market-driven rate that measures the degree of risk associated with the discounted period.

We have selected xx.x% as the discount rate. This discount rate was based upon the following factors: (1) the market capitalization rate described above; (2) the reputation of the Company in its market area, as determined by interviews of hiring managers of occupational health care clinics; (3) the strength of the education, training, and

---

11. Pratt, p. 161.
12. Ibid.
13. Ibid., p. 159.
14. Textbook for BV202, Business Valuation Methodology Course, American Society of Appraisers, October 1994, p. 42.

experience of the Company's management; (4) the Company's protocols and other positive factors increasing organizational capital;[15] and (5) the strong regional economy. We also corroborated our discount rate via the Black/Green Buildup Summation Method.[16]

The development of a discount rate using the Black/Green buildup summation method is driven by "(a) risk, and (b) actual circumstances specific to the subject company as of the valuation date. [This method considers the following factors, which contribute to risk:] competition, financial strength, management's ability and depth, profitability and stability of earnings, and economic conditions."[17] We developed a discount rate of xx.x% using this method, which serves to further support our use of a xx.x% discount rate.

Estimated Fair Market Value of a xx.x% Minority Interest in the Company: Discounted Earnings Method

We began with the projected net income based on Company management's model for the years 199x through 199x. We adjusted each projected year for income taxes, interest expense, depreciation, officers compensation, and amortization to arrive at an adjusted EBDIT of $xxx. The present value of this amount is $xxx. To this value, we added the present value of the terminal value, which is $xxx. Summing these two amounts results in $xxx, which is our estimated investment value[18] of a 100% interest in Occupational Health Care Company. The value of a xx.x% interest in the Company is $xxx, before adjustments for control and marketability. To arrive at the fair market value of the minority interest, adjustments must be made for control and marketability.

CONTROL

"Minority stock interests in a 'closed' corporation are usually worth much less than the proportionate share of the assets to which

---

15. Bradford Cornell, *Corporate Valuation: Tools for Effective Appraisal and Decision Making,* Burr Ridge, IL: Irwin, 1993, pp. 23–25.
16. Black & Isom Associates, pp. 19–23.
17. Gary E. Jones, "Using the Black/Green Approach to the Buildup Summation Method," *CPA Litigation Services Counselor,* April 1994, p. 2.
18. Pratt, p. 25. Investment value is defined as "the specific value of goods or services to a particular investor (or class of investors) based on individual investment requirements."

they attach."[19] Valuing the transfer of a minority interest in a private closely held company therefore requires the consideration of a control adjustment, which is applied to the transfer of a minority interest, to reflect the absence of the power of control.

Block of Securities Being Transferred

A xx.x% minority interest of the common stock of the Company.

Board of Directors

The Bylaws of the Company provide for two directors. The directors are Dr. Charles Chiu and Ms. Mary O'Leary.

Officers

The officers of the Company are Dr. Charles Chiu and Ms. Mary O'Leary. Together, these officers set employee compensation, determine operational policy, select the individuals and companies with whom they do business as customers and vendors, award contracts, and manage the Company.

Estimate of the Control Adjustment

A technique used to quantify the control adjustment is to determine the control premium actually paid for businesses in the same industry. The market value of a publicly traded security reflects the fact that most trades involve a minority interest. Conversely, the price of an offer seeking a controlling interest is usually higher than the price paid for a minority interest. The higher price reflects the value of the premium for control. *Mergerstat Review* reports annual figures for (1) the median market premium in which price was disclosed and (2) the average premium offered above the per share price of a minority interest for a specific industry. We began with the median market premium, and found that in 199x the median market control premium was xx.x%. We then adjusted this number by the ratio of the average health services industry control premium to the total or overall industry control premium, which is

---

19. Cravens v. Welch, 10 Federal Supplement 94, 1935.

x.x (=xx.x%/xx.x%). The result is an adjusted median market control premium of xx.x% (xx.x% multiplied by x.x). The corresponding control discount is xx.x% (Exhibit B).[20]

Having examined the level of control adjustments in the health services industry, we analyzed the Company at the time of valuation to adjust for company-specific factors. "The value of control depends on the shareholders' ability to exercise any or all of a variety of rights typically associated with control."[21] To the extent that the shares being gifted or transferred will or will not have these rights, the adjustment should be decreased or increased accordingly. The powers typically associated with control of a company include the following:

Common prerogatives of control:[22]

1. Elect directors and appoint management.
2. Determine management compensation and perquisites.
3. Set policy and change the course of business.
4. Acquire or liquidate assets.
5. Select vendors and contractors.
6. Make acquisitions of other companies.
7. Liquidate, dissolve, sell out, or recapitalize the company.
8. Sell or acquire treasury shares.
9. Register the company's stock for public offering.
10. Declare and pay dividends.
11. Change the articles of incorporation or bylaws.

As a minority shareholder with a xx.x% interest in stock, the recipient of the transferred shares of common stock will not have control over the Company. However, the articles of incorporation provide the owners of at least one-third of the common stock with certain powers. Specifically, a one-third owner has the power to elect a director to the board and to veto mergers, acquisitions, and/or the sale of treasury stock, or any other action that would dilute the percentage ownership of his or her interest below a one-third interest. These powers reduce the size of the control adjustment for the xx.x%

---

20. The formula for converting a control premium to a control discount is
     $1 - (1/(1 + \text{Median Control Premium}))$.
21. Ibid., Ch. 8, p. 18.
22. Pratt, pp. 55–56.

interest being valued. However, the hypothetical owner of a xx.x% interest does not have the power to unilaterally do any of the 11 prerogatives of control listed above.

Furthermore, the owner of a xx.x% minority interest in a California corporation has the power to sue for dissolution of the corporation under California Corporations Code Section 2000. This is a prerogative of control that the owner of a one-third shareholder interest has outright. The owner of a one-third shareholder interest can sue for dissolution under Section 2000 without having to prove wrongdoing on the part of the majority shareholders or the other shareholders in control. This gives the owner of a xx.x% minority interest more control over the Company in California.

The hypothetical owners of a xx.x% interest in the Company's common stock will have more influence and management powers of the company than a typical minority shareholder of a public company. As a result, the adjustment for lack of control for the subject xx.x% minority interest will be less than the control discount derived from the Mergerstat data. The owners of the transferred shares should have more control than a minority shareholder in a publicly traded corporation. However, the owner of the xx.x% minority interest is a minority shareholder, who does not have outright control of the corporation. Therefore, we are reducing the median market adjustment of xx.x% by xx.x% to calculate the discount for control for the shares to be transferred in Occupational Health Care Company. The final adjustment for control is xx.x% (Exhibit B).

MARKETABILITY

"By definition, ownership interests in closely held companies are typically not readily marketable compared to similar interests in public companies."[23] The degree to which this statement is true can vary materially depending on many factors: a company's stage of evolution at the time an owner of stock is transferring interest, probability of a public offering, dividend history, and size of the block. Where a company is at any one point in time in its evolutionary path is best demonstrated by the facts in evidence through

---

23. Jay E. Fishman et al., Guide to Business Valuations, Fort Worth, TX: Practitioners Publishing Company, March 1994, ¶ 815.22.

financial records and other company documents (like board of directors' meeting minutes).

There have been many studies regarding adjustments for lack of marketability (Williamette Management Associates, Robert Baird & Co., Standard Research Consultants, Maher, Moroney, Trout, Gelman, Milton, and the Institutional Investor Study Report of the Securities and Exchange Commission), circa 199x back to 196x. These studies varied in their findings with average and/or median adjustments in the range of xx% to xx%, which is strong empirical evidence that a substantial adjustment exists. The amount of the adjustment is measured quantitatively by the profile of the company being valued at the date of valuation and by how a willing buyer and willing seller will most likely negotiate a price for the shares.

The purpose is to express an adjustment to value to reflect the ownership interest in a private, closely held company which does not have an institutional marketplace for sales and or transfers.

COMPANY-SPECIFIC FACTORS AFFECTING MARKETABILITY

Probability of Public Offering

Evidence suggests that as the probability of a public offering of a company's shares of stock increases the adjustment related to liquidity of the investment decreases. However, this adjustment will most likely still be material if the shares being offered for registration must be sold prior to the initial public offering (IPO). There is also the probability that shares which remain unregistered at the time of the IPO will subsequently suffer a material adjustment from the public market price if they are sold prior to registration or if there is the maturing of some restriction on transfer.

We must look to the profile of the Company at the time of valuation. According to Company management, the Company had no discussions or prospects in the near future regarding going public. There is no market for shares of stock in a private, closely held company. Thus the liquidity of the ownership interest in the shares being transferred is materially impaired.

Restrictions on Sale

There are no restrictions on the sale of the Company stock.

Occupational Health Care Company   March 9, 199x   Page 18

Evidence of a Market

There is no market for a minority shareholder's common shares of stock owned in this Company. However, given the industry trends of merger and consolidation, it is not unreasonable to expect a greater interest in the industry on the part of companies and investors. However, we do not believe that there are currently potential purchasers interested in buying a minority interest in the Company. Therefore, there is no evidence of a market for the shares being transferred.

Dividend History

The Company did not make any dividend payments during the five-year period analyzed.

Size of the Block Transferred

At the valuation date, the Company had one class of stock. The size of the block of stock being valued is a xx.x% minority interest.

Estimation of Marketability Adjustment

The marketability adjustment related to the transfer of common stock shares owned by a hypothetical individual investor in the Company (seller) to a willing buyer is materially impacted by the Company's private, closely held nature, lack of a market, and lack of a prospect for the Company to go public at any time in the foreseeable future. The best data for the marketability adjustment come from transactions between buyers and sellers of stock.

Two types of studies have been done to quantify the lack-of-marketability adjustment. One group of studies used empirical data from the transactions of letter stocks, which are identical to openly traded stock of public companies except that the letter stock cannot be traded on the open market for a specific period of time. As Securities and Exchange Commission Accounting Release No. 113 states, "Restricted securities are often purchased at a discount, frequently substantial, from the market price of outstanding unrestricted securities of the same class. This reflects the fact that securities which cannot be readily sold in the public market place are less valuable than securities which can be sold. . . . " At the time of the letter stock transaction, the purchaser of the stock knows that at some future date (usually two years or less when the restrictions expire) there will be an established market where the shares can be traded. This is not the case for the shares of private, closely held companies such as the Company. Therefore, the marketability discount will be smaller for letter stocks than for the stocks of companies in which there may never be a market for the stock, all other factors being equal.

The second group of studies are private transaction studies, which compare the price of a company's stock during private stock transactions with the stock price at the time of the subsequent initial public offering.

The difference between the private and public price per share measures the adjustment for the lack of marketability, since no public market exists for the shares of a company's stock prior to the IPO. This technique will result in a more accurate marketability adjustment for private, closely held companies than the approach used in the aforementioned letter stock studies. However, if the private transactions took place within a few months of the IPO, there is a reasonable chance that the buyer knew about the high probability of a public market for the shares in the near future. To the extent that this is true, the marketability adjustments reported in these studies will underestimate this adjustment for the stock of the subject Company.

We believe that some of the best private transactions studies that quantified the adjustment for the lack of marketability were conducted by Williamette Management Associates and Robert Baird & Co. These studies used only transactions that were conducted on an arm's-length basis, which is appropriate for this fair market value valuation. These studies employed more appropriate and sophisticated research methodologies than other private transactions studies used to calculate the marketability adjustment.

A total of x Williamette studies were conducted over a period of x years, from 197x to 199x. The range of median adjustments in these studies was xx.x% to xx.x%.[24] In 199x, the median discount was xx.x%. More timely data are available from a study conducted by Robert W. Baird & Co., a company involved in the pricing of initial public offerings, that has performed seven marketability adjustment studies from 198x through 199x. The range of median adjustments in these studies are from xx.x% to xx.x%.[25] The most recent study was

24. Fishman, March 1995, Exhibit 8–18.
25. Ibid., Exhibit 8–17.

published in the December 199x issue of *Business Valuation Review.* This study determined a median pre-IPO discount of xx.x% for the time period from January 199x through June 199x.

We believe that the adjustment negotiated between a hypothetical willing buyer and willing seller would be approximate to xx.x%, given the specific facts and circumstances for Occupational Health Care Company. We believe that using the median adjustment is a conservative technique to estimate the lack-of-marketability adjustment for the Company, because the market evidence is from corporations that are likely to go public in the near future, which is not the case for the subject Company.

CONCLUSION

We began with the value of the xx.x% interest in the Company, before adjustments for control and marketability, of $xxx. To arrive at the fair market value of the xx.x% interest, we subtracted the control adjustment of $xxx (xx.x% of $xxx) from $xxx to arrive at a subtotal of $xxx. The marketability adjustment of xx.x% is then applied to this subtotal, which results in an adjustment of $xxx (xx.x% of $xxx). Subtracting this adjustment from the subtotal results in our estimated fair market value of a xx.x% interest in Occupational Health Care Company using the discounted earnings method of $xxx (Exhibit A).

Occupational Health Care Company   March 9, 199x   Page 20

LIMITED-SCOPE VALUATION

Valuation of
Semiconductor Corporation

Valuation date, December 31, 199x

Prepared by
ValueNomics Research, Inc.

March 9, 199x

Gary E. Jones
Certified Valuation Analyst

Dirk E. Van Dyke
Senior Quantitative Analyst

Alisa S. Marienthal
Senior Analyst

Mr. Robert Simmons, President
Semiconductor Corporation
1050 Technology Lane
Silicon Valley, CA 90000

Dear Mr. Simmons:

We have prepared and enclosed, herewith, our Ltd. Scope Valuation^{SM} of Semiconductor Corporation (a California Corporation, "the Company"), dated March 1, 199x. The purpose of the valuation is to render an estimate as to the fair market value of a x% interest in the Company as of December 31, 199x, the valuation date. The term "fair market value" is defined as:

> ... the price at which the property would change hands between a willing buyer and a willing seller when the former is not under any compulsion to buy and the latter is not under any compulsion to sell, both parties having reasonable knowledge of relevant facts. Court decisions frequently state in addition that the hypothetical buyer and seller are assumed to be able, as well as willing, to trade and be well informed about the property and concerning the market for such property[1]

This report has been prepared for the purpose of estimating the value of a x% shareholder interest in the Company for estate and gift tax purposes, and is intended for no other use.

On the basis of our study and analytical review procedures, we have concluded that a reasonable estimate of the fair market

---

1. Internal Revenue Service Revenue Ruling 59–60, Section 2, background and definitions, ¶.02.

value of a x% interest in the Company as of December 31, 199x, is $xxx (Exhibit A).

ValueNomics Research, Inc.

Gary E. Jones, President
Cupertino, CA
March 1, 199x

E X E C U T I V E   S U M M A R Y

Value of a x% interest in the Company prior to adjustments		$xxx
ADJUSTMENTS		
Equity interest before ownership and marketability adjustments		$xxx
OWNERSHIP STRUCTURE		
Lack of control as a percentage	xx.x%	
Lack of control in dollars		$xxx
Subtotal after lack of control		$xxx
MARKETABILITY		
Factors affecting marketability as a percentage	xx.x%	
Factors affecting marketability in dollars		$xxx
Estimated fair market value of a x% equity interest in the Company		$xxx

T A B L E   O F   C O N T E N T S

APPROACH TO VALUATION

Our approach has been to determine, on a Ltd. Scope Valuation^{SM} basis, an estimate of value which would provide a fair and reasonable return on investment to a buyer, in view of the facts available to us at the time. Our opinion is based on, among other things, our estimate of the risks facing the Company and the return on investment which would be required on alternative investments with similar levels of risk.

Both internal and external factors which influence the value of the Company were reviewed, analyzed, and interpreted on a limited basis. Internal factors include the Company's financial position, results of operations, and size. External factors include, among other things, the status of the industry and the position of the Company relative to the industry.

This valuation was performed under the assumption that a noncontrolling interest in the Company is being gifted. Therefore, as we are valuing a x% noncontrolling interest, we have made an adjustment for control.

For purposes of the valuation of the Company, we have included a review, analysis, and interpretation on marketability associated with the Company as of the valuation date.

LIMITING CONDITIONS

This report is based on historical and prospective financial information provided to us by management and other third parties. In this valuation, we have relied on reviewed financial statements provided by the Company's CPA and financial projections developed by Company management. Had we audited or reviewed the underlying data, matters may have come to our attention that would have resulted in our using amounts which differ from those provided. Accordingly, we take no responsibility for the underlying data presented in this report. Users of this business valuation should be aware that business valuations are based on future earnings potential that may or may not materialize.

We have no present or contemplated financial interest in Semiconductor Corporation. Our fee for this valuation is based upon hourly billing rates and is in no way contingent upon the results of our findings. We have no responsibility to update this report for events and circumstances occurring subsequent to the date of this report.

This report has been prepared for the specific purpose of estimating the fair market value of a xx.x% interest in the Company, for gift tax purposes, and is intended for no other use. This report may not be used to obtain a loan, credit, or financing in any form. Furthermore, no aspect or conclusion of this report is meant to be construed as legal advice, or any other type of professional advice or counsel (such as tax, accounting, or investment

Semiconductor Corporation   March 1, 199x   Page 1 advice), unless specifically stated to the contrary in this report. It is not to be copied or made available to any person(s) without the written consent of ValueNomics Research, Inc.

We have relied upon the representations of the Company's management and other third parties concerning the value and useful condition of all equipment, real estate leases, investments, and any other assets or liabilities except as specifically stated to the contrary in this report. We have not attempted to confirm whether or not all assets of the Company are free and clear of liens and encumbrances, or that the Company has good title to all assets. The estimate of value included in this report assumes that the existing business of the Company will achieve operational and financial goals as projected by management.

ValueNomics Research, Inc. does not purport to be a guarantor of value. Valuation of private, closely held companies is an imprecise science, with value being a matter of the interpretation of specific facts related to the company being valued, and reasonable people may differ in their estimates of value. ValueNomics® has, however, performed conceptually sound and commonly accepted methods and procedures of valuation in determining the estimate of value included in this report.

ValueNomics® and its employees are liable only to the client, and this liability is expressly limited to the amount of the fee for this engagement. ValueNomics® does not assume any liability, obligation, or accountability to any third party under any circumstances. The client agrees to hold ValueNomics® and its employees harmless in the event of a lawsuit initiated by any party other than the client.

BACKGROUND

HISTORY OF COMPANY AND NATURE OF OPERATIONS

Semiconductor Corporation was founded in 197x, with 100% equity interest owned by Robert Simmons. In 199x, Robert Simmons gave a xx% interest to John Simmons. The Company is an electronics components packaging company. Specifically, The Company offers (1) automated vision inspection for electronic components, whereby chips are optically inspected for proper labeling and setting; and (2) tape and reel, a process which transfers components from one form of packaging to another—generally from trays to plastic reels—for use in automated surface-mount assembly.

The Company began operations in Boston, Massachusetts and moved to the current Silicon Valley, California facility in 199x. Semiconductor Processing Corporation employs a total of xxx persons.

OWNERSHIP STRUCTURE

Robert Simmons   xx %
John Simmons   xx %

NATIONAL ECONOMIC REVIEW[2]

GENERAL ECONOMIC OVERVIEW

Real gross domestic product ("real GDP"), the output of goods and services produced by labor and assets located in the United States, increased at an annualized rate of x.x%, or about $xx billion, in the third quarter of 199x, according to preliminary estimates released by the Department of Commerce's Bureau of Economic Analysis ("BEA"). In the second quarter of 199x, revised growth in real GDP was x.x%, or about $xx.x billion, and higher than the originally reported annualized rate of x.x%. Growth in real GDP for all of 199x was x.x%, down from x.x% and x.x% for 199x and 199x, respectively, and the lowest since a x.x% recessionary decline in 199x. According to the BEA, the third-quarter GDP results reflected a moderation in personal consumption expenditures and a downturn in government spending.

The Composite Index of Leading Economic Indicators, the government's primary forecasting gauge, ended the third quarter with a x.x increase in September to xxx.x (198x = 100), an all-time high for the measure, according to The Conference Board. The index attempts to gauge economic activity six to nine months in advance. Multiple consecutive moves in the same direction are said to be indicative of the general direction of the economy. The index has increased x months consecutively and x of the last x months beginning with December of 199x. The increases of the last several months have been modestly lower than those measured in the first and second quarter, suggesting further moderation in growth during the rest of the year and throughout the first half of 199x.

The consensus outlook for the economy through the end of 199x suggests modest growth with somewhat increasing inflationary pressures. Growth in GDP is estimated to be near or just above x.x%, with inflation falling between x.x% and x.x% and unemployment levels remaining below x.x%.

SUMMARY AND OUTLOOK

Economic growth, as measured by growth in GDP, slowed to x.x% in the third quarter of 199x, after registering a vigorous x.x% annualized

---

2. Timothy L. Lee, *National Economic Review*, 3rd quarter 1996, Mercer Capital, 1996.

rate in the second quarter. Consensus estimates of growth in GDP for 199x are x.x%–x.x%. Inflation results for the third quarter reflected a seasonally adjusted annualized rate of x.x%, representing a respectable decrease from the second quarter level of x.x%. Inflation signals remain somewhat mixed but generally favorable enough that no eminent Federal Reserve action is expected in the near term. Many analysts and economists anticipate overall inflation levels will fall in the x.x%–x.x% range for 199x.

INDUSTRY OUTLOOK—COMPONENTS PROCESSING

SEMICONDUCTOR BOOM

Chip making has long gone through boom-and-bust cycles every three years or so, affected not only by fluctuations in the economic cycle, but also by price volatility. However, the market has been uncharacteristically strong for four consecutive years, peaking with a sales jump of xx% in 199x. And while growth in 199x is not anticipated to match that of 199x, according to the Semiconductor Industry Association, "199x shapes up as the fourth consecutive year of xx%-plus growth."[3]

Furthermore, analysts believe that the outlook is steady growth until the year 200x,[4] resulting in an estimated worldwide market of $xxx to $xxx billion.[5] "Red-hot demand from PC-oriented, communications, consumer, and other related markets is fueling an expansion already several years old that so far has defied traditional expectations of a weakening in the business cycle. While many cite the caveat that nothing can last forever, it is frequently noted that the PC-telecom-multimedia explosion has created the strongest domestic consumer manufacturing base since . . . decades ago."[6]

A key reason for the smoothing of the traditional boom-and-bust cycles has been the use of chips in a growing variety of products. In the automotive industry, for example, electronics are used for air bags, antilock brakes, and security equipment. In addition,

---

3. Robert D. Hoff and Otis Port, "Silicon Goes from Peak to Peak," *Business Week*, January 8, 1996, p. 95.
4. Ibid.
5. Bernard Levine, "Bookings Solid, but Some `Feel' Caution Needed," *Electronic News*, May 15, 1995, p.1(3).
6. Ibid.

semiconductors are used in cars for engine management, audio systems, and automatic speedometers. In fact, today's cars contain an average of $xxx of semiconductors per vehicle."[7]

Another potentially lucrative market for semiconductors is the arrival of high-definition television ("HDTV") in the United States, estimated to occur in early 199x. This technology, which yields a picture that is four to five times as clear as the image on today's television sets, is expected by many to create a wave of consumer spending for televisions. The HDTV technology is also likely to have applications ranging from medical imaging to computer graphics. The technology requires huge amounts of semiconductors, and it has been estimated that the demand for chips for this use could reach $x billion within a decade.[8]

Computers will continue to provide much of the semiconductor industry's growth in the mid–1990s. New products like the laptop computer and penetration of foreign markets mean growth for the computer industry. The semiconductor content of computers has risen sharply in the past decade. By 199x, a high-end personal computer contained $xxx worth of semiconductors, although the average was $xxx–$xxx.[9]

There are many growing applications for advance electronics—from telecommunications to computer networking to "smart" phones and credit cards—which will most likely spur strong and steady growth until the beginning of the next century.

MINITURIZATION AND SURFACE-MOUNT TECHNOLOGY

The new wave in electronics manufacturing is surface-mount technology (SMT), a technique involving soldering components directly onto the surface of printed circuit boards in contrast to the traditional method of inserting leads or wires through holes in a substrate. "In the past, a lot of parts were surface mount, but many were not. Users still needed some through-hole components, but now, more and more, boards are totally surface mount. Over the past year, it has been noticeable."[10] Indeed, surface mounting was used in xx% of

---

7. *Standard & Poor's Industry Survey*, August 3, 1995, p. E29.

8. Ibid., p. E30.

9. Ibid.

10. Bernard Levine, "Surface Mount Takes Charge," *Electronic News*, May 16, 1994, p. 1.

integrated circuits in 199x, up from xx% in 199x, according to Integrated Circuits Engineering Corp. (ICE). As recently as 199x, that figure was approximately xx%. Fully xx% of integrated circuit packages are likely to be surface mounted in 199x.[11]

Using surface-mount technology, a manufacturer is able to place components more closely together and can mount components on both sides of a board. The result is boards that can be as much as xx% smaller than conventional boards and that can weigh nearly xx% less, while providing higher performance.[12] Because surface-mount components take up less space, the technology has allowed for a new level of part downsizing to satisfy the extreme miniaturization demands of cellular phones, pagers, and other new hand-held gear. "The drive to miniaturize products in many market segments is fueling the need for technologies that deliver yesterday's performance in increasingly smaller packages."[13]

SURFACE-MOUNT TECHNOLOGY AND TAPE AND REEL

As surface-mount technology has expanded, so too has the demand for surface-mount devices that can be used in automated assembly, resulting in higher output and cost savings. New developments in surface-mount design, including miniaturization, are allowing surface-mount devices to be processed with standard "pick and place" assembly equipment: "Design advances in pick-and-place machines are broadening the types of surface-mount components that can be handled."[14] All pick-and-place machines work in conjunction with various packaging systems for holding components. The standard carrier tape-and-reel system, whereby components are placed on large reels, is "one of the most preferred packaging systems."[15]

Tape-and-reel packaging has recently been identified among leading technologies due for standardization in the National Electronics Manufacturing Initiative ("NEMI"), an effort by top

---

11. Ibid., p. E32.
12. Ibid.
13. Jeffrey Coz, "Pegging Payoffs to Four Industry P's," *Electronic Engineering Times,* August 28, 1995, p. 46(2).
14. Henry Collins and Tom Clerici, "Surface-Mount Connectors: Not the Odd Form Anymore," *Surface-Mount Technology,* July 1994, p. 36.
15. Ibid., p. 37.

electronics vendors to devise a universal road map for assembly. Furthermore, the Electronics Industry Association, a leading trade organization, has produced a set of Standards for Tape-and-Reel Processing of Surface-Mount Devices.[16]

OUTLOOK

Many large semiconductor manufacturers have incorporated tape-and-reel systems into their surface-mount component assembly processes. In addition, a number of testing houses—companies conducting electrical testing of semiconductors—appear to be moving in the direction of adding tape and reel to the services they provide. However, thus far this market has been dominated by small and midsized contractors that specialize in tape and reel and have responded most effectively to demand. In the short term, we anticipate that there will be growth in this arena by already existing vendors, particularly those that differentiate themselves either by offering superior services, such as minimized manual handling of components, quick turnaround times, and increased security protection, or by offering value-added services like vision inspection and consulting.

In the long run, if profitability and demand continue to grow for this niche service, we anticipate that any number of competitive shifts would take place: (1) the larger testing houses would focus more resources in this direction; (2) semiconductor manufacturers would strengthen this function internally; (3) end users would begin to perform internal tape and reel; or (4) a greater number of small, specialized tape-and-reel companies would enter the market. There are few significant barriers to entry. Tape-and-reel processing does not depend upon a heavily proprietary system or highly skilled labor. The largest barrier to entry is the need for technologically current machinery, requiring significant capital outlays; but leases are available for equipment purchases. Therefore, we expect competition to increase, a trend that should decrease profitability in the medium run.

We anticipate moderate to strong growth for the next three to five years, when the competitive environment for tape-and-reel services would likely see shifts as described above. Furthermore, in

---

16. Ronald Cofer, "Choosing a Tape-and-Reel Contracting Service," *Surface-Mount Technology*, May 1992.

an industry characterized by rapid technological change, there is the possibility that surface-mount processes and/or tape-and-reel packaging might be made obsolete by technological change. We used this information in our Estimate of Value section.

FINANCIAL REVIEW

We adjusted the Company's historical financial statements to present a profile of the Company's results of operations, and financial position as of the valuation date. Specifically, we made the following adjustments: (1) we adjusted officers compensation to reflect market-average living wages for a president and vice president; (2) we adjusted cost of goods sold and other salaries and wages for consistency and comparison, and to account for a classification error made during a year when financials were compiled rather than reviewed; and (3) we adjusted a one-time moving expense.

BALANCE SHEET

The balance sheet for November 30, 199x, and for the previous four years demonstrate the Company's favorable financial position. At the end of fiscal year 199x, the Company's assets totaled approximately $xxx million, up xx.x% from the end of fiscal 199x. Current assets totaled $xxx million, or xx.x% of total assets. Accounts receivable have historically been in the range of xx.x% to xx.x% of total assets, which could signal risk in the event of a question about the quality of the receivables. However, we do not believe this is a major issue, since the number of days to collect accounts receivable (an average of xx days in 199x) has been consistently declining since 199x. This means that the Company's customers have been paying their invoices at a steadily faster rate throughout the 1990s.

With respect to liabilities, current liabilities were approximately $xxx at the end of fiscal year 199x, or xx.x% of total assets. The Company's acid-test (quick) ratio of x.x:x is a very strong indicator of the Company's ability to cover its immediate liabilities (due in one year or less) with current assets.

The Company purchased $xxx worth of new machinery during 199x, for which capitalized lease obligations have been footnoted in the Company's CPA-prepared financial statements. As a result, total liabilities went from $xxx in 199x to $xxx in 199x, a xx.x% increase. Despite the fixed-asset purchases, the Company has had increased equity in recent years to offset the effect of growing liability on the balance sheet.

INCOME STATEMENT

The Company's adjusted net sales have increased over the five-year period between 199x and 199x from approximately $xxx million to $xxx million, an average annual compound growth rate of xx.x%. Sales growth has been volatile, ranging from xx.x% in 199x to xx.x% in 199x—dropping to xx.x% and xx.x% in 199x and 199x, respectively, and rising back up over xx.x% in 199x. As with the Company's revenue, growth in earnings before taxes was strong yet volatile, reaching peak growth of xx.x% and xx.x% in 199x and 199x, respectively, with more modest growth in the xx.x%–xx.x% range in between those years.

The Company's two most significant costs as a percentage of revenue are cost of goods sold ("COGS") and salaries and wages. COGS, as a percentage of revenues, fluctuated from xx.x% to xx.x% over the past six years. Salaries have also been variable, accounting for anywhere from xx.x% to xx.x% of revenues. Operating expenses as a percentage of revenue have dropped steadily over time, from xx.x% in 199x to xx.x% in 199x.

The Company reported favorable profitability over the past x years. Earnings before taxes were typically in the xx.x% range, punctuated by a low of xx.x% in 199x and a peak of xx.x% in 199x.

The Company appears to be in good financial condition, and is ready for continued profitability at increased levels of sales.

ADJUSTMENT FOR CONTROL

PURPOSE OF DISCOUNT

"Minority stock interests in a 'closed' corporation are usually worth much less than the proportionate share of the assets to which they attach."[17] Valuing the transfer of a minority interest in a private, closely held company therefore requires the consideration of a control adjustment, which is applied to the transfer of a minority interest, to reflect the absence of the power of control.

---

17. *Cravens v. Welch,* 10 Federal Supplement 94, 1935.

BLOCK OF SECURITIES BEING TRANSFERRED

Robert Simmons is gifting a x% common stock interest.

VOTING POWER

The Articles of Incorporation, dated November 29, 197x, provide for one class of shares, common stock, with no par value. The bylaws of Semiconductor Corporation, as amended on February 20, 197x, grant certain powers to shareholders with xx .x % or more of the outstanding shares. Therefore, an interest with at least xx.x% of the common stock has more power than a less than xx.x% interest.

BOARD OF DIRECTORS

The corporate bylaws provide for two directors of the company. The directors are Robert Simmons, president, and John Simmons, vice president.

OFFICERS

The officers of the Company are Robert Simmons, president, and John Simmons, vice president. These officers set employee compensation, determine operational policy, select the individuals and companies with whom they do business as customers and vendors, award contracts, and manage the Company.

ESTIMATE OF THE CONTROL ADJUSTMENT

A technique used to quantify the control adjustment is to determine the control premium actually paid for businesses in the same industry. The market value of a publicly traded security reflects the fact that most trades involve a minority interest. Conversely, the price of an offer seeking a controlling interest is usually higher than the price paid for a minority interest. The higher price reflects the value of the premium for control. *Mergerstat Review* reports annual figures for (1) the average premium offered above the per share price of a minority interest and (2) the number of transactions for certain industries. We examined Mergerstat data regarding recent acquisitions in the electrical equipment industry, and found that in 199x the market control premium for this industry was xx.x%. The corresponding control adjustment (discount) for the electrical equipment industry is xx.x% (Exhibit D).

Having examined the level of control adjustments in the electrical equipment industry, we analyzed the Company at the time of valuation to adjust for company-specific factors. "The value of control depends on the shareholders' ability to exercise any or all of a variety of rights typically associated with control."[18] To the extent that the gifted shares will or will not have these rights, the adjustment should be decreased or increased accordingly. The powers typically associated with control of a company include the following:

Common prerogatives of control:[19]

1. Elect directors and appoint management.

2. Determine management compensation and perquisites.

3. Set policy and change the course of business.

4. Acquire or liquidate assets.

5. Select vendors and contractors.

6. Make acquisitions of other companies.

7. Liquidate, dissolve, sell out, or recapitalize the company.

8. Sell or acquire treasury shares.

9. Register the company's stock for public offering.

10. Declare and pay dividends.

11. Change the articles of incorporation or bylaws.

As minority shareholders with a small amount of stock and no representation on the board of directors, the recipients of the gifted shares of common stock will not have direct control over the Company. They will be unable to exercise the prerogatives of control listed above.

We have determined that the new owners of the gifted shares will have few, if any, of the rights associated with control. We believe that the use of the median discount is appropriate in this case. The owners of the gifted shares should have approximately the same lack of control as a minority shareholder in a publicly traded corporation. Therefore, we are using the electrical equipment industry

---

18. Ibid., Ch. 8, p. 18.
19. Shannon P. Pratt, *Valuing a Business: The Analysis and Appraisal of Closely Held Companies*, Homewood, IL: Business One Irwin, 1989, pp. 55–56.

control adjustment of xx.x% as the control adjustment for the shares to be gifted in Semiconductor Corporation.

ADJUSTMENT FOR RESPONSIBILITY

PURPOSE OF ADJUSTMENT

"By definition, ownership interests in closely held companies are typically not readily marketable compared to similar interests in public companies."[20] The degree to which this statement is true can vary materially depending on many factors: a company's stage of evolution at the time an owner of stock is transferring interest, probability of a public offering, dividend history, and size of the block. Where a company is at any one point in time in its evolutionary path is best demonstrated by the facts in evidence through financial records and other company documents (like board of directors' meeting minutes).

There have been many studies regarding adjustments for lack of marketability (Williamette Management Associates, Robert Baird & Co., Standard Research Consultants, Maher, Moroney, Trout, Gelman, Milton, and the Institutional Investor Study Report of the Securities and Exchange Commission), circa 199x back to 196x. These studies varied in their findings, with average and/or median adjustments in the range of xx% to xx%, which is strong empirical evidence that a substantial adjustment exists. The amount of the adjustment is measured quantitatively by the profile of the company being valued at the date of valuation and by how a willing buyer and willing seller will most likely negotiate a price for the shares.

The purpose is to express an adjustment to value to reflect the ownership interest in a private, closely held company which does not have an institutional marketplace for sales and or transfers.

COMPANY-SPECIFIC FACTORS AFFECTING MARKETABILITY

Probability of Public Offering

Evidence suggests that as the probability of a public offering of a company's shares of stock increases, the adjustment related to liquidity of

---

20. Jay E. Fishman et al., *Guide to Business Valuations*, Fort Worth, TX: Practitioners Publishing Company, March 1994, ¶ 815.22.

the investment decreases. However, this adjustment will most likely still be material if the shares being offered for registration must be sold prior to the initial public offering (IPO). There is also the probability that shares which remain unregistered at the time of the IPO will subsequently suffer a material adjustment from the public market price if they are sold prior to registration or if there is the maturing of some restriction on transfer.

We must look to the profile of the Company at the time of valuation. According to the board of directors' meeting minutes, the Company wants to go public in the near future. The Company has been actively seeking underwriters to assist it in the process. However, as of the valuation date, the Company's stock is not sold on the open market. Therefore, the liquidity of the ownership interest in the shares being transferred is impaired.

Restrictions on Sale

There are no restrictions on the sale or transfer of the stock.

Evidence of a Market

There may be potential buyers for the entire Company. There are two potential types of companies that might be interested in purchasing the Company. The first is a large semiconductor manufacturer that wants to be able to process components in house. The second is an already existing testing house that wants to add tape-and-reel component processing to the services that the company provides. However, we do not believe that either of these potential purchasers would be interested in buying a minority interest in the Company. Therefore, there is virtually no evidence of a market for the shares to be gifted.

Dividend History

The Company has made a cash dividend distribution for each of the years between 199x through 199x. In 199x, the Company made a cash dividend of $xxx; in 199x, $xxx; in 199x, $xxx; and in 199x, $xxx.

Size of the Block Transferred

At the valuation date, the Company had one class of stock. The size of the block of stock being transferred is x% of the outstanding shares.

ESTIMATION OF ADJUSTMENT

The marketability adjustment related to the transfer of common stock shares owned by a hypothetical individual investor in the Company (seller) to a willing buyer is materially impacted by the Company's private, closely held nature and lack of a market. There is a prospect of the Company going public in the near future; however, as of the valuation date, there was no public market trading the Company's shares of stock. There are two different sources to examine when determining the size of the marketability adjustment. The first authority is common law, where "the courts have in recent years upheld discounts in the xx% area."[21] The other source of data on the marketability adjustment comes from transactions between buyers and sellers of stock.

Two types of studies have been done to quantify the lack of marketability adjustment. One group of studies used empirical data from the transactions of letter stocks, which are identical to openly traded stock of public companies except that the letter stock cannot be traded on the open market for a specific period of time. As Securities and Exchange Commission Accounting Release No. 113 states, "Restricted securities are often purchased at a discount, frequently substantial, from the market price of outstanding unrestricted securities of the same class. This reflects the fact that securities which cannot be readily sold in the public marketplace are less valuable than securities which can be sold. . . . " At the time of the letter stock transaction, the purchaser of the stock knows that at some future date (usually two years or less when the restrictions expire) there will be an established market where the shares can be traded. This is not the case for the shares of private, closely held companies such as the Company. Therefore, the marketability discount will be smaller for letter stocks than for the stocks of companies in which there may never be a market for the stock, all other factors being equal.

The second group of studies are private transaction studies, which compare the price of a company's stock during private stock transactions with the stock price at the time of the subsequent initial public offering.

The difference between the private and public price per share measures the adjustment for the lack of marketability, since no

---

21. R. E. Moroney, "Why 25 Percent Discount for Nonmarketability in One Valuation, 100 Percent in Another?" *Taxes*, May 1977, p. 320, cited in Pratt, p. 258.

public market exists for the shares of a company's stock prior to the IPO. This technique will result in a more accurate marketability adjustment for private, closely held companies than the approach used in the aforementioned letter stock studies. However, if the private transactions took place within a few months of the IPO, there is a reasonable chance that the buyer knew about the high probability of a public market for the shares in the near future. To the extent that this is true, the marketability adjustments reported in these studies will underestimate this adjustment for the stock of Semiconductor Corporation.

We believe that some of the best private transactions studies that quantified the adjustment for the lack of marketability were conducted by Williamette Management Associates and Robert Baird & Co. These studies used only transactions that were conducted on an arm's-length basis, which is appropriate for this fair market value valuation. These studies employed more appropriate and sophisticated research methodologies than other private transactions studies used to calculate the marketability adjustment.

A total of x Williamette studies were conducted over a period of x years, from 197x to 199x. The range of median adjustments in these studies was xx.x% to xx.x%.[22] In 199x, the median discount was xx.x%. More timely data are available from a recent study conducted by Robert W. Baird & Co., a company involved in the pricing of initial public offerings, which has performed seven marketability adjustment studies from 198x through 199x. The range of median adjustments in these studies are from xx% to xx%.[23] The most recent study was published in the December 199x issue of *Business Valuation Review*. This study determined a median pre-IPO discount of xx% for the time period from January 199x through June 199x.

We believe that the adjustment negotiated between a willing buyer and willing seller would be approximate to xx%, given the specific facts and circumstances for Semiconductor Corporation. We reduced the median market discount of xx% by x/x (or xx%) to estimate the lack of marketability adjustment for the Company. Our marketability adjustment of xx% reflects the prospects of the Company's going public in the future and its consistent dividend payments, factors that make a small minority interest in the Company more marketable than the comparable market evidence.

---

22. Fishman, March 1995, Exhibit 8–18.
23. Ibid., Exhibit 8–17.

DISCOUNTED EARNINGS METHOD

We utilized the widely accepted discounted earnings method to estimate the value of the Company (Exhibit B). The discounted earnings
method is an income-oriented approach, and is based on the theory
that the total value of a business is the present value of its projected
future earnings, plus the present value of the terminal value. The
projected future earnings and the terminal value are discounted back
to the present using an appropriate discount rate. The discounted
earnings method is the valuation method most frequently used in
the merger and acquisition arena for pricing/valuation issues.

Given the adjusted historical performance of the Company and
positive trends for the semiconductor and related industries, we
expect the Company's strong operating results to continue. We used
the average of the last three years' earnings to calculate a base level
of earnings. Our projections use a $xxx base level of pretax earnings.

Because of the strong link between the services that the
Company provides and the health of the semiconductor industry,
we believe projections for that industry will be a fairly accurate indicator of the Company's potential future earnings. Analysts are in
general consensus regarding growth in the semiconductor industry,
and most believe that a xx% expected growth is reasonable through
the year 199x. We have assumed a xx% growth rate commensurate
with the Company's plans to expand in 199x to accommodate a
backlog of potential customers. The terminal value is the present
value of the fifth-year earnings projected into perpetuity at a long-
term growth rate of 4%, the expected rate of inflation.

DISCOUNT RATE

The estimated earnings and the terminal value were then discounted
back to a present value by a pretax discount rate of xx.x% (Exhibit C).
The discount rate for a stream of future earnings is directly related
to the risk of the earnings. We used the build-up method to develop the discount rate. This method adds risk premiums to a safe rate
of return to calculate the discount rate. A risk premium is an excess
rate of return for a certain class of investment relative to a different
specific type of investment. Without this "risk premium" to compensate for the higher risk level for stocks relative to bonds, rational,
risk-averse investors would not invest in stocks. In other words, the

risk premium is an increase in the expected rate of return to induce investors to make riskier investments.

Specifically, the risk-free rate of return that we used is x.x%, the rate for 10-year Treasury bonds as of February 2, 199x. To this percentage, we added three risk premiums: (1) an equity risk premium of x.x% (the historical rate-of-return premium for large-capitalization company stocks in excess of the rate of return for long-term government bonds); (2) a small stock risk premium of x.x% (the historical rate-of-return premium for small-capitalization company stocks in excess of the rate of return for large-capitalization company stocks); and (3) a company-specific risk premium of x% (our estimate of the extra risk for the subject Company in excess of a small-capitalization stock). The result is an after-tax discount rate of xx.x%.

We then converted the after-tax discount rate to a pretax discount rate of xx.x%.[24] This calculation begins with the after-tax rate of xx.x%. The estimated sustainable long-term growth rate of 4%—a rate slightly higher than that of inflation—is subtracted out. The result of xx.x% is divided by 60% (1 minus the effective tax rate of 40%), which equals xx.x%. We added back in the long-term growth rate of 4%, and the sum is the pretax discount rate of xx.x%. We believe that this discount rate captures the risk commensurate with the projected future earnings.

SUMMARY

The value of the Company prior to adjustments is $xxx, which is equal to the present value of the projected pretax earnings ($xxx) plus the terminal value ($xxx). The value of a x% common stock interest in the Company before adjustments for control and marketability is $xxx, which is x% of $xxx, the value of a 100% interest prior to adjustments.

To arrive at fair market value of the minority interest, adjustments must be made for control and marketability. We subtracted the control adjustment of $xxx (which is xx.x% of $xxx) from $xxx to arrive at a subtotal of $xxx. The marketability adjustment of xx.x% is then applied to this subtotal, which results in an adjustment of $xxx (xx.x% of $xxx). Subtracting this adjustment from the subtotal results in our estimated fair market value of a x% common stock interest in Semiconductor Corporation of $xxx.

---

24. Mary Ann Lerch, "Pretax/After-Tax Conversion Formula for Capitalization Rate and Cash Flow Discount Rates," *Business Valuation Review*, March 1990, p. 18.

Bibliography

American Institute of Certified Public Accountants. *Codification of Statements on Auditing Standards.* Chicago: CCH Inc., 1995.

American Institute of Certified Public Accountants. *Communicating in Litigation Services: Engagement Letters.* New York, NY: AICPA, 1995.

American Society of Appraisers. *Principles of Appraisal Practice and Code of Ethics.* Washington, DC: American Society of Appraisers, 1994.

American Society of Appraisers. *Directory of Professional Appraisal Services.* Washington, DC: American Society of Appraisers, 1995.

Appraisal Standards Board. *Uniform Standards of Professional Appraisal Practice.* Washington, DC: The Appraisal Foundation, 1995.

Bacon, Francis. *Meditations Sacrae,* 1597.

Bailey, Larry P. *Miller GAAS 1995 Guide.* San Diego, CA: Harcourt Brace Professional Publishing, 1995, Part V, Section 17.

Black, Henry Campbell. *Black's Law Dictionary.* St. Paul, MN: West Publishing Company, 1990.

Brinig, Brian, and James McCafferty. *The CPA as an Expert Witness.* San Diego, CA: Litigation Services Institute, 1992.

CAMICO. *Loss Prevention: A Manual for an Accounting Practice.* Redwood City, CA: California Accountants Mutual Insurance Company, 1996.

California Corporation Code § 2000, Subdivision (a).

Chatfield, Michael. *A History of Accounting Thought.* Hinsdale, IL: Dryden Press, 1974.

Coffman, Edward, Raoul H. Tondkar, and Gary John Previts, eds. *Historical Perspectives of Selected Financial Accounting Topics.* Homewood, IL: Irwin, 1993.

Comerio, Mary, et al. "Postdisaster Residential Building," Working Paper 608, Institute of Urban and Regional Development, University of California, Berkeley, February 1994.

Comfort, Nicholas. *Brewer's Politics.* London: Cassell, 1993.

Cornell, Bradford. *Corporate Valuation: Tools for Effective Appraisal and Decision Making.* Burr Ridge, IL: Irwin, 1993.

Crivelli, P. *An Original Translation of the Treatise on Double Entry Bookkeeping by Frater Lucas Pacioli.* London: Institute of Bookkeepers, 1924.

"Certain-teed Faces its Vally Forge." *Business Week,* June 1, 1974, p. 29.

Cost of Capital Quarterly, 1995 Yearbook, Chicago: Ibbotson Associates, 1995.

Diamond, Michael, and Julie L. Williams. *How to Incorporate.* 2nd ed. New York: Wiley, 1993.

ESOP Association. *Valuing ESOP Shares.* Washington, DC: ESOP Association, 1989.

Federal Rules Booklet, Federal Rules of Civil Procedure, Federal Rules of Evidence. Boston: Dahlstrom Legal Publishing, January 1994.

United States Code Service. *Rules of Practice and Procedure of the United States Tax Court, Federal Tax Court Rule 143*. Lawyers Cooperative Publishing, 1994.

Financial Accounting Standards Board. *Current Text Accounting Standards, General Standards*. Norwalk, CT: Financial Accounting Standards Board, 1994.

Fishman, Jay E., et al. *Guide to Business Valuations*. 3 vols. Fort Worth, TX: Practitioners Publishing Company, 1994.

Frank, Peter B., and Michael S. Wagner. *Providing Litigation Services*. New York: American Institute of Certified Public Accounts, 1993.

Glenn, Donald A. *Advanced Family Law Topics*, California, Redwood City: CPA Education Foundation Continuing Professional Education, 1995, Ch. 3, p. 4.

Hall, Lance S., and Timothy C. Pollack. "Strategies for Obtaining the largest Valuation Discounts." *Estate Planning*, January–February 1994, pp. 38–44.

Helzel, Leo B., and friends. *A Goal Is a Dream with a Deadline*. New York: McGraw-Hill, 1995.

Imwinkelreid, Edward J., and Tim Hallahan. *California Evidence Code Annotated 1995*. Colorado Springs, CO: Shepard's/McGraw-Hill, 1995.

Internal Revenue Service. Form 8283: *"Noncash Charitable Contributions."*

Internal Revenue Service. *Internal Revenue Code*. Volumes 1–2. Chicago: CCH Inc., 1995.

Internal Revenue Service. *Income Tax Regulations*. Volumes 1–6. Chicago: CCH Inc., 1995.

Internal Revenue Service. *Revenue Ruling 59-60*. In Shannon Pratt et al., Valuing a Business, 3rd ed., pp. 644–647.

Internal Revenue Service. *Technical Advice Memorandum*, Code Section 2512.

Jones, Gary, and Dirk Van Dyke. "The Case of Contingent Tax Liability: To Discount or Not?" *The Valuation Examiner*, 1st quarter 1994.

Jones, Gary, and Dirk Van Dyke. "Using the Black-Green Approach to the Buildup Summation Method," *The Valuation Examiner*, March–April 1996, p. 6.

Kroll, Cynthia, et al., "Economic Impact of the Loma Prieta Quake: The Impact on Small Business," Working Paper No 91-187, Center for Real Estate and Urban Economics, University of California, Berkeley, 1991.

Larson, Charles B., and Joseph W. Larson. *Innovative Billing and Collection Methods That Work*. Burr Ridge, IL: Irwin, 1995.

National Association of Certified Fraud Examiners. *Fraud Examiners' Manual*. Austin, TX: NACFE, 1989.

National Association of Certified Valuation Analysts. *1995 Membership Directory*. Salt Lake City, UT: NACVA, 1995.

Pacioli, Luca. *Summa de Arithmetica, Geometria, Proportioni, et Proportionalita*, 1494.

Pallais, Don, and Stephen D. Holton. *Guide to Forecasts and Projections*. Fort Worth, TX: Practioners Publishing Company, 1990.

Porter, Michael. *Competitive Strategy*. New York: The Free Press, 1985.

Pratt, Shannon. *Shannon Pratt's Business Valuation Update*, Portland, Oregon, 1996, 1997.

Pratt, Shannon P. *Valuing Small Businesses and Professional Practices*. Homewood, IL: Irwin, 1986.

Pratt, Shannon P., Robert F. Reilly, and Robert P. Schweihs. *Valuing a Business: The Analysis and Appraisal of Closely Held Companies*. 3rd ed. Homewood, IL: Business One Irwin, 1996.

Robinson, Bruce R. *Strategic Acquisitions: A Guide to Growing and Enhancing the Value of Your Business*. Burr Ridge, IL: Irwin, 1995.

Schnepper, Jeff A. *The Professional Handbook of Business Valuation*. Reading, MA: Addison-Wesley, 1982.

Shilt, James. "Appraisal Under Corporations Code Section 2000," *Business Law News*, Summer 1985.

Tax Court Memo 1991-279. *Estate of Berg v. Commissioner*, 1991.

Tax Court Memo 1994-539. *Luton v. Commissioner*, 1994.

Tax Court Memo 1996-372. *Estate of Ross H. Freeman v. Commissioner*, 1996.

United States Department of Commerce, International Trade Administration. *U.S. Industrial Outlook*, Washington, DC: Government Printing Office, 1984–1994.

United States Office of Management and Budget. *Standard Industrial Classification Manual*, Springfield, VA: National Technical Information Service, 1987.

Williams, Jan R. *Miller GAAP Guide*. San Diego, CA: Harcourt Brace & Co., 1994.

Zier, Joe. *The Expert Accountant in Civil Litigation*. Toronto: Butterworths Canada Ltd., 1993.

ABOUT THE AUTHORS

Gary E. Jones, CPA, CVA, CFE is the President of ValueNomics Research, Inc. He serves on numerous valuation and litigation service committees, and is a highly sought-after speaker for NACVA, the AICPA, and ten different state CPA societies. Jones has received the prestigous Outstanding Member Award from NACVA, and his valuation articles appear regularly in *The Valuation Examiner*, *The Business Journal*, *CPA Litigation Services Counselor*, and other professional publications.

Dirk Van Dyke, MSBA, performs quantitative valuation analysis for private closely held companies. Prior to joining ValueNomics®, he worked as a securities analyst and a statistician. He was educated at UC Berkeley, Johns Hopkins, and the London School of Economics. Van Dyke has spoken before the NACVA, and has written for *The Valuation Examiner*.